It's not just about the hotel, it's about
the coffee shop around the corner...

# TRAVEL SECRETS

*My favourite luxury hotels and hidden gems from around the world*

Written by
Tanya Rose and Martin Turner

© 2010 Mason Rose Publishing

First published in the United Kingdom in 2010 by
Mason Rose Publishing, 8a Bradbrook House, Studio Place
London SW1X 8EL

Written by Tanya Rose and Martin Turner
Designed by Inaria, London
inaria-design.com

Printed in the United Kingdom

Although every effort has been made to ensure that the
information contained within this book is as accurate as
possible at the time of going to press, details are liable to
change. We cannot assume liability for any inaccuracies
which may be contained in the information provided.

ISBN 978-0-9566-297-0-8

# Contents

ONT

# NYA ROSE

*The voice of luxury travel*

After 25 years as a travel guru to the stars of entertainment and commerce, I am so excited to be sharing my insider travel tips with you for the first time. Memorable trips are all about amazing authentic experiences with a dash of magic to take you out of your regular day-to-day existence. Holidays are precious and each one should be exceptional.

For discerning travellers, luxury has taken on an entirely new meaning and is defined by individual taste and not by collective opinion. This is why I am often asked for my expert advice to ensure that travel plans exceed expectations. It's all in the detail. Not just which hotel, but which room? Not just which restaurant, but which table and what to order. Get it right or you can really get it wrong. We all want to feel like a knowledgeable and well-connected local, not a tourist.

Come with me on a voyage of global discovery as I share my Travel Secrets, and those of some of my well-travelled friends.

*Tanya*

**Tanya Rose**
*Founder, Mason Rose*

# THE KNOWLEDGE

—

*Once upon a time travel was elegant – and stylish. It can be again, if you seek expert knowledge to get travel plans as right as they should be. Travel Secrets is the place to start. Don't join the throng – set the pace, and bring the golden age of glamour back to travelling.*

### Forecast

Florida from July through November is hurricane season. Swimming off Hayman Island or Bedarra Island in Queensland between December and March is a 'no' to avoid tangling with a box jellyfish. Are you making a flight connection via Chicago in a February blizzard? Should a kid-phobic couple head for a resort during half-term? How about pushing your way through the Uffizi museum in July? Savvy travellers check the forecast in every sense of the word.

### Smooth ride

Flying out of Stansted? Did you know there's a lounge you can book online? www.stanstedairport.com. Better still, get yourself a Priority Pass for access to 600 lounges in 245 cities to supplement your existing airline member status. Go to the airport early to avoid queue rage and security meltdown. Wear shoes you can remove quickly and easily, limit the jewellery, laptop and toiletries bag at the ready. Avoid credit card declines by calling before you leave to let them know where you are going and for how long.

### Bags of fun

A photocopy of your passport with extra passport photos in a safe place ensures a rapid replacement in the event of a loss. Use packing cubes from www.totalwardrobecare.co.uk. Get the 'Packing List' application on your iPhone. Make sure your kids have their own rucksacks packed with things to keep them entertained, and snacks to keep them happy. Have one travel washbag, full of miniatures.

### Plane sense

Book your seats in advance, away from the galleys and the loos. Go to seatguru.com for specifics. Flying domestic USA? Order a small gourmet picnic from your hotel to collect when checking out. Dress comfortably in layers of quiet elegance to look like you belong in first class just in case you aren't already there. Upgrades are always more likely when you look the part. Planes are either icy cold or dry and hot, rarely just right. Pashminas for women, light sweaters for men, along with cashmere eye patches for you both to block out the light.

## Best hotel recipe?

1 **GENUINE RECOGNITION...**
from warm and welcoming staff

2 **A GENERAL MANAGER...**
who values their guests and is visible

3 **LUGGAGE...**
that gets to your room as quickly as you do

4 **EASY TO MANAGE...**
light switches and televisions

5 **A PROPER HAIR DRYER...**
with a plug socket adjacent to a mirror
outside the bathroom

6 **ENOUGH DESK-LEVEL SOCKETS...**
to accommodate a laptop, iPhone,
BlackBerry and iPod

7 **INTERNET CONNECTION...**
should be rapid and not require a
degree in IT (and be free of charge)

8 **LARGE BATHROBES...**
for men, not munchkins

9 **PLEASE LET ME ORDER...** *
from the restaurant menu not the room
service one, I've been here a week!!

10 **I WANT A WAKE-UP CALL...**
not a conversation at 5.45am

*\* Like you can at La Colombe d'Or!*

### Fares fair

If you know you're skiing a weekend in January and
another in February, book six months in advance
and fly out of City Airport which is almost as good
as a private jet terminal – takes at least a zero off
the ticket price. You should make your restaurant
reservations in advance, ditto your theatre bookings
if you want to be at the right table, and fifth row
centre of the stalls. If it makes practical sense,
travel without luggage and send it on ahead of
your arrival with firstluggage.com.

### Make an entrance

The trip is not just the plane journey, it's also
smooth, well-arranged ground transport at both
ends, with the driver's name and mobile number.
Load local numbers into your mobile before you
leave, or better still, in the US get a local cell phone.
Insist your hotel pre-populates your check-in card
before you arrive so it's passport, signature and
straight to the room pronto. Heading out to a
dinner appointment or the theatre? Arrange
transport in advance; don't join the line outside
your hotel for a taxi, especially on a rainy night.

# Travel secrets from some of my well-travelled friends

—

34
## ANYA HINDMARCH

*"I am forever ripping things out of magazines."*

56
## DES MCDONALD

*"For me travel revolves around sport and food."*

78
## MARIGAY MCKEE

*"Take M Labb Travel Kit and always arrive fresh."*

100
## DAVID COLLINS

*"I don't have miserable holidays."*

122
## CIARA PARKES

*"I love long-haul flights with no interruptions."*

144
## ED VICTOR

*"I do my research and I always plan everything in advance."*

166
## TAMARA MELLON

*"Trust your close friends who have the inside scoop."*

190
## NIGEL NEWTON

*"I love the hotels Winston Churchill stayed in."*

Europe

Bookings: +44 (0)20 7201 8070
masonroseprivate.com

# HOTEL AMIGO

—

## *Elegance and style flourish in Europe's capital*

A better location would be difficult to find in Brussels. The hotel is bang next to Grand Place, the most beautiful square in the country and one of the most elegant in all of Europe. It is also close to the commercial centre and is ideal for those wishing to shop for treasures and antiques in the Le Sablon district. Recently refurbished with all the refinement and style The Rocco Forte Collection is renowned for, it is recognised as the best luxury hotel in the city.

With its modern Italian food at Ristorante Bocconi, its classical references throughout in ornately carved Flemish furniture and intricate tapestries, its chic contemporary colours and textiles and its tribute to Magritte with its strategic use of surrealist prints… and then there's Tintin and Captain Haddock in the bathrooms! It's imaginative and unexpected touches such as this, which make the hotel a place that immediately welcomes the traveller and pampers the tourist.

And it is its proximity to all that is happening in the capital – galleries, boutiques (Belgium now boasts some of the hippest fashion designers) and museums that make it the ideal base for families as well as financiers.

Bookings: +44 (0)20 7201 8070
masonroseprivate.com

---

**HOTEL AT A GLANCE**

**ACCOMMODATION**
173 rooms and suites

**DINING**
Restaurant and bar

**RECREATION**
Fitness centre and children's programme

**TRANSFERS**
Brussels Airport 20mins by car, Eurostar train station 10mins by car

---

SIGNATURE EXPERIENCE

# A CITY OF SWEETNESS, CHOCOLATE AND CAKES

Brussels may be waffle central and it may have given up the best chips in the world, but it is renowned for its chocolate shops and at Hotel Amigo you are but a stone's throw from many of them – they claim 365! Names to look for – Wittamer, Neuhaus and Pierre Marcolini.

+32 (0)254 747 47
roccofortecollection.com

66
—

# The best hotel in Brussels. A stylish home away from home. As the name suggests, a real friend waiting to welcome you to its contemporary luxe arms.

**Designer sat nav**

It is essential in a new city to have someone with knowledge and style on your arm. **Linda van Waeseberghe** can be your friend for the day and steer you right to where your heart desires. No fumbling around for the right place to shop, Linda will have you in the Sablon district and buying local designer Jean-Paul Knott.

**Doing the do**

Have you found yourself in Brussels and in desperate need of attention to your locks for a dinner rendezvous? A cut above the rest is **Marianne Gray** who will massage natural products into your hair and have you exit looking elegant and ready to face the world. Because you're worth it.

**Comical**

Don't you just love Tintin? Comics are a big deal in Belgium and a visit to the **Comic Strip Museum** is a must. House d in the Waucquez Warehouses, the building itself is quite something. And if you like a museum shop as I do, the gift shop is outstanding, you'll love it!

**Moules-frites**

Moules-frites are as synonymous with Belgium as beer. Both are must-haves on the menu at **Aux Armes de Bruxelles** which has been serving since 1921. The place is crammed with locals which is always firm confirmation that you should eat here too. It's very central so perfect for resting your mules.

Bookings: +44 (0)20 7201 8070
masonroseprivate.com

# EXCELSIOR HOTEL & SPA

—

## *Palatial resort in a spectacular and historic setting*

Close enough to touch the ancient walls of Dubrovnik and yet sufficiently secluded that guests can enjoy some peace and tranquillity after a morning or afternoon's excursion in the old town. For those who have never visited Dubrovnik, this exquisite UNESCO heritage town will come as a magical surprise. Pretty and golden, set high above the bright blue of the Adriatic and with monumental walls that have protected the city for centuries – from pirates, marauders, invaders and vast armies of various kingdoms and empires.

What is so wonderful about the hotel are the views of the walls and the towers, turrets and church spires within them. But then, do make sure that early one morning, before the sun is high, you walk around them and enjoy not just the seascapes but also the tiny cobbled streets, magnificent monasteries and campanile. And then return to the hotel for sustenance or spa treatments.

**Villa Agave**, for those looking for total privacy, is a magnificent three-bedroomed summerhouse close by. With its five terraces, private beach, swimming pool, meditation room, antiques and Croatian artworks, it is a serious luxury hideaway – but still with magnificent views of the coast and city.

## HOTEL AT A GLANCE

**ACCOMMODATION**
158 rooms and suites including
Villa Agave

**DINING**
Satu Restaurant & Sushi Bar,
Prora Beach Restaurant,
Restaurant Salin

**RECREATION**
Abakus Piano Bar, private beach,
wellness and spa centre

**TRANSFERS**
Dubrovnik Airport 25mins by car

+385 (0)20 430 830
alh.hr

SIGNATURE EXPERIENCE

# WONDER AT THE JEWEL-LIKE INLETS, BAYS AND HIDDEN COVES

A boat trip along the Dalmatian Coast. The concierge will organise a little coastal cruise so that you can take in the breathtaking scenery crowned by the historic town.

"

Sufficiently apart to escape the visitors, this five-star resort provides every luxury as well as a super exclusive private residence – the Villa Agave.

**Family supper**

It's only a short walk into town, and an outside table for your whole family at **Kamenice** with a view of the statue of Ivan Gundulic the poet. Order giant plates of fried calamari, fresh oysters, and wine by the carafe. Your kids will love the popcorn fish, Dad will love the bill. So reasonably priced.

**Lokrum Island**

This gorgeous nature reserve is just a stone's throw from Dubrovnik. You'll find botanical gardens, a French fortress, an 11th-century monastery, an inland lake, incredible beaches and cliff jumping. Go in a kayak so you can navigate the island's caves, beaches, and secluded swimming spots. A great day out, wear sun block.

**In the shade**

If you need a cultural respite from the heat in mid-summer, head for the **Museum of Modern Art** located very close to popular Banja beach. The building is a large neo-Renaissance villa originally built for a local. Now it's chock-a-block with artworks from major Croatian artists. Cool in more ways than one.

**Hats on**

**The Ronchi Hat Factory** set up shop in 1858 and has been covering the heads of the stylish ever since. Heiress, owner and designer Marina Grabovac Ronchi is still using the same technology to turn out the most exquisite creations. Go and get a piece of history, the hats are unique and fabulous.

Bookings: +44 (0)20 7201 8070
masonroseprivate.com

# ANASSA

—

## *Dripping in glamour this fashionable hideaway is fabulous all year round*

It is rather fitting that in ancient Greek; Anassa means 'Queen' as this super-stylish resort definitely commands the top spot on the island.

The location is stunning; with the mountains and pine forests of the unspoilt Akamas Peninsula as the backdrop the Anassa has a wonderful seclusion. In keeping with this glorious landscape the entire complex has been designed to resemble a traditional Byzantine village; think white-washed walls, shutters and pathways of bougainvillea leading down to the best beach to be found. What's more there is a whole host of things to do from a sublime spa and exceptional watersports to the superlative kids' club and crèche with the brilliant Baby Go Lightly services. For families and escapists alike this hotel is a natural choice.

Subtle, soothing and very smart, the guestrooms are deliciously cool white expanses with marble floors and louvred shutters. All have spacious balconies looking out over the azure sea. For an extra slice of heaven go for a room with your own terrace and private plunge pool; at night these are romantically lit by candles.

Equally chic are the four restaurants; whether alfresco by the heavenly infinity pool or a gourmet dinner in an intimate stone cavern, the dining is a taste sensation.

As Mediterranean retreats go Anassa is hard to beat.

Bookings: +44 (0)20 7201 8070
masonroseprivate.com

---

**HOTEL AT A GLANCE**

**ACCOMMODATION**
175 studio rooms, suites and
villa residence

**DINING**
4 restaurants

**RECREATION**
Spa with indoor pool, 3 outdoor
pools, watersports, PADI dive centre,
powerboats, tennis, sailing, nearby
golf, kids' club and crèche

**TRANSFERS**
Paphos International Airport
45mins by car

+357 26 888 000
thanoshotels.com

---

SIGNATURE EXPERIENCE

# RELAXATION COMES IN MANY FORMS

The Thalassa Spa takes tranquillity to a whole new level. From one-off treatments to detoxifying Organic Pharmacy programmes this Roman-style Thalassotherapy spa is quite simply one of the best you will ever find. All manner of luxurious therapies will leave you feeling totally zoned out. This is a spa retreat in the truest sense.

*Tanya's travel secrets…*

❝

——

A year-round destination of golden
sunshine, local warmth, and genuine
hospitality. A luxurious Mediterranean
destination. Aphrodite is the goddess
of love and beauty and synonymous
with Cyprus… need we say more?

**Heavenly wine**

Wine can be a religious
experience in the right location.
If you need time away from
the sun lounger organise an
air-conditioned car and driver
to take you to **Panagia
Chrysorroiatissa Monastery**,
with its important collection
of Byzantine icons. Try saying
that after a bottle or two of
the best vintage wine in Cyprus
from the winery located at
the Monastery. Heavenly.

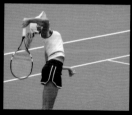

**Love, set and match**

Having trouble convincing the
other half about a languid sun
and sand vacation? Channel
their John McEnroe tantrums
into all-star **tennis**. The hotel
has two flood-lit courts on
which you can take private
lessons with a pro. Book your
sessions for morning or late
afternoon/early evening so
that mid-summer you don't
self-combust in the heat!

**Herculean feats**

Are your teenagers
superheroes with endless
energy and appetites? Or
are they sitting about being
generally moody and tapping
endlessly on their mobiles and
iPods? From July 1 to August
31 you can check them into
**Hercules Teens Club**. Sailing,
tennis, scuba diving, movie
nights, kayaking, banana boat,
ten pin bowling, table tennis,
waterskiing, squash, cooking
lessons, snorkelling and
Cyprus nights… you'll
forget they even exist.

**Mysterious**

If you spend a week in a
hotel, you do need to venture
out now and then for some
authentic local flavour. Go to
the **Mystery Family Tavern**
located in the town of Polis.
Dinner is served late into the
evening, famous for its meze.
Imagine feasting on calamari,
eggplant, artichokes, tzatsiki
and tahini lovingly prepared
by Nasso Rossides, mother of
the Mysteriosis Brothers who
run the place. The mystery is,
will they have any fresh fish
caught that very day for your
dinner? Go now and find out!

Bookings: +44 (0)20 7201 8070
masonroseprivate.com

# THE AUGUSTINE

—

## *Ecclesiastical elegance meets city-centre simplicity*

A place oozing history, comfort and opulence, The Augustine, just around the corner from the Charles Bridge, is comprised of seven buildings which include the 13th-century St Thomas Augustinian monastery. And although true to its origins in the decor – huge vaulted ceilings, dark wood, rich shades of crimson, purple and emerald – it also offers everything the modern traveller requires. The design, spearheaded by Olga Polizzi for The Rocco Forte Collection, merges monastic simplicity with furniture and artefacts of early 20th-century Czech cubism – a marriage that works magnificently.

Most of the rooms, and no two are the same, look out onto serene courtyards or the spires and rooftops of the city, including views of the Castle, while the public rooms are spacious and serene. For instance, The Monastery restaurant is in a glass-encased courtyard and Tom's Bar is in a barrel-vaulted hall with high ceilings and outside seating in the cloister terrace. It also hosts live music performances on certain days throughout the summer.

The monastery once housed its own brewery, so the Brewery Bar is a modern reminder of that with a wide choice of locally brewed beers… including its own.

And while the hotel has a fully equipped fitness centre, its Augustine Spa is the place to go to chill out after a day's sightseeing.

## HOTEL AT A GLANCE

**ACCOMMODATION**
101 rooms and suites

**DINING**
Restaurant and 2 bars

**RECREATION**
Spa, gym and
children's programme

**TRANSFERS**
Prague Ruzyne International
Airport 30mins by car

SIGNATURE EXPERIENCE

# A NATURAL REMEDY TO HELP YOU RELAX AND REFRESH

The spa offers a number of natural remedies based on one of the things the monastery was once famed for – beer. So indulge yourself with a St Thomas Beer Signature Body Forming Treatment, where finely ground hops are used to exfoliate, then a dark beer is used to nourish and detoxify before the final massage.

"

Prague is a fairytale town where time appears to have stood still in its historical architecture. But beneath that well preserved facade lurks luxuriously cool design. Better still, there's something special about it in any season.

### Civilised nightlife

If you want some nightlife that doesn't start at 3am, has style, and attracts a knowing fashionable crowd, then go to **Manesova**. Located in Vinohrady one of Prague's most desirable upmarket residential neighbourhoods, you will feel you have stepped right into a deluxe private club. Open during the civilised hours of 5pm-3am instead of the opposite.

### The boots are made for walking

If you need to escape your monastery for a little retail therapy, then head to **Beltissimo** for shoe heaven. Accessories also abound, and they have stylish footwear for men too. Featured in many of the world's fashion magazines, buy now, you'll walk all over the competition.

### Viewfinder

The King Charles Bridge is the centrepiece of the fairytale magic of Prague. Best seat is the **Kampa Park** terrace in warm weather for the view. That is Matt Damon over there. If you have a sweet tooth order the Fresh Strawberry Capuccino dessert, your kids will love it too. Candlelit dinner in winter with the bridge seen through the windows is pure romance.

### Treasures

Are you a lover of classical music? Then go to **Lobkowicz Palace** and see Beethoven's original scores for the 4th and 5th symphonies, and Mozart's revisions of Handel's Messiah. Completely inspiring, and alongside Canalettos and a Pieter Brueghel, it's so worth the visit. And it's located within the walls of Prague Castle. The fairytale continues.

# CHÂTEAU DE BAGNOLS

—

*Grand hotels don't come much grander than this 13th-century château*

There are some places in the world you want to visit and visit again – Château de Bagnols is one of them. It has a unique magic and incomparable style.

Firstly there is the setting of a charming French village surrounded by hillsides crammed with vines, in the very heart of the Beaujolais countryside. Then there is the breathtakingly beautiful château with its warm honey-coloured stone, magnificent turrets, dry moat and a drawbridge which leads you to this outstandingly fine hotel.

Château de Bagnols was transformed from derelict castle to glorious splendour through the inspired vision of Lady Hamlyn. The result is so stunning that this extraordinary château is both a major historic monument and a luxurious hotel. Rooms are filled with fantastic decoration, particularly the bedrooms. For these are salons of romance and self-indulgence; many feature fanciful four-poster beds from Lady Hamlyn's own collection. If the gardens were not so divine and the dining so delicious you would be tempted never to leave them.

Whether being warmed by the fire in winter or sitting on the terrace under the 100-year-old lime trees you will find dining one of the most pleasurable experiences. Each dish is a tour of the wonderful flavours of the region and the wine list is incredible.

This is a sumptuous world; where the exceptional is the norm.

## HOTEL AT A GLANCE

**ACCOMMODATION**
20 rooms and suites, 1 apartment

**DINING**
Restaurant

**RECREATION**
Outdoor pool, spa services, biking, hiking, horse riding, horse and carriage ride, wine tasting, cooking classes, private guided tours, hot air ballooning, nearby tennis and golf

**TRANSFERS**
Lyon Saint Exupéry Airport 20mins by car; Frontenas Airport 10mins by car

+33 4 74 71 40 00
chateaudebagnols.co.uk

**SIGNATURE EXPERIENCE**

# A COLLECTOR'S FLAIR

Under Lady Hamlyn's guidance hundreds of specialist craftsmen restored Renaissance frescos, original sculpted stonework and ornate plasterwork to their former glory. She gathered rare and beautiful antiques and commissioned a specially designed collection of objects inspired by the 17th and 18th centuries to create the finishing touches that make the Château de Bagnols so very special.

Once upon a time a travelling Prince and Princess checked into their own fairytale moated, luxury castle twinkling under a Michelin star, and lived happily ever after.

**Tip toe**

A night out at the theatre in a foreign country can be challenging unless you are a linguist. Dance is the answer, and lovers of the art will adore the **Lyon Dance Theatre** whose programme covers the spectrum from classical to contemporary. Always something new and exciting to see. I could have danced all night.

**Medieval**

Absolutely wear flats for a visit to the hilltop medieval town of **Pérouges**. The town is preserved by the Beaux Arts Commission. With noble and craftsmen's houses side by side, you can see why the town has been featured in many French films. Try the local speciality '*galette de sucre*', a thin sugar pancake, simply delicious.

**Antique**

Go to **rue Áuguste Comte** in Lyon's Antiques Quarter. In the spring there is Tapis Vert, and in the autumn Tapis Rouge. A huge carpet is laid out on the street and all the galleries and shops display their wares. A plethora of amazing treasures you'll want to decorate your home with. An antique bargain bonanza awaits the savvy shopper.

**Gourmet mecca**

You could mortgage your house and eat in Lyon forever, but at least one pilgrimage is in order. The facade of **Paul Bocuse's** restaurant is an history of gastronomy which speaks volumes about what you'll experience inside. Order the Bresse chicken, or the famous black truffle soup, and stop for a cookbook in the boutique shop on the way out. Mission accomplished.

> **"**
> ——
>
> *Travel as well as you can afford. It's worth it.*

*Designer Anya Hindmarch MBE is famed for her unique handbag and luggage collections.*

**TR** *Your favourite hotels and why?*

**AH** I travel a lot for business in the Far East and my favourite hotel is the Park Hyatt in Tokyo. It has breathtaking views of the city and Yoyogi Park. Another favourite but for personal reasons is the Hôtel du Cap in Cap Ferrat as it is where I married my husband James. It has the most divine saltwater swimming pool with the most amazing swimming teacher. He has been there forever and has taught the most incredible people to swim from the David Niven days. He feels like a bit of history and has taught all my kids to swim.

**TR** *Your favourite restaurants when travelling and anything special on the menu that you always order or recommend?*

**AH** Freemans in New York is such a great restaurant. So low-key and tucked away at the end of Freeman Alley in the Lower East Side, it really does feel as though you are discovering a place no one else knows about. And the food is divine. I have enjoyed a few late nights here with friends – it is so cosy it is difficult to leave.

**TR** *What do you love and hate about travelling?*

**AH** As a designer, travelling is essential in giving me inspiration for my collections, whether it is a beautiful building or an intricate tile. I hate travelling without my children but it means they get great presents when I get home.

**TR** *Whose recommendations do you trust?*

**AH** I tend to go with friends' recommendations and I am forever ripping things out from magazines.

**ZIP IT!**

Use Anya Hindmarch 'loose pockets' to organise your money, one for each currency and one for each cities receipts. It makes it so much easier on your return.

Available exclusively online: anyahindmarch.com

*Anya's*

**WORDS OF TRAVEL WISDOM...**

1 **SLEEP EASY**
Take Aromatherapeutics sleep enhancer to inhale in-flight as it helps you to sleep

2 **FEEL FRESH**
Try to fly during the day if you can. Melatonin helps me sleep when I am jet lagged and doesn't make you feel groggy

3 **CARRY ON**
Take a great tote bag in flight with a little 'comfort kit' your own socks, eyeshades, moisturiser, eye cream etc

Bookings: +44 (0)20 7201 8070
masonroseprivate.com

# HÔTEL LE BRISTOL

—

*A tranquil home and garden of understated elegance and personal service with the best address in Paris*

In this city of chic, Hôtel le Bristol is the favourite place to stay for the most fashionable of crowds. Seductive sophistication and timeless luxury abound. An individual, intimate comfort characterises the rooms, some of the most spacious to be found in Paris. For the best views of the glorious garden of Paris itself, choose a suite with a private terrace.

The indoor swimming pool, a rarity in Paris, is a delight. Designed to resemble a Belle Époque yacht, this small but beautiful pool opens up to a solarium offering an incomparable vista over the city rooftops towards Montmartre. Extra pampering is guaranteed with the personalised aromatherapy treatments of the Anne Sémonin Spa.

The 'in crowd' of Paris adore this hotel, in particular the famed cuisine of the 3 Michelin star restaurant. The new lively 114 Le Faubourg restaurant, housed in the new wing of the hotel, is a fabulous addition. Both restaurants are run by the legendary chef Eric Frechon.

Located on the rue du Faubourg Saint-Honoré, Le Bristol is moments away from the fashionable boutiques and artistic delights of Paris. For the more adventurous hire one of Bristol's Smart cars to nip around in style.

A true Parisian treat awaits you.

38     France
Paris          Bookings: +44 (0)20 7201 8070
masonroseprivate.com

**HOTEL AT A GLANCE**

**ACCOMMODATION**
187 rooms and suites

**DINING**
2 restaurants and bar

**RECREATION**
Indoor swimming pool, spa,
fitness centre and private garden
with courtyard

**KIDS**
Children's VIP facilities

**TRANSFERS**
Charles de Gaulle Airport 45mins;
Orly 30mins; Gare du Nord 20mins

+ 33 1 53 43 43 00
lebristolparis.com

SIGNATURE EXPERIENCE

# HIGH TEA MEETS HIGH FASHION

There is nothing quite so chic as afternoon tea, particularly when it is accompanied by some of the world's greatest fashion designs. Le Bristol, synonymous with haute couture, transforms Le Bar into the most elegant of catwalks. As models parade the latest creations, sip on delicate teas or indulge in the most delicious pastries created for these monthly events.

"

Paris epitomises romantic dreams and joie de vivre. Who can fail to be moved by the diamond glitter of the Eiffel Tower and the effortless chic of Parisian fashion? My heart belongs to Paris.

**Taste**

When the evening is warm the terrace at **Brasserie de L'Ile St-Louis** is the place to be overlooking the Seine and Notre-Dame. Opened in 1870 and still going strong, it says a lot for its coq au Riesling, cassoulet, and choucroute garnie. Skip dessert and head to Berthillon close by for ice cream!

**Sweet tooth**

Can you imagine the delectable experience of biting into a chocolate and passion fruit macaron made by Pierre Hermé, dubbed the 'Picasso of Pastries'? On display now at **Pierre Hermé Paris**.

**Seduction**

Since 1976 a little light green shop in St Germain has been the place for fabulous lingerie. Movie stars and models have been wearing **Sabbia Rose's** gorgeous lingerie for years – now you can too. Make sure you buy a lingerie bag in silk.

**Flame**

Light your next dinner party with candles from the official supplier to Versailles under Louis XIV. Founded in 1643, **Cire Trudon** was where Napoleon shopped and you can too – their scented candles launched in 2006 are divine.

# GRAND-HÔTEL DU CAP-FERRAT

—

*A place which provides a mega-stylish sojourn for sybarites*

On a peninsula between Nice and Monte-Carlo, the hotel boasts some of the best views of the Mediterranean, particularly if you view them from the edge of the infinity pool. Many people have fallen in love with this particular pool, deeming it the most spectacular on the planet.

But then there is much to wonder at in this really grand hotel, from its acres of landscaped gardens decorated with a profusion of flowers, to the hedonistic heaven that is its new wing. The hotel was recently refreshed and refurbished, which is when the new wing emerged complete with eight amazing suites, all with their own private pools, a further 16 sea-view suites with their own terraces and a magnificent spa.

It is the sort of place where you might rent a Ferrari to take you along the coast to the delights of Nice and Cannes, or a baby Bugatti to head for the hills or indeed the hotspots of Monte-Carlo. Those wishing for a slower tempo can take a yacht to explore the bays, islands and coves of this magical coastline. But those with most sense will never stray from the hotel and its myriad of luxurious enticements.

**HOTEL AT A GLANCE**

**ACCOMMODATION**
73 rooms, suites and villa

**DINING**
3 restaurants and bar

**RECREATION**
Spa, wine salon, club with infinity pool, cooking classes, tennis, kids' club and bicycle rental

**TRANSFERS**
Nice Côte d'Azur Airport
25mins by car

SIGNATURE EXPERIENCE

# LIVE LIKE A TRILLIONNAIRE – EVEN IF IT'S ONLY FOR A DAY

Become a total hedonist and do not move far from the garden and the pool. Float and relax, soak up the atmosphere from the depths of a lounger or book one of those sexy cabanas at Club Dauphin. Order a naughty cocktail and enjoy the good life.

+ 33 (0) 4 93 76 50 50
ghcf.fr

66
—

Grand occasions, grand romance, grand views. Cap-Ferrat is synonymous with classic elegance that is simply timeless. The view is breathtaking, it's all just magnifique.

**Water features**

No, not the pool, but the truly spectacular fountains at **Ephrussi de Rothschild Villa** in Beaulieu. A water dance of epic proportions in the most incredible garden. With the Mediterranean on both sides, it's just dreamy. Special events are the evening show choreographed to Mozart, Vivaldi, and Bach. Guaranteed to cast a spell of romance over you.

**Swim icon**

Who taught Charlie Chaplin's children to swim? **Pierre Gruneberg,** that's who. He's been teaching people to swim at the Club Dauphin pool since 1950. Celebrate his 60th anniversary by splashing out and taking a lesson from the master. From here to infinity in the Olympic-sized pool. A stroke of genius.

**Plage right in**

As you float in the crystal-clear water off Plage Paloma, look back to shore to take in some of the most spectacularly expensive real estate in the world. Rent your towel-size acreage sunlounger at the **Paloma Beach Club** for shoulder-rubbing with the stars, deeply chilled rosé, and lunch with a view. Is that Jack Nicholson over there?

**Running on air**

Cap-Ferrat is so beautiful, the fitness fiend will be in **jogging heaven**. Rise early in the summer and take off along the shoreline in the quiet of the morning. It's the perfect way to start the day with fresh sea air before the sting of sun sets in. You'll feel guilt-free when you approach the breakfast buffet.

Bookings: +44 (0)20 7201 8070
masonroseprivate.com

# BEAUVALLON PRIVÉ

—

## *Classic Côte d'Azur elegance*

Enjoy all the fun but none of the frenzy of St Tropez from this beautifully restored classic palace a mere eight-minute boat ride away. A Belle Époque dream, available only for exclusive hire, the palace is set in beautifully landscaped gardens overlooking the Bay of St Tropez with its own private beach and an 18-hole golf course just behind it.

It's where the discerning holidaymaker likes to stay – discreet and tranquil, and yet close to the action. Apart from the golf course, guests have access to the Beauvallon tennis club while riding and polo can also be arranged. Next to the hotel beach is the sailing club where both children and adults can learn to sail and windsurf, while adrenalin-seekers can head off in the hotel's own navette to Port Grimaud where they can hire the high excitements of jet-skis and water-skis.

But back at the palace all is calm with unobtrusive, yet admirable service, even for the tiniest guests. To make yummy mummy life easier the palace has its own maître de bébé (baby butler) who will take care of all baby's needs. Adults can just relax and chill out by the pool or the brand-new spa or simply linger on the terrace of Le Salon Sud after a late breakfast or early brunch admiring the grand yachts in the distance.

---

**HOTEL AT A GLANCE**

**ACCOMMODATION**
50 rooms and suites

**DINING**
Dining room

**RECREATION**
Clubhouse, private cinema and
atelier, wine room, spa services,
beach club, private yacht and
Belle Époque ballroom

**TRANSFERS**
Nice Côte d'Azur Airport
1hr 30mins by car

+ 33 (0) 4 94 55 78 88
lebeauvallon.com

SIGNATURE EXPERIENCE

# A TRULY EXCITING LEARNING CURVE

If you've never tried windsurfing and have always longed to,
the hotel will organise a discreet and private lesson next door
at the sailing club… with a sympathetic teacher. Once you've
got the hang of it, it is simply exhilarating.

"

---

Best people-watching in the world married with French style, food, fast cars, and mega yachts. Stay in a confection of classic proportions and elegance overlooking a bay of great beauty.

**Chauffeured speedboat**

The last thing you need in summer is to sit in the most expensive car park in Europe. How about a private speedboat at the end of the garden to take you into St Tropez in 8 minutes? Or charter a **Sportmer Cigarette Boat** directly to Le Club 55 with no parking to deal with? Imagine the faces as you alight with your hair tied back with an Hermès scarf, large Jackie O sunglasses firmly in place.

**Bar with a view**

Yachts, supercars, models, men, a feast for the eyes. All seen from the best dress circle seats at **Hotel Sube** above the **Café de Paris**. Watch the boats and the boobs bobbing up and down from a front row seat that cannot be booked – so come early!

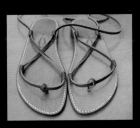

**Original style**

There is only one place in St Tropez to buy the original **'sandales tropéziennes'**. The Rondini family still own and operate the shop that first opened in 1927 and each sandal is still made by hand, piece by piece. Telling the real apart from the others is easy. The original Rondini doesn't have a buckle!

**And on that farm**

If your eyes are hurting from the bling bling of Le Club 55 and Nikki Beach and you need to return to authenticity, go to **Ferme Ladouceur** in the village of Ramatuelle. Imagine dining under the stars instead of next to them. The real scent of olive and pine trees instead of expensive perfume. You'll feel like you've stepped into the pages of 'A Year in Provence'.

# LA COLOMBE D'OR

—

## *Possibly the most famous hotel in the world*

How did a small café become such an institution that it has attracted artists, writers, film-makers, musicians, sculptors and ceramicists from all over the world? Originally it was just a simple café but with such warmth and style that it attracted a growing band of both locals and visitors, until in the later 1940s and early 50s it became a home away from home to some of the most stellar beings on the planet. It had by then become a hotel where, in memory of its humbler beginnings, artists would often pay their bills with something to put on the wall. Where else will you find a Léger, a Matisse, a Bonnard and a Miró, a Braque and a Picasso – all of whom have stayed here, eaten here, played here? And the tradition continues with the latest work of art designed for the swimming pool area by Irish artist Sean Scully.

And while it may be the favourite hostelry of the rich and famous, it is also home from home for families and friends who return year after year, first on their own, then with their children and then their grandchildren. Of course, the welcome is legendary, the food beyond delicious and the location as near perfect as you can get in Provence.

---

**HOTEL AT A GLANCE**

**ACCOMMODATION**
13 rooms and 12 suites

**DINING**
Restaurant with garden terrace
and private room

**RECREATION**
Swimming pool, sauna and
art collection

**TRANSFERS**
Nice Côte d'Azur Airport
20mins by car

SIGNATURE EXPERIENCE

# MOVIE STAR MEMORIES FOR TASTES THAT NEVER CHANGE

Enjoy a Simone Signoret and Yves Montand moment – book the table they sat at each time they visited – against the wall for warmth, comfort, and the best views of the restaurant and the other guests. Start with hors d'oeuvres de la Colombe d'Or and be sure to order the soufflé flambé au Grand Marnier for pudding.

"

---

If they could bottle La Colombe d'Or, it would be the magic elixir that makes a hotel great. Authentic quality that is not about perfection, but genuine hospitality with exquisite taste and style.

**Heart of glass**

Most men like a good set of jugs. And **Biot** has some exquisite ones to go with their gorgeous glasses. You can watch them being made at **La Verrerie de Biot**, then choose your set in any number of colours and ship home. So chic for your dinner party table.

**Art Shangri-La**

Calder on the lawn, mosaics by Chagall and Braque, Miró ceramics. Kandinsky, Léger, Matisse on the walls. Bronzework by Giacometti. It's just astonishing. Pick up an original lithograph by Chagall on the way out. Art heaven, showing now at **Fondation Maeght**.

**Rare drop**

Be careful on the steep steps into the 14th-century wine cellar **La Petite Cave de Saint Paul**. Sample the rare wines from Le Clos Saint Paul, a vineyard of only seven acres, or Île St-Honorat's local monastery. A wonderful inventory of wines from Provence and Alpes-Maritimes.

**La grand dîner**

While you might find the slightly eccentric Madame Ruby and her service team at **La Petite Maison** a little overwhelming, it's worth every minute of the drama. Order the delicious succulent roast chicken with just-right crispy skin, and stuffed with foie gras. Fresh sweet peaches served on ice with crème fraîche, simple and heavenly. Quietly packed with stars, it doesn't need any Michelin ones.

Bookings: +44 (0)20 7201 8070
masonroseprivate.com

# HOTEL DE ROME

—

## *A monument to power, culture…*
## *and sophisticated luxury*

This glorious hotel which is in the former headquarters of
the Dresdner Bank has one of the most desirable addresses in Berlin.
It's on the Bebelplatz next to the State Opera and a short walk to
Museum Island, one of the greatest cultural quarters in Europe,
as well as a mere ten minutes from the Brandenburg Gate. While
retaining all the architectural splendour of the 19th-century building,
with its high ceilings and classical proportions, the designers of
The Rocco Forte Collection, headed by Olga Polizzi, have imbued
the hotel with contemporary chic – all vibrant colours, rich fabrics
and flower decorations the size of small forests.

From its imposing entrance hall a huge lobby lounge studded
with vast velvet-backed sofas, the whole experience is one of splendour.
This is echoed in the sheer size and opulence of the rooms and suites,
some of which have fantastic views of the Platz and beyond to Unter
den Linden, and also the grandeur of the public rooms, including
the restaurant and the roof terrace which is used for al fresco dining
in the summer.

Downstairs in the walk-in former jewellery vault is a gem
of a spa complete with fitness centre and a swimming pool whose
walls are decorated with gold-flecked mosaics.

## HOTEL AT A GLANCE

**ACCOMMODATION**
146 rooms and suites

**DINING**
Restaurant, roof terrace,
bar and lounge

**RECREATION**
Spa, indoor swimming pool, gym
and children's programme

**TRANSFERS**
Tegel International Airport
20mins, Schönefeld International
Airport 40mins; both by car

**SIGNATURE EXPERIENCE**

# THE SOUND OF MUSIC, IN THE GRAND CITY OF MUSIC

Experience the sound of the city – beg, borrow, steal or simply ask the concierge to get you tickets for Sir Simon Rattle and the Berlin Philharmonic. No other orchestra has that oomph!

+ 49 30 4 60 60 90
roccofortecollection.com

You can bank on style at this former Dresdner headquarters now luxury hotel. Splendour with a contemporary twist makes for the perfect residence in a city of intellectual chic.

### Design

In the upcoming district of Friedrichshain you will find **Berlinomat**. If you want Berlin design, it's all here. Icke Berlin, Magaco, Presque Fini, Nix amongst the 150 in stock. Minimalist space and scads of modern chic, so you'll instantly feel cool in this rare atmosphere. Clothing, jewellery, furniture, it's all here.

### Cabaret

Life is a cabaret, so sang Sally Bowles in Bob Fosse's legendary film. Also legendary is **Bar Jeder Vernunft** where you can experience amazing musical extravaganzas from song and dance to comedy. Curtain up in an Art Nouveau mirrored tent that dates to 1912, just stunning. Come to the cabaret, old chum, it's simply wunderbar.

### Coffee culture

If you like a really good coffee go to **Bonanza Coffee Heroes**. Worth the wait for sublime coffee from talented baristas. The perfect blend, creamy and punchy, I can smell its aroma now. It's on the edge of Mauerpark with outside seating for good weather and great on Sunday when the market is in full swing.

### Beer garden

It seems only natural that you should experience a beer garden and **Prater** has been serving up since 1837. Everyone goes, and with every beer imaginable on tap and fabulous food to go with it, then if the sun is shining, go. Families and trendy locals are all side by side at the wooden tables. Bottoms up!

# DES
## ON TRAVEL

"

*For me travel
revolves around
sport and food.*

*Des McDonald, CEO of Caprice Holdings, presides over the finest stable of restaurants and private clubs in the world.*

**TR** *Any truly memorable moments you can share from your travel experiences?*

**DMD** Being flown by helicopter to the Fiordland National Park in the South Island of New Zealand to board a boat for a day of fishing. We caught rock lobsters, hooked up the BBQ and tucked into the freshest asparagus and seafood I have ever eaten in my life. It is one of the most magical places in the world where the weather changes constantly to reveal a spectacular landscape.

**TR** *Any examples of how you have combined your love of sport and food?*

**DMD** On a trip to Biarritz we stopped in Arcachon near Bordeaux and went sand-surfing followed by sucking oysters in a beachside shack while drinking incredible wine. In Biarritz, we surfed and checked into a grand hotel on the seafront where we could hear the incredible sound of the waves crashing onto the beach. We went to the rugby too, so really a perfect week for me.

**TR** *You like to stay in good hotels. Do you always eat in fine restaurants too?*

**DMD** In Marrakech, I was staying at La Mamounia but I couldn't wait to get to the souk where in the evening the food stalls come alive and are magical. Great mussels and mutton sausages. You need to get into the street for phenomenal local experiences.

## FAVOURITES

London, New York, Los Angeles, Miami

Cecconi's, Caprice, Soho House… where everyone knows your name

## Des'

**TAKE ON AUTHENTIC ESCAPISM**

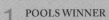

1 **POOLS WINNER**
Spend quality time with your kids in rockpools looking for crabs at the beach, or horse riding… you don't need a kids' club, they just want to be with you

2 **PEDAL POWER**
Get involved and do something for charity, like the London to Paris bike ride for the British Heart Foundation

3 **MR SANDMAN**
Stay in shape – pack your gym gear and hit the beach for an early-morning run

58      Greece
           Crete                 Bookings: +44 (0)20 7201 8070
                                   masonroseprivate.com

# AMIRANDES
## GRECOTEL EXCLUSIVE RESORT

—

*The ultimate five star island resort
on Crete's verdant coast*

Imagine a vast sandy beach being lapped by gentle blue
waves, an Olympic-sized outdoor sea-water pool, an indoor pool and
60 private 'Star' pools with their own villa, cottage or suite attached…
then you have some idea what this luxury water wonderland is like.
Add to that a network of gentle lagoons dissecting the landscaped
gardens, and a school where various watersports can be taught or enjoyed.

On the north coast of Greece's magnificent island of Crete –
with its rugged mountains, dramatic gorges, wild hinterland and huge
caves (including the one where Zeus was born) – you begin to sense
why this is called the isle of the gods. Add to that the Minoan palaces
and archaeological wonders of Knossos and you will understand that
in order to experience all of these riches you may need to extend your
holiday… more… and more. Then there are all the joys of the resort
to experience from its seven restaurants, including a faux-boho
beachside restaurant, its spa and wellbeing centre, tennis courts,
fitness area and a five star children's club.

Bookings: +44 (0)20 7201 8070
masonroseprivate.com

## HOTEL AT A GLANCE

**ACCOMMODATION**
212 rooms, suites, bungalows
and villas

**DINING**
7 restaurants and bar

**RECREATION**
Spa, sandy beaches, indoor and
outdoor pools, children's club, nearby
golf and bespoke experiences

**TRANSFERS**
Heraklion Airport 20mins by car

SIGNATURE EXPERIENCE

# MAKING YOUR STAY EVEN MORE MEMORABLE – GET MOVING!

The concierge will organise and help you (you might even want
a guide) to take a walk along the Samarian Gorge. It is not for the
faint-hearted and takes between four to seven hours to complete,
but the views and the experience are unforgettable.

+ 30 28970 41103
amirandes.com

*Tanya's travel secrets...*

"

—

A Cretan palace to sleep in. Ancient history alongside modern design. And a genuine warm hospitality that truly says 'welcome'. You'll feel like a god, which seems only natural as made Crete their home.

**Oil slick**

If you need help unwinding on arrival, book into the spa for the **Sirodhara** treatment. Half an hour of soothing massage followed by the Kerala treatment of a steady stream of medicated oil on the forehead. You will melt and sleep like a baby. Languid and lavish.

**Palatial**

Make plans to visit **Kuossos** the famous Minoan palace. It is the most stunning archaeological site with its ruins beautifully preserved and surrounded by oak, cypress and olive trees. Go early morning or very late in the day (the site closes at 7.30pm) for the best light. Stop for a refreshing drink in one of the tavernas just outside the gates. It's an historic experience.

**Organic**

Step back in time to the **Agreco Farm** which has revived organic farming alongside hospitality. This replica of a 17th-century lodge features an olive press, flour mill, village square and a zoo! Enjoy food on the terrace in the shade of the pergola overlooking the sea. Featured in Vanity Fair as Best Organic restaurant.

**Grape vine**

You heard it here – go to the **Boutari Winery** outside Heraklion which is beautifully located to combine with your visit to Knossos. It's state-of-the-art: you can have a tour and then sample the red varieties of Kotsifali and Mantilari, as well as Malvasia Aromatica and Moschato Spinas. Drop in for a drop, and book a driver.

Bookings: +44 (0)20 7201 8070
masonroseprivate.com

# VILLA SAN MICHELE

—

## *High point for high culture*

On a hill in Fiesole, this exclusive resort has mouth-watering views over the city of Florence and the Arno Valley – sit in the shade of the spacious loggia, prosecco in hand, and gaze at one of Italy's most beautiful cities. The great thing about a stay here is that you are sufficiently removed from the heat and visitors of the season and yet can be in the midst of it in less than 20 minutes.

For the rest of your stay enjoy the rooms, views and space of this former monastery turned Renaissance villa turned super-luxury hotel, with its frescos, including one of the Last Supper, a hidden chapel turned honeymoon suite in the gardens and glorious food. Should you need a reminder of how great the food is, spend a morning at the hotel's cookery school learning the ease of pasta-making and the joys of Florentine tastes. You get to eat it too!

In between times you have the entire Uffizi and its treasures waiting for you, the glamour of the designer shops and the enticing jewellery stores of the Ponte Vecchio, while the concierge can organise tours and visits to the wineries of Chianti, local olive oil producers or the magical towns of Siena and San Gimignano.

Bookings: +44 (0)20 7201 8070
masonroseprivate.com

## HOTEL AT A GLANCE

**ACCOMMODATION**
46 rooms and suites

**DINING**
2 restaurants and 3 bars

**RECREATION**
Pool, gym, cookery school,
mountain bikes, nearby golf,
tennis, and horse riding

**TRANSFERS**
Florence Airport 20mins by car

**SIGNATURE EXPERIENCE**

# IF YOU'VE GOT IT, FLAUNT IT

Go in early summer to wonder at the wisteria which covers one
entire wall of the hotel – it looks as if it's wearing a lace dress.
Or ask the concierge to plead for you to visit the Vasari Corridor
which runs between the Uffizi and the Pitti Palace. It's like a
Renaissance skywalk filled with extraordinary views and pictures
and can only be seen by special arrangement.

*Tanya's travel secrets...*

66

---

Florence immediately conjures up a romantic voyage of dreams. It lives up to all of its cliché, dazzling even the most jaded traveller with its history, style and elegance. The Medicis and Michelangelo, simply marvellous.

**NBF**

Spend the day on the arm of **Heather from NewTours,** who is a veritable encyclopedia. Fast track to Michelangelo's David. Whizz through the Uffizi. See the interior design of the Medicis' private library and be led to the most buttery leather gloves you can imagine. Your 'nuova migliore amica'.

**Food on stage**

Lively, crazy, madness. A buffet of pastas, grilled meats and salads. Keep eating but stake your place early (7.30pm). At **Teatro del Sale** chairs turn to the stage at 9.30pm for tonight's surprise musical or theatrical performance. It's an unexpected buzz of local life.

**Belle donne**

Go and visit the wonderful **Loretta Caponi** and her daughter Lucia for the most exquisite linens. Pyjamas, nightgowns, silk, cashmere, cotton… it's a giant pillow of couture elegance and refinement. The baby gift items are too gorgeous for words. Via delle Belle Donne – how appropriate!

**Costume clout**

The world of film and television has discovered the fabulous costume jewellery of **Angela Caputi**. Buy a statement piece that will be a knockout at your next cocktail party. It's a fantasy of sophistication and elegance you don't have to mortgage the house to buy. Accessorise uniquely.

# GRAND HOTEL A VILLA FELTRINELLI

—

*Where history and luxury*
*meet style and serenity*

BEST FOR

LUXURY

★ ★ ★ ★ ★

Possibly the most opulent ever hôtel du lac… this seriously grand lake side villa was built at the end of the 19th century for the exceptionally rich Feltrinelli family. No expense was spared in either its construction, decoration or upkeep. A grand pink palace set amid eight acres of manicured lawns, landscaped gardens, lemon terraces and olive groves, all leading down to the lake. So desirable was it that Mussolini used it as his war-time hideout.

The hotel was sold and refurbished at a cost of millions almost twenty years ago. It was as much a labour of love as an awesome undertaking, maintaining all its grandeur and luxury but with major modern additions such as vast bathrooms with heated marble floors. The frescos and furniture were restored, the gardens re-planted and the glorious La Contessa, the largest privately owned yacht on the lake, was introduced. The attention to detail throughout the hotel is extraordinary as is the reverence for historical accuracy… and yet it is as comfortable as it is opulent… a place for truly spoilt sybarites.

68     Italy
        Lake Garda        Bookings: +44 (0)20 7201 8070
                          masonroseprivate.com

**HOTEL AT A GLANCE**

**ACCOMMODATION**
21 rooms and suites

**DINING**
2 restaurants and bar

**RECREATION**
Outdoor pool, croquet, gardens, boat trips on the lake and personal guided tours

**TRANSFERS**
Verona Airport 1hr 15mins and Milan airports 2 to 3hrs by car

SIGNATURE EXPERIENCE

# DRINK IN THE BEAUTY OF THE LANDSCAPE AND ITS SURROUNDINGS

Gargnano, the small town which is home to this grand villa… should not be ignored. Pretty and gentle with cobbled streets and lemon-painted houses, it is worth a gentle morning's stroll. Sit at a cafe and admire the mountains around you and the views of the lake in the distance. D H Lawrence described the area as one of the most beautiful anywhere – we think you may agree.

+ 39 0365 798 000
villafeltrinelli.com

66
—

Quite simply one of the best hotels in the world. A total fairytale with hotel service that you only dream about. Homemade pasta, herb garden, gelato by the pool, pure perfection.

**Stellar cellar**

The hotel has the most incredible **wine cellar**. Splash out and take it privately for a wine-tasting and candlelit dinner for two. If you have friends with you it's perfect for a small dinner party. A thousand bottles of premium wine surround you while you dine on **Stefano Baiocco's Michelin star food**.

**La Contessa**

**La Contessa** is the hotel's utterly beautiful private salon boat and is at your disposal. You're on Lake Garda, so the best way to see your location is from the water. Timing is important in the Lakes, so check with the concierge for weather conditions to maximise the experience and romance. Stop at **Locanda San Vigilio** for lunch under the trees, it's stunning.

**Cocktail kiss**

Settle in at the bar and order a **Disaronno Kiss cocktail**. A heady concoction of Disaronno and pomegranate juice topped with prosecco. Six of these later and you may be asked not to entertain the guests with your version of O Sole Mio.

**Verona**

A good 45-minute drive away, but worth the effort for some **Romeo and Juliet** romance. Make sure you touch the bronze statue of Juliet for good fortune. She is in the courtyard of the house that was supposedly owned by the Capulets. And of course attending the **Opera** in Verona is a must on life's to do list. Book a driver.

# HOTEL DE RUSSIE

—

## *Eternal elegance in the city of la dolce vita*

Rome to most of us conjures up visions of fountains, cathedrals, great piazzas, ancient monuments, classical ruins, galleries and glitz. Well, this is the place to stay while you explore all of them. An amazing central location gives you almost immediate access to the Spanish Steps and the Piazza del Popolo with a handful of basilicas within a stone's throw and all the designer emporia of the Via Condotti at your feet.

And yet… The Rocco Forte Collection's Hotel de Russie is one of the most tranquil spots in the entire city because of its lushly planted terraced gardens, which provide the ideal retreat to come to refresh and repair by sipping a prosecco after a hard day's sightseeing. Quiet and cool and gloriously elegant, both the gardens and the rooms are ideal for the stressed-out business traveller, for lovers on a romantic break and for families exploring the riches of Rome together. Most of the rooms and suites have enchanting views over the Secret Garden and the famous Rome rooftops.

And should you wonder at its name, well it is a reminder of how, in a previous incarnation, it was the favoured place of the Imperial family and the greats of Russian art and ballet – hence there is still the Nijinsky suite and Stravinskij Bar where the Martinis are legendary.

## HOTEL AT A GLANCE

**ACCOMMODATION**
122 rooms and suites

**DINING**
Restaurant and bar

**RECREATION**
Garden, wellness zone, gym,
and children's programme

**TRANSFERS**
Rome Fiumicino Airport
40mins by car

SIGNATURE EXPERIENCE

# WATCH LATTER-DAY GLADIATORS AT THE CITY'S GREAT FOOTBALL STADIUM

Become a Roman for the evening and head off to Stadio Olimpico to watch a footie match – Lazio if you can. It will change your views about football and its supporters for good – Highbury will never be the same. Remember Nancy?

*Tanya's travel secrets...*

"

Between the Spanish Steps and the Piazza del Popolo, only moments from Via Condotti...could it get any better? Indeed, with terraced garden and plush pastel parlours it's truly bellissimo.

**Gladiator**

Do you fancy wielding a sword and shield? Enrol now at the **Scuola Gladiatori**. It's a terrific workout, and your kids will love it too. No one gets wounded, except for some egos. Drop husband and children off while you wield your handbag and credit cards on Via Condotti.

**Behind the scenes**

By special arrangement you can diviate from the tourist track for a specially planned visit to the private palazzos of some of Rome's noble families. Imagine the art in these private collections. The concierge can even get you a private visit to the **Sistine Chapel**. No crowd scenes, exclusive access!

**Designer discount**

If you want lashings of designer swag, but want to avoid plastic meltdown, head to the **Castel Romano Designer Outlet** just 25km from Rome. Dolce & Gabbana, Valentino, Salvatore Ferragamo, La Perla, Zegna Outlet, Etro, CK Jeans at permanently discounted prices. It has the look and feel of imperial Rome with views of the Tyrrhenian Sea. It's retail heaven.

**Caffè and Coliseum**

In the BARmuda triangle of Rome you will find **Caffè della Pace,** populated by monied locals and visiting celebs. With your Campari and orange, settle back in your wicker chair beneath the ivy for absolutely first-class people-watching. This establishment is as much a fixture of Rome as the Coliseum, and like the eternal city in which it is located, eternally trendy.

# FORTE VILLAGE RESORT

—

*A dazzling wonderland fringed by powder-soft sand and a translucent emerald sea*

BEST FOR

FAMILIES

★★★★★

Award after award has been heaped on Forte Village; rightly so as it is the ultimate family destination in the Mediterranean.

Under a shady canopy of pine and palm trees, this sprawling village-style resort is set in acres of luxuriant banana trees, flamingo ponds and colourful sub-tropical gardens. Nestled amidst this gorgeousness are eight superlative hotels; from secluded beachfront bungalows to fabulous family-friendly accommodation, you are definitely spoilt for choice. You can have lunch and dinner in a different restaurant every day of the week if you so desire. Like a journey around the world the cuisine is infinite in its flavours, from traditional Sardinian to Japanese, Indian or Brazilian; there are simple beachfront eateries, pizza and pasta joints, spectacular buffets and extraordinary fine dining. For nocturnal action head to the Piazza lined with fashionable boutiques or sip a Mojito at the beachside Blue Moon Jazz Bar.

Days are filled with endless possibilities; a luxury play zone with go-kart track and ten-pin bowling, tennis coaching by stars, innumerable pools and a raft of watersports. The swanky Thalassotherapy spa deserves a special mention. Tucked away in a quiet corner, it is an enclave of serious pampering and therapeutic relaxation.

Family holidays will never be the same again; peace and luxury for parents whilst children have a really, really good time.

## HOTEL AT A GLANCE

**ACCOMMODATION**
8 hotels with 766 rooms, suites
and bungalows

**DINING**
21 restaurants and 11 bars

**RECREATION**
Spa, watersports, diving, swimming
pools, gym, tennis courts, bikes,
football academy, go-karting, kids'
clubs, nightclub, bowling and golf

**TRANSFERS**
Cagliari Elmas airport 35mins
by car, 15mins by helicopter

**SIGNATURE EXPERIENCE**

# IMPECCABLE FOOTIE CREDENTIALS

If you have a budding Beckham make sure you sign up for the
Football Academy run by the coaches of Chelsea FC. Every
summer, week-long courses are like a mini Championship League;
training is serious and daily matches competitive. You will lose
them for hours but they come home happy and the graduate
goody bag is pretty cool too!

+ 39 070 92171
fortevillageresort.com

From the sublime to the ubiquitous, Sardinia is see and be seen, or not seen at all. Soft sand, crystal water, it's heaven on earth. It's perfection for families. It's a vacation no brainer.

**Body doctor**

Checking into Forte Village for two weeks and want to go home a goddess? Commit to sessions with the **Body Doctor – David Marshall**. He promises you'll drop two dress sizes in six weeks. Start now and go home glowing from workouts, therapy, sunshine and healthy food. Who needs boot camp?

**Healing therapy**

The most renowned Italian families know good therapy when they feel it. Which is why they fly out to Forte Village Sardinia just to see **Guido,** healer and masseur extraordinaire. Book two hours of treatment every morning and arrive at lunch on a cloud of serene wellbeing.

**The best table**

**Guiseppe** is the man to know at the Cavalieri and Beachcomber restaurants. For a quarter of a century Guiseppe has been making sure yours is the right table. He knows the wine you like, and his personal welcome and care remind us what real hospitality is all about.

**Wine**

Not familiar with Sardinian wines, and want to try something local? You can't go wrong with a crisp refreshing white from the **Arigolas** estate to complement that lobster. Located in the north of Sardinia, you will also love the complex reds they produce. The sommelier is bound to compliment you on your choice.

> *Take the M-LAB
> Travel Kit wherever
> you go and arrive fresh!*

*As head of beauty and fashion at Harrods, Marigay McKee has her finger on the pulse of what's new and hot globally.*

**TR** *What are your favourite hotels?*

**MMK** In Paris the Vendôme which is very central to the St Honoré stores and my appointments in the 8th. It's near my favourite vintage stores, opposite Wolford for emergency hosiery, and Bucellati my girlfriend's jewellery store. The Carlyle in New York, is a great jazz haunt and close to Central Park. The Beverly Hills Hotel in LA is paradise, with music underwater in the pool, fluffy-towelled loungers, and each guest-room an oasis. It's kitsch and cool, and makes me feel glamorous.

**TR** *Where is food heaven?*

**MMK** Contravapore is my favourite in Milan. Cristina the owner is fabulous, the steak is heavenly as are the fresh truffles. In New York, I love the Waverley Inn on Bank Street and West 4th – it's super and all the tables are full of known faces. The Bellinis are great and the mac and cheese is superb. In LA The Ivy for lunch has the best mixed fish platters. Cecconi's for dinner – Jason is a great maître d' and it's celebsville. Ago is a true favourite for pizza or pasta.

**TR** *What do you love and hate about travelling?*

**MMK** Love the chance to catch up with vendors with whom we have long-standing relationships, and the chance to spend time one-on-one with my buyers. I hate being away from my children whom I miss terribly while I am on the road. The result is an astronomical phone bill!

**TR** *A few of your favourite places?*

**MMK** My house in Spain is the place for downtime and family. La Mamounia is Arabian Night's glamour every day. Peninsula Hong Kong for its green Rolls Royces and the views which make me feel like a Bond girl every time.

**BEFORE I GO**
I buy my weekly sessions at Urban Retreat. It's all primping and preening and Clarins body-shaping supplements

## Marigay's

**FOUR DESERT ISLAND STAPLES**

1 **PRETTY FEET**
My Essie polished toes look sensational in a pair of Zanotti flats for summer chic. They are jewels for the feet and SO comfy!

2 **SWIMWEAR**
A Pucci bikini with a kaftan or coverup to match is essential

3 **SHADES**
A large cool pair of Rayban classic aviators that never date

4 **MIND, BODY & SOUL**
Ginger by Origins, my favourite energiser scent, and the M-LAB travel kit for cleansing, toning and moisturising on the go

# VERDURA GOLF & SPA RESORT

—

## *The luxurious side of sport, spa, sea and sun in Sicily*

One of the newest and most exciting resorts in Europe, Verdura is the latest addition to The Rocco Forte Collection. Here on the southern coast of Sicily on a vast estate a pleasure playground for all ages has grown out of the island's red soil. Sicily is a place of treasures – all you have to do is look for them. There are amazing beaches, wild interiors, charming villages, historic towns such as Sciacca, the nearest one to Verdura and once a trading post, and beautiful archaeological finds such as the Temple of Concordia just a short drive away in Agrigento.

But then it is also an island full of surprises – delicious wines and olive oil; the most active volcano in all of Europe, Mount Etna; and now Verdura – a resort that seduces both grown-ups and children. With its two 18-hole championship golf courses and small 9-hole version, a host of tennis courts complete with pro's, almost two kilometres of private coastline caressing the blue Mediterranean, a vast infinity edged swimming pool, running trails through magical lemon and olive groves, a state-of-the art fitness centre and the best spa on the island. The spa boasts with its four open-air Thalassotherapy pools, steam, sauna and a comprehensive list of treatments, many of which use local ingredients, as well as a selection of programmes for weight loss, detox and fitness. And then there is the children's club with its own pool and full programme of events – it's what we all need for a heavenly holiday.

## HOTEL AT A GLANCE

**ACCOMMODATION**
203 rooms and suites

**DINING**
8 restaurants and bars

**RECREATION**
Golf, spa, kids' club, teens club,
watersports, tennis, swimming
pools, bikes, nearby riding and
cycling trails

**TRANSFERS**
Palermo and Trapani Airports
1hr 30mins by car, Cantania
Airport 3hrs by car

+ 39 0925 998 180
roccofortecollection.com

SIGNATURE EXPERIENCE

# GOOD ENOUGH TO EAT

Olive oil, lemons and blood oranges – no, not the resort's salad dressing but the local olive oil blended with essence of lemon and orange, used in the spa for the signature treatment. Even the smell makes you feel great.

66

——

Rocco's forte is to get it right. With limestone, terracotta and wood, it is design delight. Verdura's warmth embraces parents and children alike in a concoction of sun, sea, sand, spa, golf and impeccable service.

**Temples**

Go to Agrigento's UNESCO World Heritage site, better known as the Valley of the Temples. Organise a driver so you don't get lost and head for the **Temple of Concordia**, it's a real stunner. The secret is to go in the evening when you can experience the grandeur of this 2400-year-old building in the glow of a setting sun and out of the heat.

**Chardonnay**

Not a footballer's wife, but what you should order from **Planeta Winery**. Alessio, Francesca and Santi Planeta have attracted worldwide attention in wine circles with their fine Segreta Bianco, Alastro, and Cometa. Visit their 16th-century country house for wine tastings amid the vineyards and ancient olive grove. Only established in 1995, but with the perfect climate they are producing a classic drop.

**Best mates**

At an altitude of 870m you will find the beautiful little village of **Caltabellotta**. The fresh air in mid-summer is a refreshing respite that complements the incredible view. Drop into **M.A.T.E.S.** for the most delicious regional Sicilian cuisine made from the freshest local ingredients. It's a museum dedicated to food and wine traditions too! Gastronomic.

**Local charm**

A visit to **Sciacca** is a must to stroll the rambling streets of its ancient town centre. You'll find artisans workshops, antiques, and lovely ceramics. Go in the late afternoon, and then stop by **Bar Barbagianni** for a Campari and orange and some appetisers. Located near the Palazzo Signorile, you'll immediately recognise there is an elegant local crowd populating this stylish wine bar.

# GRAND HOTEL TIMEO

—

## *High times and high style, high on a Sicilian hill*

The newest acquisition in the Orient Express stable. They have taken an existing iconic property, and given it their own inimitable twist of style and service. Being the first luxury hotel built on Sicily it has the best location, with great views of the Mediterranean, Mount Etna bubbling away and one of the most remarkable ancient monuments on the island – the Greek Theatre. Little wonder that such a dramatic setting has, over the years, enticed an über-dramatic clientele with all the major Italian screen stars rubbing shoulders with those from Hollywood. Indeed the visitors' book looks like a dream Oscar party.

And while the rooms are spacious and deeply comfortable, and most have terraces or balconies, for guests looking for extra peace and quiet the Villa Flora, a chic country-house-style retreat is available for exclusive use, just 50 metres from the main building. Guests there can enjoy all the facilities of the hotel too, with its fine dining focusing on Sicilian and Mediterranean specialities and of course its terraced pool which is surrounded by lavishly planted gardens. Wherever you are within the hotel or its environs the views are mouth-watering, while the indoor bar gives the impression of being in an enchanting 19th-century winter garden.

Guests can also use the beach of a sister property a short drive away and Timeo offers a free shuttle bus service to and fro… hence giving you the best of both worlds.

## HOTEL AT A GLANCE

**ACCOMMODATION**
70 rooms and suites

**DINING**
Restaurant, bar with terrace,
pool bar

**RECREATION**
Wellness centre, swimming pool,
private beach and fitness centre

**TRANSFERS**
Catania Fontanarossa
International Airport 40mins
by car

+ 39 0942 627 0200
grandhoteltimeo.com

SIGNATURE EXPERIENCE

# PLAYING WITH FIRE – OR SIMPLY ENJOY ALL THE HEAT AND DUST

Whether you hike, drive, take a taxi or a broomstick – see Etna
from the top. Don't wear white though.

*Tanya's travel secrets...*

"

—

# Luc Besson's cult film 'Le Grand Bleu' begins your romance with Taormina. The rugged landscape drops into the most incredible azure sea under a dazzling sun.

**To the mattresses**

I do prefer a chocolate at turndown to a horse's head. But you cannot afford to miss the **Godfather tour**. You'll be whisked to the medieval village of Castelmola with a view of Etna. Visit the church of St Lucy where Apollonia and Michael wed. Watch the movie again before you go.

**Passeggiata**

Better known as an after-dinner constitutional stroll. And it is mandatory that while wandering you partake of a **Granita** in lush flavours like almond or basil. The lemon Granita is fresh palate-cleansing zing. **Bam Bar** in Taormina purports to serve the best Granita in town.

**Flipper**

Put one on each foot and hop into the Timeo's own boat for a cruise down the coast. **Isola Bella**, also known as the Pearl of the Ionian Sea, is an enchanting little jewel. The sea is teeming with fish which make for a technicolour view through your goggles. The water visibility is astonishing. Grotta Azzurra's blue water is breathtaking. Dive in.

**Roots**

Imagine the town way up in the mountains where Domenico Dolce of Dolce & Gabbana was born. **Polizzi Generosa** is also home to the family of film director Martin Scorsese. It's away from the glamour of Taormina, but bursting with character, and cooled by fresh Madonie mountain air. An authentic Sicilian experience in a village of great charm and ambience. Take your camera.

Bookings: +44 (0)20 7201 8070
masonroseprivate.com

# CASTEL MONASTERO

—

## *An exquisite Tuscan experience to delight the most experienced traveller*

The beautiful Ombrone Valley with its rolling hills, rich vineyards, chestnut forests and long rows of cypresses is home to Castel Monastero. Not so much a hotel but an entire village, this refined rural retreat is so picturesque you can imagine Rapunzel letting her hair down. Masterful restoration has transformed this 11th-century "borgo" into an exclusive idyll of charming Italian hospitality and luxurious sophistication.

Guestrooms are scattered throughout the village; some overlook the castle's courtyard whilst stand-alone cottages are more secluded. In the garden there is a spectacular two-storey villa with its own private chef and butler. These are grown-up romantic havens designed true to their Tuscan roots, with painted old wooden beams, comfortable leather sofas, Rubelli silk curtains, terracotta floors and shutters to fling open. Adding to the ambience of relaxation is the sleek spa. With its specialist detoxifying and rebalancing programmes by world-renowned Dr Mosaraf Ali, pioneering saline pool, charming tea room and delicious spa cuisine this is a place to rediscover your wellbeing. If you just wanted to chill at one of the terraced infinity pools you will be rewarded with the most sublime views.

The star attraction has to be the authentic and delectable dining; Gordon Ramsay has the gourmet spot set-up in the village square whilst the castle's ancient wine cellar hosts a more intimate restaurant.

Bookings: +44 (0)20 7201 8070
masonroseprivate.com

## HOTEL AT A GLANCE

**ACCOMMODATION**
75 rooms and suites and one villa

**DINING**
2 restaurants and bar

**RECREATION**
Spa and wellness centre, cookery
school, library, 3 swimming pools,
fitness facility and tennis

**TRANSFERS**
Florence Airport 55mins by car

**SIGNATURE EXPERIENCE**

# KICK YOUR COOKING
# SKILLS UP A NOTCH

Gordon Ramsay and the super-talented Head Chef from Castel
Monastero have created classes in the art of Tuscan cuisine. Aspiring
cooks can learn the secrets from the masters; from gnocchi di Baccala
to delicious gelato, the flavours and ingredients of the region are so
inspiring you can be sure your next dinner party will be a triumph.

+ 39 0577 570001
castelmonastero.com

*Tanya's travel secrets...*

"

——

'A Room with a View' meets 'Under the Tuscan Sun'. With gourmet food, Dr Ali, spa, and warm attentive staff, it could not be more fabulous. A truly tantalising Tuscan Dream.

**Dr Ali**

You may have read about **Dr Ali** and his work with HRH The Prince of Wales. A renowned therapist who has performed what some deem to be close to miracle cures. Dr Ali's detox, slimming and revitalising programmes are available at Castel Monastero. A divine place to heal.

**Giddy up**

Plan your visit well in advance to experience the **Palio di Siena**. On July 2 in honour of the Madonna di Provenzano and on August 16 in honour of the Assumption of Mary. It is essential that you are ensconced above the crowd in a private viewing room for this crazy horse race. It's a once-in-a-lifetime experience and thrilling to watch.

**Start wining**

Tuscany is synonymous with great wine, and you are right in the heart of its rich bounty. Visits can be arranged to **Chianti, Brunello di Montalcino** and **Vernaccia di San Gimignano**. The entire area is about 90% proof. The hotel will arrange a driver so you can savour the wine.

**Retail therapy**

Take a visit to **The Mall**... I know it sounds hideous...but wait until you see the treasure trove of bargains. The Mall is a gallery of select, top luxury brands and quality merchandise including Armani Jeans, Balenciaga, Bottega Veneta, Ermenegildo Zegna, Fendi, Giorgio Armani, Gucci, I Pinco Pallino, La Perla, Loro Piana, Marni, Pucci, Salvatore Ferragamo, Sergio Rossi... outlet heaven. Wear flats and big sunglasses.

Bookings: +44 (0)20 7201 8070
masonroseprivate.com

# HOTEL CIPRIANI

*A visual feast in the lap
of luxury*

BEST FOR

ROMANCE

★ ★ ★ ★ ★

Defined by its extraordinary location which is in the heart of
a city… and yet quite separate from it. The Cipriani is directly across
from St Mark's Square with its palaces, campanile, cathedral and
thousands of visitors… and yet there is a water's breadth between
them. You can look, but you cannot touch until you take your liveried
launch across. It is a hotel that offers the best of both worlds –
being there, and not being there. How wonderful it is after a day's
sightseeing, shopping, savouring delicacies and sipping Bellinis to
retire from the madding crowd and return to the cool elegant environs
of the Cip, as it is known to aficionados.

Here, bathed in the golden light of sunset, or escaping from
the heat of the day, guests can relax by the pool or in the Casanova
Spa before preparing for lunch or dinner at any of the hotel's three
restaurants. Small potentates and princesses repair to the Smile Club
@the Cip where they will be amused while their parents relax. Those
looking for a little extra seclusion can head through the gardens to the
suites of the Palazzo Vendramin where butlers await to cater for their
every whim. If super-luxury has a name it is Cipriani.

Bookings: +44 (0)20 7201 8070
masonroseprivate.com

---

**HOTEL AT A GLANCE**

**ACCOMMODATION**
79 rooms and suites; 16 rooms and
suites at Palazzo Vendramin

**DINING**
3 restaurants and bars

**RECREATION**
Wellness centre and kids' club

**TRANSFERS**
Venice Marco Polo International
Airport 30mins by water taxi

---

SIGNATURE EXPERIENCE

# DRAMA, MYSTERY, ROMANCE

The best way to see Venice is from the water so take your own
private cruise through the canals. Do it in the early morning as
Venice wakes and ask the concierge to organise the hotel's boat
for you. Return to the smell of great coffee and breakfast on
the terrace.

+ 39 041 520 7744
hotelcipriani.com

"

———

# Make a little romance and kiss under the Bridge of Sighs at sunset. Piazza San Marco, the swish of pigeons taking flight, a gondolier serenading lovers glides gently by… just heaven.

**Legendary**

Once in your lifetime you must experience Claudio Ponzio serving you a Bellini in **Harry's Bar** – he's been pouring them for over 30 years. Book a corner table downstairs as did Ernest Hemingway, who set scenes in this very bar in his books 'Across the River' and 'Into the Trees'. Make your own romantic scene and continue the legend.

**Sir Lunchalot**

On the island of Torcello a humble wine and oil shop became what is now **Locanda Cipriani**. Go by private speedboat for lunch on the terrace. The place is run by Bonifacio Brass, nephew of Harry Cipriani. Perfect dining and hospitality definitely runs in the family. Savour Carla's version of John Dory or the herb risotto, and gaze at the 11th-century Cathedral. Unforgettable.

**True grit**

After dinner wander down to the **Hotel Gritti Palace** and get a grip on some grappa. A 16th-century palazzo with the most enchanting view overlooking the Grand Canal. The romance of it all will melt your heart as you sit where royalty and other illustrious visitors have sat and been mesmerised too.

**Veg out**

If you love vegetarian food you'll cross the world to dine at **Osteria La Zucca**. The potato cake is spud heaven. Or order the pumpkin flan, which is so utterly delicious it leaves pumpkin pie in its gondola wake. Save some room for the dark seduction of their chocolate mousse or the zing of the mint semi-freddo.

# HÔTEL
# DE PARIS

—

## *Nothing becomes a legend like Monte-Carlo*

An iconic hotel in an iconic principality right on Casino Square and decked out with a finery and opulence that is synonymous with the glamour and glitz of this Belle Époque palace, with its panoramic views over the Mediterranean.

Arrive by limo, helicopter or yacht and your welcome will be as warm as it is impressive. On arrival each guest is issued with a Carte d'Or which gives access to some of the most privileged spots in Monte-Carlo – the Casino, a private beach and of course the legendary Thermes Marins complex with its healthcare and wellness programmes, Hammam, sauna and fully equipped fitness centre, as well as the Monte-Carlo Country Club with its 23 tennis courts and golf club with heavily discounted green fees. This is the place to live like a king, play like a prince and be pampered like a princess.

It is a veritable temple of all that is luxe with great marble halls, silken sofas, vast chandeliers, frescoed walls and gold-leaf ceilings. The rooms are plump and luscious, so much so that aficionados return year after year for more spoiling. Dining is beyond delicious with four restaurants to choose from, including Alain Ducasse's 3 Michelin star restaurant, Le Louis XV, and the hotel bar is rated one of the best in the world year after year. Witness and enjoy what a really grand hotel is like – the Hôtel de Paris is the place to be.

---

## HOTEL AT A GLANCE

**ACCOMMODATION**
182 rooms and suites

**DINING**
3 restaurants and 1 bar

**RECREATION**
Healthcare and wellness
programmes and spa, fitness
area, indoor and outdoor pools,
sea sports, nearby tennis, golf
and casinos

**TRANSFERS**
Nice Côte d'Azur Airport 30mins
by car; by helicopter 7mins

+ 377 9806 3000
hoteldeparismontecarlo.com

SIGNATURE EXPERIENCE

# SPLASHING, BATHING, HOSING, FLOATING, PULSATING

For all the joys of water, head for the splendid Les Thermes Marins, one of the best Thalassotherapy spas on the planet where the minerals and salts of sea water, weeds and muds are harnessed to beautify you and your body.

"

Shaken and stirred in a destination that just oozes glamour. Just say you're in Monte-Carlo and suddenly you are on a movie set that could not be more stunning. Guaranteed to sparkle and shine.

**Bond... James Bond**

If your man wants to walk with authority and style into Alain Ducasse's Le Louis XV or into the Casino, he needs to look the part. Before you leave for Monaco go to **Society Club** in the Metropole, and get your man his **Tom Ford** spy kit and daytime linen. This is a destination where the jacket and tie are de rigueur and dressing up for men and women is a must.

**Boogie nights**

There is only one place in Monte-Carlo that has always been the place to strut your stuff on the dance floor and people-watch. **Jimmy'z** has been packing them in for 30 years and never fails to please. Have the concierge organise your booking in advance so you can glide in with recognition. Don't sit near the dance floor.

**Air hel air**

There are only two ways to arrive in Monte-Carlo, by helicopter or on a mega yacht. So unless you are cruising into town with Abramovich's ship AKA yacht… you must travel by helicopter. **Heli Air Monaco** is the way to get from Nice Airport in about ten minutes. You'll feel glamorous as soon as you are zooming down the coast above the ocean.

**Le sportif**

Can you only manage so much novel-reading by the pool and spa treatment before you get twitchy? Head on over to the **Monte-Carlo Beach Club** and try out some Sea Scooter outings, wakeboarding, parachuting, flyfishing… and more. People don't need the gym here: they get all the exercise they need walking with all their gold on.

66
—

*Always pack in advance, not at six in the morning to avoid stress and the wrong wardrobe.*

*David Collins is the world-renowned architect whose bars, restaurants and hotels are the ultimate in cutting-edge chic and elegance.*

**TR** *Do you manage to get away from it all when travelling?*

**DC** The days of getting away from it all have passed. Not many of us really want to get away from it all. We are quite addicted to being in touch. I always carry my mobile phone with me. You know that when you come back from holiday you will have to catch up. So the question really is – do you switch on when you are on vacation?

**TR** *Are you a good planner?*

**DC** I have discovered that as I get older I leave less and less to chance. I tend to research where I am going to, and find out a little more about where I am going. Holidays are precious. I research hotels in advance. I wouldn't buy something without trying it on. However I do not obsessively read reviews and I am rarely influenced by them. I trust Mason Rose, Wallpaper and word-of-mouth.

**TR** *Do you return to the same destinations and hotels?*

**DC** I go every year to the Belvedere in Mykonos. I laugh about how expensive it is but the way they look after me it's worth it. I've rented the same house in Ibiza at the end of May or early June each year, and the reason I love it is that it is low-maintenance, and exactly where I want to be ten minutes from town. Also the Ellerman House in South Africa – it's absolutely what I want.

**TR** *Any restaurant recommendations?*

**DC** Eat Café on Madison Avenue in New York for the delicious toasted raison bread. I love the Wolseley. Blakes in London, although it needs something done to it, don't we all! Café de Flore in Paris.

# David's

**DESIGNS ON TRAVEL**

Arrive at
Gare du Nord by
Eurostar and avoid the
horrendous taxi queue by
calling G7 taxis:
**+33 14 739 4739**
They'll pick you up at Café de
la Paix across the road –
five minutes later you
are en route

**1 NICE LUGGAGE**
Pack neatly, label clearly, edit everything down to two colours so you can mix and match

**2 TECHNO GEEK**
iPad for watching the movies I want to see rather than the airline choice, and the TV shows I love

**3 BOARD GAMES**
Keep yourself entertained with Travel Scrabble and a pack of cards – easy and portable entertainment that fits perfectly into your luggage

$G_2$ $O_1$

# HOTEL ASTORIA

—

## *Imperial grandeur in an historic setting*

     Monumental is a word that could help describe this hotel and its setting – the building is big and strong and indeed has witnessed much. It opened just before the Bolsheviks began their rout on the Romanoffs and since that time has hosted presidents and plutocrats, and cultural and historical icons.

     Therefore, guests are in no doubt that this is a serious hotel – which can be witnessed in the comfort of the rooms, the authentic cuisine in the Davidov Restaurant (especially in the choice of vodka and caviar) and the levels of service throughout. The Astoria is part of The Rocco Forte Collection bringing with it all that implies, which includes attention to detail in everything from design and decor to delivery. There is, for instance, a Kandinsky original in the Kandinsky Bar.

     And, of course its location is spectacular – in St Isaac's Square right next to St Isaac's Cathedral with its vast dome and richly decorated interior, just around the corner from the Winter Palace and the Hermitage, but a short distance from the Marinsky Theatre. A visit to all of these is a must. The hotel's concierge will organise tickets for the ballet or opera… but ask for these when you book your room, not when you arrive, to ensure you are not disappointed. After such exigencies you will of course need to recover with a perfect vodka or two in the lobby or bar.

Bookings: +44 (0)20 7201 8070
masonroseprivate.com

---

## HOTEL AT A GLANCE

**ACCOMMODATION**
210 rooms and suites

**DINING**
Restaurant, bar and lounge

**RECREATION**
Spa and gym

**TRANSFERS**
Pulkovo International Airport
30mins by car

---

SIGNATURE EXPERIENCE

# COSSACK CHIC – LEARN THE RUSSIAN WAY TO DEAL WITH THE VAGARIES OF WINTER

Amber and a Cossack fur hat – two of the must-haves. Ask the concierge to guide you to the right traders, although the shop at the Hermitage is good for the former.

+ 7 812 494 5757
roccofortecollection.com

66

___

Step back in time and glide into a city that still evokes its imperious past. You can almost hear Lara's theme from 'Dr Zhivago' providing the soundtrack to your imperial romance with glorious St. Petersburg.

**Tsars and stars**

The **Marinsky Theatre** has been in existence for over 200 years. Anna Pavlova, Vaslav Nijinsky, Rudolf Nureyev and Mikhail Baryshnikov have all danced on its stage. Have your own magical evening of classical music, opera or ballet in the Tsar's Box. Utterly dreamy.

**Guiding light**

Your new best friend in St Petersburg is **Tania Illingworth** whose magic touch will whisk you past the line of tourists to the VIP-only section of everything. Tania is your passport to the cognoscenti's local experience. St Petersburg gold pass.

**If you must**

If you want the finest souvenirs, then go to **Onegin**. You will find the best in lacquer boxes, Fabergé, matryoshkas (Russian dolls), amber and porcelain. Do it quickly on your way out of the Russian Museum. Bystraya (fast)!

**Vodka and caviar**

Synonymous with Russia, and where better to sample the goods than at home? In this case in **Davidov** which will ply you with the finest... and you can just go upstairs and lie down afterwards. Fabuloski darling.

# HOTEL VILLA MAGNA

—

## *Classic charm and sophistication in the Spanish capital*

Villa Magna could not have a better location, a better address. Right in the heart of the swishest neighbourhood of Salamanca, this is a hotel that only rubs shoulders with kings and corporate chiefs, princes and heads of state. The King of Spain is practically a neighbour, and every visiting dignitary passes through its doors.

Its service is discreet and elegant while its dining experiences are of the gourmet variety. As many guests are in Madrid for business its business centre is renowned for its helpful multi lingual staff. But best of all, and especially for culture vultures, its location right at the heart of the Madrid Art Triangle is ideal for those visiting some of the most important galleries in Europe. And when you need respite from Velasquez and El Greco, the hotel is but minutes away… and here you can sink into true contemporary comfort. Of course everything else you may need to visit is in the neighbourhood too – from boutiques to bars, clubs and restaurants as well as designer salons.

But the recently refurbished hotel will draw you back throughout your stay… and the minute you enter it you will be cocooned in a glorious scent – Sierra – which was especially created for the hotel by Blaise Mautin. Should you need further seduction there is a spa and fitness centre.

Bookings: +44 (0)20 7201 8070
masonroseprivate.com

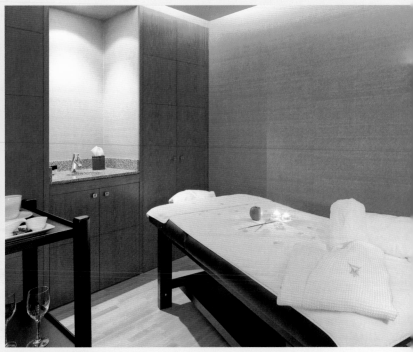

## HOTEL AT A GLANCE

**ACCOMMODATION**
150 rooms and suites

**DINING**
2 restaurants, 2 bars and lounge

**RECREATION**
Wellness area and fitness centre

**TRANSFERS**
Madrid Barajas International
Airport 20mins by car

SIGNATURE EXPERIENCE

# RICH ROYAL REMEDIES FOR TENSE AND TIRED BODIES

The spa by Kiara Kare offers a wide choice of treatments for face and body – rich in unguents and fragrance. There is a wondrous body ritual, the Ceremony of Gold, which uses 24-carat gold in the treatment – spoil yourself, you know you're worth it.

+ 34 915 871 234
hotelvillamagna.com

"

---

Magnificent Madrid, the perfect European city escape on a grand scale. Not just flamenco, bullfights and football. Epic museums and galleries complement the fashion style and exuberant spirit that punctuate the days and nights.

**Sedate cocktail**

Don't have the stamina for nights out that start at midnight? Head to the **Casa de América** for the fabulous outdoor bar set on the terraces. It's all palms and pillows under canvas with a cool vibe. Order a Mojito and people-watch. It wraps up around midnight so you can leave the jungle early for bed.

**Dedicated follower**

Do you adore fashion? Then go to the temple of **Museo del Traje**, the fashion and costume museum. One of the rooms is dedicated just to the great couturier Balenciaga and another to Spanish haute couture. Enlightenment, romanticism, Belle Époque, it's all here. Perfect for a rainy afternoon, and you can rest your Choos at the cafe.

**Made for walking**

If you are going to hit the old town anywhere in Europe, you know that you are going to hit cobblestones. Stilettos are lethal in this environment, so you need stylish flats. **Monica Garcia** can sort you out with just the right pair at her fabulous shoe haven. Buy several pairs, they don't exactly take up luggage space.

**Triple-decker**

Chueca is the hub of the fashion scene and the **Mercado de Fuencarral** is the place to be. Three storeys jammed with everything urban and trendy. While she shops, he can kick back on the sofas in the WiFi cafe in the basement and catch up on cybernews.

# HOTEL PUENTE ROMANO

—

## *Lavish sporting estate on the Costa del Sol*

Designed as an Andalusian village, the hotel is lush and luxurious right on the beach between Marbella and Puerto Banús, one of the most glamorous areas in all of Spain. It has acres of landscaped gardens, at the centre of which is the ancient Roman bridge from which the hotel takes its name. But although it is home to antiquities its amenities and service are timeless, which is what attracts guests to return year after year.

Spacious and beautifully laid out, the resort never feels crowded with its large expanse of beach, not to mention its three swimming pools, renowned tennis club (which has hosted world-class tournaments) where beginners, amateurs and hopefuls can play, be taught and seriously improve their game. There is an 18-hole golf course, a watersports centre on the beach for jet-skiing, sailing and paddle-boating, and riding stables for equestrian enthusiasts. The mountains behind the hotel have a glorious choice of trails for both riding and hiking. During the summer months a kids' club is available for four- to ten-year-olds… and, along with the usual amusements, there are both swimming and tennis lessons for tots.

If all this sounds like too much activity, there is ample space and opportunity to just lie down and enjoy the sun, and when a little extra pampering is needed the Thalasso Spa just a few hundred yards away at the Marbella Club is available for guests.

---

**HOTEL AT A GLANCE**

**ACCOMMODATION**
285 rooms and suites

**DINING**
4 restaurants, 2 bars and
beach club

**RECREATION**
Tennis, golf, spa, 3 swimming
pools, horse riding, fitness club,
watersports and nearby skiing

**TRANSFERS**
Malaga International Airport
40mins by car

SIGNATURE EXPERIENCE

# HAVE THOSE WIMBLEDON DREAMS

This is truly the place to take up, improve or simply enjoy your
tennis. Book a couple of private lessons, and you will be astonished
at your progress. Turn your dream into a reality.

+ 34 952 82 0900
puenteromano.com

66

———

My bella Marbella. Guaranteed glam, fast cars, vertiginous heels, and endless sunshine. Gigantic yachts and big diamonds. Everything is racy and sleek, like your swimsuit. Blingtastic!

**Suite dreams**

Such joy! The very fashionable and hugely popular **Suite** is located right on your doorstep at the hotel. The resident DJ's keep the crowd on its feet in a stylish frenzy of glamour. Attentive staff make it even dreamier. Disco inferno.

**Fashion mountaineering**

**K2** is not a mountain in Marbella, but one of the most exclusive boutiques. High fashion altitude, they stock a range of designer brands with just the right look for the Costa del Sol. Fashion scale:10.

**Culture vultures**

Could there be anything more divine than a Picasso? Art aficionados visit the **Picasso Museum** in Malaga. Let me frame this for you… a building with his work and Phoenician, Roman and Moorish remains from the 7th-Century. A veritable feast.

**Rock on**

If you are feeling adventurous Gibraltar is only an hour away. Go to the apes' den: no, not a local bar, but where the Barbary apes live. You'll go ape over the Cajun prawns at the **Queensway Quay Marina** which has the best marina and sea view for lunch. Jungle VIP.

Bookings: +44 (0)20 7201 8070
masonroseprivate.com

# MARBELLA CLUB HOTEL

—

## *A princely resort with all the ensuing glamour*

Hohenlohe has its own definition of luxury but to Prince Alfonso von Hohenlohe, the founder, mentor and instigator of the Marbella Club, it was very definitely 'a blend of privacy and gardens'.

This is an all-year pleasure garden where guests have every amenity close at hand… a wide choice of bars and restaurants – buffet lunch at the Beach Club is a must while cocktails under the trees in the early evening make this the most glamorous place on this ritzy coast, complete with the most glamorous guests.

The golf course is only for hotel guests but staying here gives access to five other top courses along the coast. The resort has its own riding stables and one of the best spas in the Mediterranean. The Thalasso Spa is adjacent to the beach and is a mosaic-studded temple of health and wellbeing with steam rooms, saunas, Hammam and a plethora of face and body treatments. It also offers a number of packages dedicated to slimming, rejuvenation and de-stressing.

However, a gentle walk around the grounds to the beach is a stress-buster on its own. The gardens are lushly and lavishly planted, designed by the Prince himself, and are one of the great joys of the resort. Opt for one of the villas to enjoy a garden, with pool, all to yourself.

## HOTEL AT A GLANCE

**ACCOMMODATION**
135 rooms, suites and villas

**DINING**
5 restaurants, 6 bars and
beach club

**RECREATION**
Golf, spa, horse riding and use
of Puente Romano facilities

**TRANSFERS**
Malaga International Airport
40mins by car

+ 34 952 8222 211
marbellaclub.com

SIGNATURE EXPERIENCE

# A BEAUTIFUL WAY TO USE SEASHELLS ON THE SEASHORE

You are spoiled for choice the minute you enter the Thalasso Spa, with one of the most comprehensive spa menus on the Med. Ingredients include seawater, minerals, rose oil, mud, salts and seashells. Indulge in the signature Thalasso Sea Creation – a luxury rejuvenating facial including active deep-sea elements and an exquisite seashell massage. The ultimate in self-gratification.

*Tanya's travel secrets...*

"

—

# A chic resort that is the Marbella address to aristocrats and tycoons who jet into town and appreciate discretion, spacious accommodation, gorgeous gardens and great service.

**Racy**

It doesn't get any sexier or more turbo-charged than the **Ascari Race Track**. The adventurous can find themselves behind the wheel of a Lotus or a BMW marque touring car. Push your driving skills to the limit round the track under expert tuition, or take a passenger seat in a Radical SR3 for a white-knuckle ride at race speed. You star in 'Top Gear'.

**Disco ball**

The **Babylonia Palace** is legendary when it comes to Marbella nightlife. Billionaires stroll in with an entourage of models and GQ men to dine on gourmet food and shimmy on the dance floor. This really is Babylon circa 2011. Go late at the weekend for people-watching that's off the scale, and crack a bottle of Champagne to refresh yourselves.

**Horsey**

Self-exiled Brit James Hewitt's reinvention has kicked off in fine style with the **Polo House**. It conveniently houses bar, restaurant and club under one roof. After devouring some of the Chukka Tukka you can move to the dance floor populated by the 30+ bracket who are cutting their shapes to music they recognise.

**Pamper afloat**

Here come the girls, on their bling-erama hen weekend. Marbella is about excess so rent a **Sunseeker** and head out to sea for spa treatments afloat. Buffed, polished and truly kneaded, the entire posse can step ashore at any number of glam beach bars. Cosmos on the way home, heels off for the walk back up the jetty, girls!

# GSTAAD PALACE

—

*It's a Palace… think royalty… that will be you*

FAVOURITE FOR

SKIING

★ ★ ★ ★ ★

Ever since opening in 1913 the Gstaad Palace has been the star attraction of this ultra-glamorous village. This legendary 'grande dame' is a magnet for high society, rock stars and celebrities; just about everyone hangs out here.

There are many reasons why this fairytale castle is so acclaimed; not least the fact that it has been owned by three generations of the charming and gracious Scherz family. The setting is not to be sniffed at either; with the glorious Alps around you this mountain resort is perfect all year round. In winter indulge in a wealth of wintersports right on your doorstep; in summer as the mountains burst into life you can picnic Heidi-style in flower filled-meadows or learn tennis from a renowned pro.

Make sure you book some time at the striking new spa, it not only has craveworthy treatments but a unique Hammam experience, private spa suite, indoor and outdoor Jacuzzis – all overlooking the sweeping Alpine vista. Treatment complete, you will be ready to hit the exclusive GreenGo nightclub.

As you can imagine this is definitely a place for a room with a view; outside the Alps and inside elegance abounds. There are heaps of restaurants but for traditional Swiss cuisine with a touch of class, think fondue with a hint of truffle, try La Fromagerie.

**HOTEL AT A GLANCE**

**ACCOMMODATION**
104 rooms and suites

**DINING**
5 restaurants, 2 bars and nightclub

**RECREATION**
Spa, indoor and outdoor pools, tennis, wintersports, hiking, white-water rafting, mountain biking, Alpine coasting and nearby golf

**TRANSFERS**
Geneva Airport 2hrs by car
Zurich Airport 2hrs 30mins by car

+ 41 33 748 50 00
palace.ch

SIGNATURE EXPERIENCE

# MAGIC IN THE MOUNTAINS

Come the summer months head up the mountain to the Palace's utterly charming Walig Hut. The beauty of this old mountainside lodge is its lovely traditional feel; all wooden floors, animal hide rugs and cosy atmosphere. Then there are the views, simply mind-blowing. This gorgeous mountain retreat is perfect for lunch or dinner; you can even stay overnight.

Mountains of glamour in a town that twinkles with a stellar reputation and celebrity. It's a Palace of mountain chalet chic with a contemporary twist. You'll appreciate the royal treatment.

**Dashing through the snow**

There is nothing more magical than a star-filled night in the **Alps**. Imagine travelling in a horse-drawn sleigh, a fur thrown over you, cool air on your face, and romance in your heart.

**Mountain by night**

A private opening of the **Eggli** chairlift will get you and your friends to the top of the mountain for a fondue party. And then, with guides, you can career down the mountain through the woods in soft snow on a toboggan. Or how about skiing lit by flame torches? Toast the success of your descent around a roaring fire, Schnapps in hand. You'll be giddy with exhilaration.

**Front-row fashion**

Do you want to look elegantly fabulous on the slope, at dinner, in the bar, on the dance floor… well, everywhere really? Head to **Lorenz Bach's** exquisite boutique for velvet, cashmere, and streamlined über-chic for the slopes. He has it all and more.

**Say cheese**

You'll be grinning from ear to ear when you tuck into the gooey delicious fondue and raclette at **Café du Cerf**. Located in the village of Rougemout, it's an institution that has been packing in the A-listers and locals for years. With live Swiss folk music on Friday and Saturday nights, it's brimming with mountain atmosphere. Take the whole family for smiles all round.

66
—

*I like to really experience
life in the country I've
chosen to visit.*

## Ciara Parkes, Chairman of Public Eye.

**TR** *How do you escape from the crowds?*

**CP** I like to have an idea of where I am going before we start travelling, especially if we are driving around and exploring. So I try to choose four to five places to visit and book something in each so it keeps our plans partly organised, but to a lazy regime.

**TR** *Any remote hotel recommendations?*

**CP** A hotel we visited recently was the Picoaga in Cusco, Peru where we spent New Year's Eve. After that we really had an adventure by taking off on a 4,000km drive around the country passing through the Sacred Valley. The hotel was relaxing, unpretentious and the rooms beautifully decorated with huge bathrooms and soft everything.

**TR** *Whose advice do you seek to plan these out-of-the-way trips?*

**CP** Absolutely has to be people who also have the same sense of adventure about travel that I do. I'm not one for long beach holidays with nothing to do.

**TR** *Has travel ever been part of a birthday celebration?*

**CP** In a way it was! Many years ago I had the most delicious duck shepherd's pie at Balthazar in New York and became slightly obsessed with it, so I had it prepared for my 40th birthday by a chef here in England from exactly the same recipe.

### CLOUD NINE
I love long haul flights with no interruptions

## Ciara

**ALWAYS TRAVELS IN STYLE**

1 **ESCAPE**
The independence of a boat or car is a passport to freedom. With no timetable to adhere to, the days are your own and you can really escape the rat race

2 **PIT STOP**
I like to get to the airport early so I'm not hassled and I head to the Caviar House for a glass of Chablis and smoked salmon blinis

Bookings: +44 (0)20 7201 8070
masonroseprivate.com

# BAUR AU LAC

—

## *Elegant excellence in its own parkland*

For more than 165 years this elegant hotel has been top of the luxury list in one of Switzerland's most demanding and fastidious cities. Visitors to Zurich know that it prides itself on its civility and service – both of which are hallmarks of the hotel. Yet both the city and hotel have evolved into the very models of modern metropolitan style and sophistication.

The city has great shops, chic cafes and terrific restaurants, while the hotel has a gastronomic restaurant, the Pavillon, chic terrace and the cosmopolitan Rive Gauche Restaurant & Bar, as popular with the locals as it is with the guests.

All of this is helped by the hotel having one of the best of settings overlooking the lake, nestled in parkland and yet caressed by the nearby Alps. Little wonder that it has welcomed the discreet, the discerning and the decidedly demanding over the last century or so, which includes kings (Ludwig II) and Bonds (Daniel Craig) and has never once let its standards slip. In fact it constantly updates its rooms, suites, public areas, bars and restaurant which is why it is not only home from home for the corporates and banking kings… but also for the jeunesse dorée of Zurich.

**HOTEL AT A GLANCE**

**ACCOMMODATION**
120 rooms and suites

**DINING**
4 restaurants and bars

**RECREATION**
Fitness centre

**TRANSFERS**
Zurich Airport 20mins by car

SIGNATURE EXPERIENCE

# HAVE A HEAD, AND BODY, FOR HEIGHTS

The view from the rooftop will take your breath away, especially if you choose to workout in its state-of-the-art fitness centre… but all in a good cause – your wellbeing.

+41 44 220 50 20
bauraulac.ch

66
—

A city that is as precise as you would expect. A panoramic vista, an old town. And then, she sneaks up on you with hip design, techno chic like an elegant spy in a Bond film.

**Transformer**

The hotspot in Zurich is **0815/2**, which transforms throughout the day. Breakfast cafe cool becomes lavish lunch, before divine dinner and hip bar kick in after dark. Music, architecture, fabulous food and design under one roof with a star crowd. Everything is truly scrumptious including the staff.

**Unmissable**

The Museum of Fine Arts, better known as the **Kunsthaus**, is the most stunning building to look at in its architectural cool on the edge of the lake. But it's the plethora of 19th- and 20th-century art that will amaze, it's brimming with Picasso, Gaugin and van Gogh. Perfect for a cold winter day, and the shop is marvellous.

**Three apples?**

**Trois Pommes** is not three British people in Australia, but a chic boutique in Zurich. Design discount is apparent when you see how reasonable the prices are for Dolce & Gabbana and Jil Sander. They have opened another outlet next door, where you can pick up something out of season but classic for even less. Beauty, mate!

**Quiet inspiration**

You don't have to be a church-goer to appreciate the ecclesiastical majesty of the stained glass at **Fraumünster**. In the bright morning sun you will gaze at the Chagall windows in wonderment. Blue, green, yellow, red… the colour is incredible. Totally divine in every sense of the word. A quiet moment of solitude and light.

# PERA PALACE

—

*A true travellers' rest. A hotel built for travellers now welcomes them back after a glorious overhaul*

Heavy with the glamour of history, this iconic hotel in the heart of Istanbul's social and cultural centre has for over 100 years welcomed politicians and princes, millionaires and megastars as well as writers, artists and travellers. And especially the latter, as it was originally built as the place for passengers of the Orient Express. It really came into its own when Atatürk, the founder of modern Turkey, began to stay on his frequent visits to the city. Now, resplendent in its recent refurbishment, there is an Atatürk Museum full of the great man's memorabilia.

The refurbishment and restoration were carefully monitored by the Turkish authorities to ensure the hotel remained true to its fusion of Art Nouveau, Oriental and Neoclassical beginnings, and has been recognised as a triumph of restoration. Even though it has every modern amenity from a fully equipped fitness centre to a state-of-the-art spa, it has been cognisant of its past and many devotees. Everyone of note who visited Istanbul stayed here including Greta Garbo, Jacqueline Kennedy, Zsa Zsa Gabor, Ernest Hemingway and Agatha Christie who, it is claimed, developed the plot for 'Murder on the Orient Express' whilst staying. Today, there is an Agatha Christie suite – room 411, her favourite – and a Hemingway suite.

Close to everywhere a visitor needs to be in this glorious city, this palace has truly reinvented itself.

## HOTEL AT A GLANCE

**ACCOMMODATION**
115 rooms and suites

**DINING**
Restaurant, patisserie, bar
and lounge

**RECREATION**
Spa with indoor pool, Hammam,
steam bath and Jacuzzi

**TRANSFERS**
Atatürk International Airport
30 to 45mins by car

SIGNATURE EXPERIENCE

# TIMELESS GLAMOUR, AWESOME GLITZ

Emeralds! Sadly not in the hotel, but do ask the concierge to organise a tour for you of the Topkapi Palace – not too far away. He will know the best time to go, and the best tickets you need to give you all the time possible to marvel at these vast green stones – some the size of dinner plates! Magnificent isn't a big enough word to describe them!

+ 90 212 377 40 00
perapalace.com

"
—

# Who can resist a Turkish delight? And Istanbul is full of them. JFK and Jackie O honeymooned here which speaks volumes. Stretching across two continents, brimming with exotic mystique and sensuality, it never disappoints.

**Hot summer nights**

With its amazing views it is no wonder that **Sortie** is known as one of Istanbul's hottest clubs. After a long day, dress up and watch the sunset over the Bosphorus whilst dining with friends. Then join in with the entertainment and let the rhythm of the music take you into the early hours of the morning.

**Cruising**

There's no better way to see the fabulous Ottoman villas that line the Bosphorus than from the water. Take a **private yacht charter**, pack chilled wine and canapés and sail out in late afternoon to experience the glow of the sunset on castles, fortresses, fishing boats and sometimes dolphins. A magical evening afloat.

**Food with a view**

It doesn't get more opulent than the **Sunset Grill & Bar** which maximises the Bosphorus views lavishly. The sushi is incredible, as are the beef kebabs with velvety yoghurt. It literally sizzles with romance and has to be one of the world's best locations for that important proposal.

**Hangover cure**

It worked for Cameron Diaz and any number of royals... you have to experience a real Turkish bath once in your life. This is not a remake of 'Midnight Express' but the last great Ottoman Hamman **Cağaloğlu**. Steaming out the creases since 1741. It's grand an opulent, and it will cure your hangover.

# THE ROYAL CRESCENT HOTEL

—

## *For a super-indulgent weekend this hotel ticks all the boxes*

The Royal Crescent Hotel offers an abundance of style and elegance but also a delicious sense of being in an exclusive retreat.

The beautiful situation of The Royal Crescent, Bath's renowned 18th-century design masterpiece, creates a splendid setting for this most graceful of hotels. From the moment the liveried doorman whisks away your bags, you realise you are in for a treat. Far more than a remarkable collection of buildings, this hotel is all about luxurious grandeur, memorable interior design and serious service.

The gorgeous rooms and suites are exceptional not just in their stunning surroundings but also because of the special little touches. All are individually appointed, with a delightful mix of sensitive contemporary styles, and restored antiques. The suites are to die for, some even have their own airy conservatory dining room looking onto the garden and for the ultimate in privacy there is the secluded Garden Villa.

At the end of the garden, stone villas house the spa and the Dower House restaurant. There are few locations as agreeable as this for enjoying a meal but the chef's innovative modern British menu makes every meal a supremely pleasurable experience. In the summer the outdoor dining terrace is extremely popular and rightly so. Make sure you sample the traditional afternoon teas complete with homemade Bath buns.

Bath's fashionable Georgian heyday lives on.

---

**HOTEL AT A GLANCE**

**ACCOMMODATION**
45 rooms and suites

**DINING**
1 restaurant

**RECREATION**
Spa, gym, garden, 1920s river
boat, tours of Bath

**TRANSFERS**
London Paddington to Bath
by train 1hr 30mins
Bath rail station 10mins walking
Heathrow Airport 90mins by car
Gatwick Airport 3hrs by car
Bristol International Airport
40mins by car

+ 44 (0)1225 823333
royalcrescent.co.uk

SIGNATURE EXPERIENCE

# ROMAN BATH MEETS TRANQUIL RETREAT

An absolute 'must do' is the Bath House, a chic spa housed in the former coach house and stables of the hotel's gardens. Experience the restorative tradition of Bath as many of the huge range of divine treatments use the city's renowned natural spa water. The relaxation pool heated to body temperature is heavenly. Top tip – make sure you book in advance.

Gracious curves. Bubbles in the bath and the glass. Grand genes and jeans. Incomparable elegant sweeping class. The perfect car-free getaway for everyone in an easy to reach town steeped in history.

### Rainy afternoon

Slip romantically into the Art Deco splendour of the **Little Theatre** for quality cinema from around the world. In operation since 1936, it's a gorgeous little piece of nostalgia in the middle of Bath with state-of-the-art comfort and technology. With popcorn and someone you love it's the recipe for a brief encounter you will adore. Tickets please.

### Humpty Dumpty

Sand in my Shoes, Creepy Crawly Calypso and Pirate School are just some of the fantastic theatre workshops for 2.5- to 6-year olds at **The Egg Theatre**. A wonderful family-friendly place oozing with creativity and happiness. The cafe on the ground floor is a great place to hang out while your kids shout, sing, bang tambourines and hoist the mainsail.

### Potato head

**Demuths** was awarded Best Vegetarian Restaurant for 2010 in the Gourmet Britain Awards. There are plenty of vegan, wheat-free dishes and gluten-free options. Vegetables, breads and cheeses are sourced from local suppliers. Pick up the cookbooks Green Seasons and Green World, or attend the Demuths cookery school to wow your veggie friends. The baked hazelnut

### Booked

I love a good shop, and **Topping & Company** in the heart of town is a beacon in the intensely literary world of Bath. Alan Bennett, Nigella Lawson, David Attenborough and Stephen Fry have all made personal appearances. With 30,000 titles there's lots to choose from, and you can even have a cup of tea or coffee. Take a leaf out of my book and go!

# LOWER SLAUGHTER MANOR

—

*For the most cosseted country living imaginable and tranquillity with a capital T*

Lower Slaughter Manor is picture-perfect, set in what is regarded as Gloucestershire's prettiest village; this incredibly beautiful manor is quintessentially English.

It has that classic country-house chic at its best; burnished antique furniture, beautiful paintings and soft sofas that demand to be sat on. In one room the décor is a deluge of crystals, in another a sea of cushions. Guestrooms are personal boltholes of immense style – no chintz but rather bold contemporary design meeting 17th-century grandeur. Their seductive tone makes them perfect for the relaxing in-room beauty treatments.

The restaurant exudes smart sophistication, from its cool design to the innovative cuisine of modern English enriched with a French twist. The impressive cellar is filled with vintage Champagnes and prestige wines, all carefully selected for your pleasure, and for the whisky-lover there is a dream menu. In the summer, lunch on the terrace is a must as the gardens are gorgeous. Magnificent beech and chestnut trees, perfectly manicured lawns, a secluded walled garden and an ancient dovecote create a serene paradise. On one side you overlook the gently flowing River Eye and on another the old village church; this is the Cotswolds at its best.

Calm and immensely relaxing, Lower Slaughter Manor is a place of wish-fulfilment.

## HOTEL AT A GLANCE

**ACCOMMODATION**
19 rooms and suites

**DINING**
1 restaurant

**RECREATION**
Outdoor dining and lounging area,
tennis courts, croquet lawn, in-room
and beauty treatments

**TRANSFERS**
London Paddington to
Moreton-in-Marsh by train 90mins
Birmingham International
Airport 1hr 10 mins
Heathrow Airport 2hrs
Helipad on site

+ 44 (0)1451 820456
lowerslaughter.co.uk

SIGNATURE EXPERIENCE

# A ROMANTIC IDYLL WITH ITS OWN HOT TUB HEAVEN

For an extravagant weekend of romance book a room in the
refurbished Georgian Coach House. Highly recommended is the
decadent Valentine Strong suite with a huge bathroom featuring
twin rolled-top baths and French doors leading to a private garden
complete with hot tub. With the delicious gourmet room service
you might never leave.

*Tanya's travel secrets...*

"
———

Audrey Forbes-Hamilton would
be quite at home at this 17th-century
house set in an idyllic location on
the edge of one of England's loveliest
villages. To the manor born.

**All that jazz**

The **Cheltenham
International Jazz Festival**
saw a line-up in 2010 that
included Paloma Faith
headlining in an exclusive
performance with The Guy
Barker Big Band, plus Elaine
Paige, Eric Bibb, Imelda May,
Liane Carroll, and Natalie
Williams. Guest Director was
Jamie Cullum. Performances
take place in the Town Hall
and Everyman Theatre or
more intimately in bars and
clubs around town. Musically
magnificent.

**Connoisseur**

**Sudeley Castle** was home to
Katherine Parr, the the last
surviving wife of Henry VIII.
A connoisseur tour takes you
into parts of the castle not
seen by most visitors including
the Stone Drawing Room, the
Library and the Billiard Room.
Art by Rubens, van Dyck and
Claude Lorrain abounds. Make
sure you see the love letter to
Katherine penned by Sir
Thomas Seymour.

**Vintage headturner**

Fancy pootling about the
countryside in a 1963 Austin
Healey or a 1970 E-type Jag?
Take the train to Stratford-
upon-avon or Warwick and
pick up your vintage car from
**Open Road Classic Car Hire.**
Drive in open-top style through
the unspoiled villages of
Chipping Campden, Stanway,
Stanton and Snowshill.
Picture-perfect, and Hermès
scarf firmly tied a must.

**Organic**

If you have experienced
**Daylesford Organic** in Pimlico
or Notting Hill, it's wonderful
to visit the home of this
fabulous brand. The cookery
school in a converted barn is
truly exceptional. From baking
bread to the gourmet delights
of fish and pastry, there is
even a class for children where
they learn about harvesting
their own vegetables and
collecting eggs from the farm.
Truly organic.

# CLARIDGE'S

—

## *A priceless London classic of impeccable heritage and timeless glamour*

Staying at Claridge's is like stepping into a world of timeless glamour. You get a thrill just entering through the bronze and gilt revolving doors, fingerprinted over the decades by the rich and famous.

Claridge's is London's authentic Art Deco gem. More fashionable than ever, it attracts everyone from catwalk models to media moguls. The hippest hangout is Claridge's Bar; a favourite with the 'in crowd', this seriously chic bar is styled with luscious lipstick, red leather banquettes and a fabulous silver-leaf ceiling. The bijou Fumoir has a more sensual allure with its original René Lalique panels and marble-topped horseshoe bar where you sip 1930s-themed cocktails. Further upping the buzz quotient is the Michelin-starred Gordon Ramsay restaurant, where exquisite modern European dishes are served in designer splendour.

The subtle aura of decadence continues in the elegant guestrooms; styled with either Art Deco or Victorian touches, everything you can think of is here making these havens of comfort into ultra-sophisticated spoiling worlds. The Linley suites are a Deco delight, with sofas in the softest leathers, walnut tables and brilliantly bold dressing-rooms. If the bustle of chichi Mayfair gets too much, head to the Claridge's beauty and fitness suite on the sixth floor for a deliciously soothing treatment.

Claridge's is definitely a place to see and be seen.

---

**HOTEL AT A GLANCE**

**ACCOMMODATION**
203 rooms including suites and
2 penthouses

**DINING**
2 restaurants and 2 bars

**RECREATION**
Beauty and fitness suite and private
dining rooms

**TRANSFERS**
London Heathrow Airport
45mins by car or 1hr by tube

SIGNATURE EXPERIENCE

# SUITE STYLE

When a fashion icon comes to a 'grande dame' you can be assured
you are in for a treat. And the new Diane von Furstenberg collection
of rooms and suites does not disappoint. Her trademark glamour
abounds; signature prints, bold colours and specially crafted furniture
adorn these haute-couture guestrooms. DVF's first interiors are a
stunning triumph of fashionable flair.

"

—

Rule Britannia! And it doesn't get more British than this hotel. You feel instant social credibility with one of the finest addresses in London. It's a home with a heart, pedigree and loads of style.

**Royal warrant**

Established in 1698, **Berry Bros. & Rudd** have been the purveyors of fine wine to the royal family since King George III's reign. Attend a wine-tasting evening in their magnificent cellar in the heart of St James. An exclusive and enjoyable way to stun your friends with your wine-list savvy and knowledge.

**Treasure trove**

Could there be anything more awe-inspiring than gazing upon Fragonard's gorgeous 'Swing'? The **Wallace Collection** on one of London's grand squares is a jewel box that is sometimes overlooked. Lined with Titian, Rubens, Rembrandt, Canaletto Gainsborough, it's a sea of treasures. Stop for the French afternoon tea in the elegant cafe, it's magnifique!

**My kingdom for a horse**

Have you ever wanted to travel regally on horseback through Hyde Park surveying your kingdom? Set the alarm and head over to **Hyde Park Stables** where you can board your fur-clad carriage and head on out into the Park to see London from 16 hands up. Giddy up!

**Off with her head!**

A private drinks reception in the home of the Crown Jewels? Privately experience the Ceremony of the Keys which has taken place every night for 700 years? All possible by private arrangement at the **Tower of London**. Imagine yourself right at the heart of English history.

# ED
## ON TRAVEL

"

*I love luxury
and part of
travel is luxury.*

*The legendary and ultra-successful literary agent Ed Victor, is the most invited guest on both sides of the pond.*

**TR** *The first step in planning a trip?*

**EV** The single most obvious thing about air travel is to arrive when there is no traffic. If I have just flown seven hours across the Atlantic do I really want to spend three hours getting into town? I will always take a flight that avoids that. The day flight back to London is perfect for missing the peak hour and you end up sleeping in your own bed. It's not enough to book your plane or train; you need to think about when you land. You'll need to get somewhere so arrange ground transport; this is as much a vital part of your planning as getting there.

**TR** *Is travel advice from other people a good thing?*

**EV** Never recommend a hotel or restaurant to me unless you are going to tell me which room I should stay in, where to sit in the restaurant and what I should order. You can go to a great hotel and have a lousy room, or go to a mediocre hotel and have a great room. Be specific with people, say 'Room 85 it has a balcony and a view, and the dish you should order is the calamari; it's fabulous.'

**TR** *You travel for business constantly; where do you like to eat?*

**EV** In New York I like Michael's, it's full of my media crowd. I go to the Minetta Tavern for great steak. I still love Elaine's where I have been going since the sixties; the best thing to eat there is the veal chop. Katz's Deli on Houston is a must; they filmed the famous scene from 'When Harry Met Sally' there. In Paris sit down at Café Flo for a kir then cross the street to Brasserie Lipp, and go to Voltaire for lunch. In LA try The Ivy at The Shore or Jeffries north of Malibu for Sunday lunch and order the lobster cobb salad.

## Ed's
### OBVIOUS TRAVEL TIPS

**NO.1 RULE**

Never , ever, ever, go to a hotel that is recommended to you by someone you know and trust but they have not been to

**!!!**

2 **STRETCH**
For tall travellers like me seat 63K on the upper deck of the 747 Club Class on British Airways is the seat to book. Just don't be on my flight. If you are driving in a foreign city and are lost, stop a taxi, tell them where you are going, pay the driver and follow them

1 **OZO CAR**
Arrive in the city by eco-luxury. A private car service in New York which is all hybrid cars. Ask for Roman, driver number 1661

Bookings: +44 (0)20 7201 8070
masonroseprivate.com

# ST JAMES'S HOTEL AND CLUB

—

## *A cosseting institution with just the right flicker of cool*

BEST
KEPT
SECRET
★★★★★

Once a gentlemen's club, the St James's Hotel and Club has undergone a complete transformation. Classic London meets 21st-century chic in a stylish modern way.

Not only does it have a superb location, in a quiet cul-de-sac in the heart of Mayfair, but heaps of personality. Interiors are brimming with urban sophistication and hushed opulence. Dramatic touches abound, particularly with the outstanding artwork from the Rosenstein Collection dotted throughout the hotel. This distinctive flair makes for gorgeous guestrooms – they are individual masterpieces of soft subtle palettes enhanced by luxurious finishes, swathes of sensuous fabrics and stunning Murano chandeliers. Exceptional comfort mixed with every mod-con. A great plus is that many have a balcony or terrace, some with great views over the rooftops. With the vast Penthouse Suite you get your own personal piece of skyline from a deck so large you can entertain all your friends.

The decadent design extends to the intimate gourmet restaurant where you are treated to impeccably 'haute' cuisine. For top-notch cocktails the bar is definitely the place to go. On top of all this the staff are unbelievably helpful and courteous yet unobtrusive.

With its relaxed and discreet privacy it is not hard to see why this elegant townhouse hotel and club is a firm favourite with celebrities.

Bookings: +44 (0)20 7201 8070
masonroseprivate.com

---

**HOTEL AT A GLANCE**

**ACCOMMODATION**
60 rooms and suites

**DINING**
Restaurants and bar

**RECREATION**
Access to nearby gym and spa,
local shopping, sights, culture
and galleries

**TRANSFERS**
London Heathrow Airport
45mins by car, 1hr by tube

SIGNATURE EXPERIENCE

# A MASTERPIECE OF TASTE

The hottest ticket in town is a table at the hotel's Seven Park Place restaurant. Chef-in-residence is the super-talented Michelin starred William Drabble. This culinary genius is one of London's brightest shining stars; his creative cuisine is a mouth-watering combination of modern French style with the best of British ingredients.

"

—

London, who can tire of it?
It's the right address, interior-designed
exquisitely in great comfort. Take the
Penthouse in summer and have a party
on the roof terrace.

**The royal treatment**

A night to remember at the **Royal Opera House**. Treat your guests to a world-class performance; start with an exclusive backstage tour, before Champagne overlooking the stunning auditorium, seats in the Royal Box and dinner served by your butler in the Royal Retiring Room. At the end of the night, watch the cast take their bows from the wings and take home wonderful memories of an extraordinary evening.

**London through the lens**

Explore London's East End with a teacher from the **London School of Photography** who will coach you on how to capture those amazing urban shots of London's colourful neighbourhoods with your digital camera. Stun your friends with your amazing work.

**Café deluxe**

Since 1987 The River **Café** has been cooking up a storm, earning a Michelin star in 1988. It was the learning ground of several famous chefs including Jamie Oliver. It's all about the ingredients in the kitchen and the wild mushroom risotto will not disappoint. The service is second to none. Ruthie Rogers is an icon. Culinary magic.

**Royal parks**

A private walk around **St James' Park** with a historical expert who will show you the gorgeous view across the lake, originally laid out during the reign of King Charles II. The hotel will supply a bag of bread to feed the ducks and pelicans. Quack quack. No ugly ducklings here.

# THE BERKELEY

—

*Utterly fashionable, incomparable
service, so now... and forever*

Knightsbridge, home to Harrods, Harvey Nichols and
every luxury brand known, is the perfect location for The Berkeley.
This sophisticated, cosmopolitan hotel is so on trend that it fizzes
with style.

Take the delectable Prêt-à-Portea, a fashionista afternoon
tea service straight from the catwalk. Inspired by the changing fashions,
it is a veritable roll-call of must-have designers, from Burberry to
Chanel. It is a mini fashion week. After dark the 'it crowd' hits the
Blue Bar. A vision in mesmerising inky blue glamour, this swish
hangout is the ultimate cocktail paradise.

Guestrooms are equally chic; their individual style offers
lashings of contemporary comfort in a sexy understated way. The
collection of designer suites is spectacular; fabulously spacious, they
are like having your own pied-à-terre and the views from the
conservatory suites are stunning. Up on the rooftop you find a hip
chill-out zone with spa and a pool that is alfresco in the summer
months. Next to the spa is a little courtyard terrace that at times
turns into an outdoor movie theatre complete with popcorn.

Good taste abounds and particularly in the Marcus Wareing
fine dining restaurant. The ambience with its hypnotic lighting and
rich dark claret colours creates a clubby backdrop to savour Michelin
starred cuisine from one of Britain's most talented chefs.

---

**HOTEL AT A GLANCE**

**ACCOMMODATION**
214 rooms and suites

**DINING**
3 restaurants and 1 bar

**RECREATION**
Rooftop pool, health club and spa

**TRANSFERS**
London Heathrow Airport 45mins
by car or 1hr by tube

**SIGNATURE EXPERIENCE**

# A CULINARY COUP

Super-chef and super-legend, Pierre Koffmann's return to the London scene is a delicious delight for foodies everywhere. His eponymous restaurant is a masterstroke; the cuisine is a divine blend of his signature dishes. Think pistachio soufflé with pistachio ice cream, with a more relaxed brasserie style highlighting provincial Gascon classics.

+ 44 (0) 20 7235 6000
the-berkeley.co.uk

"

Fashionista Britannia! In the heart of fashion central with a pool on the roof? Is that Kim Cattrall in the lobby… Madonna in the bar? Ladies who lunch, men doing business, they're all here. Absolutely fabulous!

**Theatre under the stars**

Imagine a glorious summer evening in London sitting in the Rose Garden of Regent's Park sipping a glass of Champagne. How about front-row seats for this evening's performance at the **Regent's Park Open Air Theatre**? With a throw over your knees and the breeze rustling through the trees around you, it's not just the show that will transport you.

**On point**

It needles me that I just can't pinpoint what it is that is so great about a good acupuncturist. **Annee de Mamiel** is a complete wonder. Her expertise in Chinese medicine, aromatherapy, physiology and acupuncture is second to none. She will help you achieve balance and a sense of emotional well-being. It's a moving and wonderful experience.

**Style central**

At **Neville's** have your locks tended to by Stephen whose scissor hands touch the manes of celebrities and Londoners in the know. For colour, ask for Donald. The stunning and glamorous Elena is the face of the salon and will welcome you with her well-known Italian warmth and grace. You are in Knightsbridge, so look like you are!

**Pub soldiers**

Want a bit of London pub culture with style? Try the **Grenadier** which was the original mess of Wellington's Grenadier Guards. It's tiny, but you won't mind having your Bloody Mary while admiring the historical surroundings and ebullient crowd. Bottoms up!

# THE CONNAUGHT

—

## *A legend reborn into contemporary luxury*

There is something discreetly grand about the Connaught; rather like the home of a rich friend; it has always been a place of great taste and exquisite hospitality. A recent revamp by über-decorators has sprinkled even more fairy dust on this palatial pad making it one of the hottest places to stay.

Its location is so in vogue you will find practically everything on your doorstep. Although once inside you might not want to leave as the Connaught really knows how to treat its guests. Rooms come with that must-have accessory of a personal butler who, from sunrise to sunset, will cater to your every whim. Gorgeously designed, they are filled with layers of pampering in a truly cosseting and elegant style. Topping them all is The Apartment, which is like a private residence and has two fabulous garden terraces overlooking the rooftops.

Masterminding the cuisine throughout the hotel is the culinary superstar Hélène Darroze, and her Michelin starred restaurant is another world, a little Narnia of gourmet delights. Adding to the pleasure are the ultra-stylish designer bars. The ultra-slick Connaught Bar is an Art Deco extravaganza – order a signature Martini and enjoy the theatre of a mixologist creating the perfect cocktail at your table. Then there is the Coburg Bar, whose rich velvet wingback armchairs and quirky décor create the perfect modern drinking den.

HOTEL AT A GLANCE

**ACCOMMODATION**
121 rooms and suites

**DINING**
2 restaurants and 2 bars

**RECREATION**
Aman spa, indoor pool
and exercise room

**TRANSFERS**
London Heathrow Airport
1hr by car or 1hr by tube

SIGNATURE EXPERIENCE

# BLISS OUT WITH AMAN

A real treat awaits you with the fabulous new Aman spa; their first
and only one outside of an Aman resort. Its sleek Asian aesthetic
oozes soothing serenity whilst the enticing menu of treatments
and healing therapies from around the world will transport you to
pampering heaven. Add in the divine indoor pool and you have
the perfect de-stress antidote.

+ 44 (0) 20 7499 7070
the-connaught.co.uk

*Tanya's travel secrets...*

66
—

Cool Britannia! Wow, what a fabulous makeover. Could she be more elegant and plush? Even the garden is a design stunner. A classic is reborn with a large dash of vogue style.

**The birds and the bees
the flowers and the trees**
Take a train to gorgeous
Richmond on the outskirts
of London, and there you will
find **Petersham Nurseries**.
Not just a multi-coloured blaze
of flowers and plants, but
home to a café and teahouse
frequented by the cognoscenti.
How about tea in a real English
garden, a cooking workshop, or
'how to be an urban farmer'!
Quintessentially British.

**Harrods**

**H A Rods** the corner shop, that
would be Harrods to the
locals… and the only way to
negotiate this retail palace is
by appointment with a
personal shopper. Think of it
as the VIP queue-jumping
pass at Disneyland. Imagine,
someone bringing you things
to try on, and you don't have
to touch anyone. Champagne
and Chopard, who could want
for more?

**Bag a bespoke**

Go immediately to Pont Street
and visit **Anya Hindmarch
Bespoke** for the ultimate in
luxury and quality in which
you can have a hand in your
own design. Imagine knowing
you own something exquisite
and personal, that harks back
to a London when craftsmen
created individual pieces.
The range has items for both
women and men, offering
you the most unique gift to
take home.

**Nuts about Nuttall**

Once upon a time there were
craftsmen who made special
and unique furniture with
exquisite fabrics. **Amber
Nuttall** and her sister **Gytha**
have created a little piece
of heaven in Chelsea which
is a treasure trove of such
exquisite taste you can't help
but want something for your
home. Just a whiff of their
furniture and accessories, and
you'll see why they are made
to enjoy for generations. Store
up for winter.

# CLIVEDEN

—

*A legendary stately home with*
*a blue-blooded history and a*
*frisson of political scandal*

Think renowned hospitality, extraordinary extravagance
and a glamorous past and you have Cliveden in a nutshell. Everyone
who is anyone has stayed here, the most famous hostess of all being
Nancy Astor.

The surroundings are so impressive you could be on the set
of 'Atonement' or 'Brideshead Revisted'. The long gravel drive leads
you through 376 acres of parkland and magnificent formal gardens to
the lavish grandeur of the house. Glimpses of the vast marble fountain
and stunning thousand-yard parterre are a foretaste of the incredible
curiosities that fill the beautiful gardens.

Every design detail of the splendid décor is so carefully
thought through, that you feel like one of Nancy Astor's house guests.
The bedrooms, each named after a prominent figure from Cliveden's
past, are richly decorated and come equipped with four members of
staff, so flawless service is guaranteed. The Nancy Astor suite, one of
the grandest in the world, certainly lives up to the celebrated style
of its namesake.

For over three centuries Cliveden has been a byword for fine
dining, a tradition that continues in delightfully individual settings.
Classic cuisine in the grand Terrace Dining Room; remarkable
contemporary menus at Waldo's; and the Duke of Westminster's
personal stables converted into an informal gastropub.

Staying at Cliveden is the pleasure of sheer luxury.

---

**HOTEL AT A GLANCE**

**ACCOMMODATION**
39 rooms and suites

**DINING**
3 restaurants

**RECREATION**
Boathouse, spa, outdoor and
indoor pools, tennis courts, gym
and National Trust gardens

**TRANSFERS**
Central London 40mins by car
London Heathrow Airport
20mins by car,
London Gatwick Airport
50mins by car,
Helipad on site

+ 44 (0)1628 668561
clivedenhouse.co.uk

SIGNATURE EXPERIENCE

# A RIVERBANK SECRET

Right on the edge of the tranquil River Thames and nestled in the
woods is Spring Cottage. Originally built as a secluded summerhouse,
this charming hideaway was much frequented by Queen Victoria who
loved to take tea in the gardens. Now it is the most peaceful place to
stay and it even comes with its own personal butler.

*Tanya's travel secrets...*

"

Have your own Profumo Affair in aristocratic luxury, and add your name to the guest list which has included Joseph Kennedy, George Bernard Shaw, Mahatma Gandi, and F. D. Roosevelt. Historically and architecturally spectacular.

**Floating**

The Thames is irresistible, and no better way to ply its waters than aboard one of the magnificent restored vessels at Cliveden. My favourite is the **Liddesdale**, an electric canoe commissioned by Lady Astor. Its silence contributes to the tranquillity and allow's you to hear the lap of water as you sip Champagne. It floats my boat.

**Chukka**

If you've ever fancied the idea of polo and would like a taster of the sport, it behoves you to contact **Cool Hooves** who will make the plans. In the prestigious environment of the Royal Country of Berkshire Polo Club you'll learn to swing a mallet and ride a polo pony. Privately, in a small group, or en famille, it's so much fun.

**Doggies**

Do you love your pooch so much you just don't want to leave them at home? Bring them to Cliveden, they love **dogs**. Their tails will wag off when you tell them in a demented voice about 250 acres to bound through and rabbits to chase. Chef will cook up canine cuisine, and dog sitters will pat your pet while you dine quietly. Woof woof!

**On the ball**

Ladies and gents who love a round of golf must go to the lovely **Burnham Beeches Golf Club** for local prestige. An elegant clubhouse complements the championship course which measures 6,458 yards. A par 70 course, it's one of the region's best golfing challenges. Head back to Cliveden in time for tea off with cakes.

Bookings: +44 (0)20 7201 8070
masonroseprivate.com

# SHARROW BAY

—

*This is a place where you can
do nothing all day and feel
fulfilled at the end of it*

BEST

ENGLISH
ESCAPE

★★★★★

If heaven is a good novel, a comfortable sofa and the best
view in Britain then Sharrow Bay is heaven. From the moment you
arrive you almost sink into Sharrow Bay's unhurried all-embracing
calm, so perfectly matched to the sublime landscape of the Lake
District. It is rare to find a hotel where the view is an equal partner,
but that is the case here. From every corner of the extensive gardens,
woodlands and lake frontage you will be treated to breathtaking
panoramas of ever-changing beauty.

Such a dream setting creates the perfect backdrop to enjoy
the mouth-watering cuisine. It is no surprise that the restaurant is
Michelin rated as every meal is a feast for the senses with tantalising
menus combining tradition and contemporary flair. Another highlight
is breakfast; classic full English at its very best.

This is a hotel about individual style and the bedrooms
showcase this better than anything. They are not about the latest
trends but a heartfelt love for timeless comfort filled with quirky
charm and character. Adding to their ambience are their locations
which range from the main house, and garden to the Edwardian
Lodge gatehouse and the secluded Bank House.

Loved by generations Sharrow Bay excels at the country-
house hotel style it pioneered 60 years ago.

## HOTEL AT A GLANCE

**ACCOMMODATION**
24 rooms and suites

**DINING**
1 restaurant

**RECREATION**
Jetty, boathouse, 12 acres
of gardens and woodlands

**TRANSFERS**
Penrith rail station 15mins by car
London Euston to Penrith by train
3hrs 30mins
Newcastle Airport 1hr 45mins
Manchester Airport 2hrs

+ 44 (0)1768 486301
sharrowbay.co.uk

SIGNATURE EXPERIENCE

# TEMPTATION ON A PLATE

Sharrow Bay has always been famed for its desserts, and rightly so, but it is the sticky toffee pudding that is the most celebrated. Invented in the 1970s by the then owner Francis Coulson, this is a pudding for the gods. A sponge so light, a texture so succulent and a sauce to die for – no stay is complete without sampling this delicious treat. Now available to buy at Harvey Nicks.

"

A Michelin star and so many awards and accolades, you would go for the food alone. Breathtaking views and hospitality that's warm and genuine. It's a lake view and dinner not to be missed!

**Potty for potter**

Many of Beatrix Potter's 'little white books' were inspired by and written in the Lake District. Buy your children the books, watch the movie with Renee Zellweger, and then take them to the **World of Beatrix Potter**. Take a stroll in the Peter Rabbit Garden designed by Chelsea RHS Gold medal winner Richard Lucas.

**Go ape**

Have your teenagers got energy to burn and are they bored with the lake view? Take them to **Whinlatter Forest** and let them swing through the trees. Get a thrill from riding a zip slide under skies, over water and through England's only true mountain forest. Over 18s Gorillas, under 18s Baboons. I'm the king of the swingers, yeah, the jungle VIP… brilliant.

**Bond cars**

Get your motors running and head out on the highway for the **Bond Museum**. There are cars from most of the Bond movies including the Aston Martin DBS from 'Quantum of Solace', and the Vanquish V12 from 'Die Another Day'. How about the DB5 from 'Goldfinger'? More cars than Q branch to ogle, really astonishing and not just for the boys. OK with you, Moneypenny?

**Punchy**

Champagne by the glass, foreign draught and bottled beers, an impressive wine list in a pub? The **Punchbowl Inn** is a great place to stop for a break on a day trip for fabulous food and a read of the papers by the beautiful stone fireplace. Pub of the year in the Michelin Best 200 Pubs, it's worth a detour.

# TAMARA
## ON TRAVEL

❝
—

*For recommendations only trust your close friends who have the inside scoop.*

*Tamara Mellon OBE is world-renowned for the amazing global Jimmy Choo shoe empire.*

**TR** *Where do you call home when travelling?*

**TM** The Peninsula in LA would be a great example, it's a second home for me. I have lots of friends in LA and love the laid-back lifestyle. The spa is really amazing.

**TR** *Any menu recommendations?*

**TM** You must have the chopped grilled vegetable salad at The Ivy in LA. When Minty is with me I like to treat her to the assorted cookie platter. In London I just love Mark's Club, Scott's and Harry's Bar.

**TR** *Any favourite islands?*

**TM** I try to get to St Barts as often as my schedule allows. I go with my close friends and daughter to unwind and to get away from it all. It's always totally relaxing. The water and beaches are breathtaking and I always leave there completely rejuvenated.

**TR** *How do you maintain your good looks while travelling?*

**TM** Lots of water to keep my body hydrated and lots of cream and lotion. And sunglasses for when I arrive at my destination, preferably not off a red-eye flight!

**TR** *Any travel tips for shoes?*

**TM** I travel with my shoes in separate dust bags all contained in my new black mock croc Roy Shoe Case from the Jimmy Choo 24:7 luggage range.

## ROYAL ADVICE

Don't forget Zip-lock bags for swimwear from PracticalPrincess.com

# Tamara's

**TRAVEL THOUGHTS FOR THE WELL-HEELED**

**1 UGG**
Jimmy Choo Ugg Boots are snuggly comfort for the feet with a touch of glam

**2 24/7**
Fiona Choo's 24/7 flat sandal is perfection for daytime with sarongs, kaftans, shorts and capris

**3 TOTE**
The Jimmy Choo Babeth is the versatile must-have for all the stuff Minty and I need on the plane or the beach

# VON ESSEN FAMILY SET

—

*Not just family-friendly, but family-celebratory hotels throughout the country*

BEST FOR

KIDS

★ ★ ★ ★ ★

Just because there are children around, there is no reason not to enjoy luxury, super comfort, great food, fine wines and still have the time and energy to have fun with your children. This is the philosophy behind von Essen's family set of hotels. Each one has space to play, kick a ball, bounce on a trampoline, cycle through the grounds. Each one recognises that children need teddies as well as PlayStations, and each recognises that parents need the same space and similar entertainment… while both ages want to be looked after and spoiled during a family break to remember.

More than anything both the hotel group and its guests have the same idea of the type of childhood they want to portray – a quintessentially English one with lots of fresh air, lots of space and buckets of things to do. Children are more than simply tolerated here – they are honoured guests with their own areas, own meals and mealtimes too.

So whether you choose the Jacobean splendour of Woolley Grange in Wiltshire, the Queen Anne elegance of The Elms in Worcestershire, the coastal beauty of Fowey Hall in Cornwall, the architectural extravagance of Suffolk's Ickworth Hall and Apartments with its huge rotunda, or the Georgian grace of Moonfleet Manor in Dorset, you and your family will instantly recognise that this will be a family holiday to remember.

## HOTEL AT A GLANCE

The Elms, Worcestershire
+ 44 (0)1299 896 666

Fowey Hall, Cornwall
+ 44 (0)1726 833 866

The Ickworth Hotel &
Apartments, Suffolk
+ 44 (0)1284 735 350

Moonfleet Manor, Dorset
+ 44 (0)1305 786 948

Woolley Grange, near Bath
+ 44 (0)1225 864 705

luxuryfamilyhotels.co.uk

SIGNATURE EXPERIENCE

# STEAMING AND SHOWERING IN A WARM AND SCENTED ENVIRONMENT

The Spa at the Elms is rightly considered one of the best in Worcestershire with its own pool, delicious spa cuisine, a Rasul room made for two and more than 40 treatments to choose from. Opt for the signature face and body reviver.

Is there anywhere as magical as the English countryside for families? These hotels highlight just that throughout the year – bluebells and lambs in the springtime, the golden days of summer walks and bike rides, the conkers and berries of autumn and the happy sledging and snowballing of winter.

## The Ickworth Hotel & Apartments, Suffolk

Holiday heaven for children of all ages at Ickworth Hall and Apartments in Suffolk. Small children and babies head for the **Den**, an Ofsted-registered nursery with 24-hour access and lots of structured activities during the school holidays. Older children head for Club Blu which offers everything from table football to computer games while the grounds are ideal for biking, hiking, nature trails and a huge adventure playground.

## Fowey Hall, Cornwall

Beep! Beep! Close your eyes and you can almost hear him coming along the drive, the irrepressible Mr Toad. For Fowey Hall on Cornwall's south coast was the inspiration for **Toad Hall** in Kenneth Grahame's 'The Wind in the Willows'. Close to the sandy cove of Readymoney and the sailing centre at Fowey, the hotel has a glorious walled garden and fab spa. Head for the outdoor hot tub with views of the sea.

## Moonfleet Manor, Dorset

Full of wonder, beauty and history, the location of Moonfleet Manor leaves much to be explored and remembered. Not far from Chesil Beach with its tales of wreckages, piracy and legends… and close enough to the Jurassic coast for all types of **fossil foragers**.

## Woolley Grange, near Bath

Savour the grandeur of staying in a Tudor manor which was home to the **Hervey family** for over 200 years, and while the house is laden with history, antiques and architectural gems, the gardens are what draw visitors time and time again. There's a small walled garden near the church, a kitchen garden, a formal Italian garden, a gold and silver garden and of course 1,800 acres of parkland partly cultivated by Capability Brown. Magnificent!

# Asia

SIA

Bookings: +44 (0)20 7201 8070

masonroseprivate.com

# PARK HYATT BEIJING

—

## *Futuristic style statement high above China's capital city*

Modern, monumental, dynamic, awesome – the words used to describe Beijing's highest hotel are in themselves epic. For there is nothing ordinary about the place, which is located slap in the city's central business district and opposite the China World Trade Centre. A colossal symbol of the new China, it is but fifteen minutes from the wonder that is the Forbidden City.

An ideal place to stay to savour the seriously modern alongside the ancient and traditional. A structure of glass, steel and glittering black stone, it is a mere 66 floors high with the China Grill, one of its five eating and drinking experiences, reigning as the highest restaurant in the city and offering magnificent 360-degree views of the city.

Add to this a vintage wine bar, live jazz and both a Dynamic Fitness Centre and Tian Spa both of which have indoor lap pools. And it is in the area of wellbeing that ancient and modern meet again… with the fitness area having state-of-the-art equipment and the spa basing many of its treatments on centuries-old traditional Chinese medicine. While the Podium area has a mouth-watering array of luxury boutiques and designer shops.

Bookings: +44 (0)20 7201 8070
masonroseprivate.com

## HOTEL AT A GLANCE

**ACCOMMODATION**
237 rooms and suites

**DINING**
4 restaurants and bar

**RECREATION**
Spa, fitness and wellness centre
and 2 indoor pools

**TRANSFERS**
Beijing Capital International
Airport 40mins by car

SIGNATURE EXPERIENCE

# IT'S ALL ABOUT A PERFECTLY BALANCED BODY

Head for the Tian Spa and book a Yin and Yang Jade Restoration treatment which will highlight the vagaries of the body's energy, or chi, and then help restore its balance… so that you can enjoy your visit to Beijing even more.

+ 86 10 8567 1234
beijing.park.hyatt.com

"

The majesty of the Forbidden City and the grandeur of the Great Wall transport you back in time. The epic growth of modern design and luxe chic catapult your forward to the future. Wow!

**A dove**

**Paloma Sanchez's** given name means dove in Spanish, and you will find this little bird in some of her amazing jewellery. Her lovely boutique is a treasure trove of amethyst, smoky quartz and ametrine. A wonderful designer whose one-off pieces will spark immediate interest. Rough stones with a twist.

**Hang it up**

Mr Fang Fang of **Star Gallery** deals exclusively in Post 70s artists. This is the place to go if you want to see the rising talent of the Chinese art world. Many of the exhibitions come directly from the students of the Central Academy. Take home something completely unique and modern from the new China.

**The wall**

One of the manmade objects you can see from outer space. That and my home at Christmas. You simply have to go to say you've been. Dodge the worst of the crowds, never go on the weekends and plan to arrive in the early morning or late afternoon. **Badaling** is an hour from the city, so carve out the time for the commute.

**Candy shop**

One thing you can count on Philippe Starck for, and that's lashings of design clout. And when you drape the best eye candy in Beijing over it, you have yourself at the very top of the Twin Towers in glam central – **The Lan Club**. The cocktail prices are as vertiginous as the location, but worth the price for the ogle factor alone.

# THE PULI HOTEL AND SPA

—

## *Style haven and fashionista heaven in downtown Shanghai*

Feted as China's first urban resort, the PuLi Hotel boasts a fantastic location right in the middle of wherever you want to be in this ever-expanding metropolis. It's in the centre of the Jing An District with access by a sky bridge to shops, offices, restaurants and cafes. Best of all it overlooks Jing An Park so is one of the few places in the city where you look out onto trees!

It is already the hotel of choice of the cognoscenti while the Long Bar is the favourite of the city's fashionistas for cocktails or late-night meetings. The Jing An restaurant is where you will find visitors and locals alike enjoying the fab fusion food on offer. Make sure you book for lunch and dinner.

Style is everywhere within the hotel, including the automated sunshades in each room which are designed to adapt to different times of the day, hence not just looking after your comfort, but being ecologically savvy too. While throughout the hotel there is a modern take on traditional Chinese design with the use of furnishings and materials which are a synthesis of new and old – such as the Sung-dynasty-style headrests in the bathrooms, and the tiles on the lobby floor which were made by the same company who made those for the Forbidden City.

## HOTEL AT A GLANCE

**ACCOMMODATION**
229 rooms and suites

**DINING**
Restaurant and bar

**RECREATION**
Spa, gym, sauna, steam rooms,
infinity pool and library

**TRANSFERS**
PuDong International Airport
50mins, HongQiao Airport
20mins by car

SIGNATURE EXPERIENCE

# REPAIR, REFRESH AND TOTALLY RELAX

The Spa on the third floor has a host of pampering treatments inspired by the renowned healing properties of tea – the centuries-old beverage that has always been important to Chinese culture. For example the detoxifying properties of green tea, the balancing and anti-ageing forces of white tea, the health-giving properties of chrysanthemum tea or the beautifying properties of rose tea.

+ 86 21 3203 9999
thepuli.com

66
—

Shanghai is the cool metropolis, the Paris of the East, now pulsing with futuristic optimism and newfound wealth. The Bund at night glitters with grace. The stylish sister of Beijing.

**Style icon**

Texan Sarah Villareal studied in China, fell in love with the place and stayed. Lucky us, as she opened **The Villa** in the French Concession area. Contemporary luxury abounds in this retail space featuring contemporary and classic designers. Cocktail dress to t-shirt, it's all here in spades. The Shanghai boutique with everything.

**Shanghai feast**

Want to eat Chinese food you recognise in an elegant restaurant? **Fu 1088** is the answer. Located in a three storey Victorian mansion, it smacks of old Shanghai. Order the wild king prawn and baked codfish. This is the best place to sample Shanghainese cooking in a place of great period charm. Fortune cookie say go now.

**Hair-raising**

Penelope Cruz, Sophie Marceau, Naomi Campbell Diane Krueger won't split hairs with you over who should tend your tresses in Shanghai. **Franck Provost** is the place to go for effortless chic and a shampoo in luxury. Personal attention and stylists who listen ensure no hair disasters. You've got to look divine for your sensual night out in sexy Shanghai.

**1920s inspiration**

If you're trying to find the Shanghai of the 1920s you need to dig. The opening of **Chinatown** is a beginning. With its rich wood and dark velvet lining of what used to be a temple, you can sample the combination of burlesque, Moulin Rouge and Vegas. Naughty but nice.

# RAMBAGH PALACE

—

## *A jewel of a residence in India's gem capital*

From the riches of the Moghuls to the magic of the Maharajahs this is a palace hotel sans pareil. From its magisterial entrance, sweeping driveway, grand 47-acre garden complete with peacocks strutting their stuff on every pathway, musicians on the lawn and magnificently turbaned staff, this is where guests get first-hand experience of what it is to live like a prince.

The marble corridors lead to vast heritage suites with jewelled lights, deep sofas and rich rugs all reminiscent of days when this was one of the premier palaces of the Jaipur royal family. The vast dining room hosts paintings of their grandest Durbars and festivities, while the Polo Bar is a repository of many of the trophies won by the Maharajahs through the years. It also serves fantastic cocktails and diet-spoiling snacks. For a real Rajput experience opt for a Thali dinner on the lawns one evening where traditional music and dance provide the entertainment, while the pathways are lit with hundreds of little oil lamps giving the whole place a fairytale finish.

The Jiva tented spa continues the royal pampering while sports and fitness enthusiasts have access to indoor and outdoor pools, a gym, a jogging track and a mini-golf course on the premises. There is also an 18-hole golf course nearby.

## HOTEL AT A GLANCE

**ACCOMMODATION**
79 rooms and suites

**DINING**
3 restaurants and 2 bars

**RECREATION**
Spa, golf putting & pitching greens, nearby golf, indoor and outdoor pools, fitness centre, yoga pavilion, table tennis, polo and vintage car tours

**TRANSFERS**
Sanganer International Airport
20 to 25mins by car

+ 91 141 221 1919
tajhotels.com

SIGNATURE EXPERIENCE

# TENTED SEDUCTION IN SCENTED SWEETNESS

Cocoon yourself in the grandeur of the Jiva Spa in one of its spacious Rajasthani royal tents… and there, amidst the scent of jasmine and the sweet sound of a sitar, indulge in a face or body treatment – or indeed both. But do try the Champak Facial with its essences of marigold, rose and sandalwood.

"

The Jewel of Jaipur and former residence of the Maharajah should say it all. But if you are thinking decaying palace, wrong. It could not be more luxurious, a total stunner.

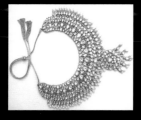

**Jewel box**

**Gem Palace** is home to the priceless jewels of the Maharajahs of Rajasthan who were forced to sell in 1972. They are now owned by the Kasliwals and on display along with the most amazing jewellery to buy. Shoppers have included Princess Diana, Sir Paul McCartney and now you. A real sparkler.

**The pink pamper**

In the garden of the Narain Niwas Palace you will find **Hot Pink**. Gorgeous clothing by Rajesh Pratap Singh and Manish Arora. Accessories and textiles from 25 hot Indian designers in one cool style haven. Great menswear, and some home items that will have you buying another suitcase. Truly fabulous.

**The future**

Do you wonder about yours? Make an appointment to see Dr Vinod Shastri, Professor of **Astrology and Palmistry** at Rajasthan University. At about USD$70 for ten minutes, it's not cheap. I see a hole in your wallet in your future. But I do love a reading… booking well in advance essential.

**Energy food**

If you need to stop for lunch while shopping, go where Bollywood goes – **Niros**. Order the laal maas or the creamy kormas which go perfectly with an ice-cold beer. The soundtrack is pop music and it's kitsch, but the food is so delicious you must go. Curry in a hurry, simply too yummy for words.

# UMAID BHAWAN PALACE JODHPUR

—

*Strong, proud, monumental –
India's last great palace*

Hotels do not get any grander than this monumental building which was only completed in the middle of the last century. With its magnificent public rooms, vast 105-foot-high cupola and 26 acres of landscaped gardens it is the embodiment, like its host city, of the power of India.

Jodhpur, 'the blue city', is as strong and masculine as Jaipur, 'the pink city', is pretty and feminine. Jodhpur is the last stronghold before travellers meet the rigours of the huge Thar Desert so it is a city that inspires strength and power, and its palace underlines that.

But it is also the place where magnificence becomes nurturing – its food is delicious, service warm and friendly and welcome memorable – it is after all still a home. The current Maharajah lives there with his family in their own quarters so, impressive as it is, it has the ambience of somewhere loved and lived in.

Take tea on the terrace and look out across the lawns, watch the changing of the mounted guards just below you, while way in the distance is Jodhpur's jewel, Mehrangarh Fort, sitting proud and forbidding on its hilltop. Have dinner there and for an evening think you are lord of all you survey – and be sure to visit the Mehrangarh Fort museum chronicling the history of the city and its family.

Bookings: +44 (0)20 7201 8070
masonroseprivate.com

## HOTEL AT A GLANCE

**ACCOMMODATION**
64 rooms and suites

**DINING**
2 restaurants and bar

**RECREATION**
Tennis, squash, croquet, health club, nearby golf, horse riding, polo on request, indoor and outdoor pools, palace museum and library

**TRANSFERS**
Jodhpur Airport 15mins by car

SIGNATURE EXPERIENCE

# SUBTERRANEAN WONDERLAND – IDEAL FOR SYBARITES

Downstairs the palace is host to the Jiva Grande Spa which has been built around the most glamorous circular swimming pool in India – each part of it decorated with the stars and constellations. The spa treatments are a sensuous mixture of east and west with great ayurvedic specialities.

+ 91 291 251 0101
tajhotels.com

A huge palace with a lavish interior of Art Deco decadence that will make you feel like a glamorous star. The Maharjah of Jodhpur is still in residence – and you, of course.

### Camels

A total flash of colour and excitement to be found every November is the **Pushkar Camel Fair**. Put Ascot and Glastonbury in a blender, add camels, pilgrims, and lots of bright colour, and you have the fair. A photographer's dream, and a visual sensory experience unequalled. Get a red ribbon Pushkar passport for your wrist.

### Silver lining

Go to the **Girdikot and Sardar Market** and prowl through this colourful bazaar. The narrow lanes are crammed with gorgeous little shops teeming with textiles and handicrafts. Not to be missed is the delicate and exquisite Rajasthani silver jewellery. Buy some for the ladies with style in your life – the pieces make wonderful gifts.

### Ghost story

A spooky excursion to the ruins of **Bhangarh** is a day-time activity; like the locals, don't go at night. Built in the 1630s and suddenly abandoned under mysterious circumstances…The story turns on an evil magician who cursed a queen. Don't go alone, take your friend Caspar.

### Village safari

Combine seeing wildlife with village life. A safari to the villages of **Bishnoi, Gudha Raika and Salawas** is as authentic a travel experience as you can get. You might even see blackbuck and chinkara in the wild en route to your appointment to join in a village opium ceremony. Lordy!

# NIGEL
## ON TRAVEL

66
—

*I love the hotels*
*Winston Churchill*
*stayed in.*

*Nigel Newton, Founder and Chief Executive of Bloomsbury Publishing which launched upon the world the phenomenon of Harry Potter.*

**TR** *How important is a specific room in a hotel?*

**NN** Extremely. The Pierre in New York is a good example of where knowledge pays. Only three rooms look directly over Central Park – rooms 1102, 2202 and 3202, all with wonderful views. They also have really comfortable beds and duvets.

**TR** *Is the décor important?*

**NN** I like good furniture in a hotel. The Savoy had the nicest everything before its recent refurbishment… beautiful shower heads, clocks, Art Deco… I love all those features. The Danieli in Venice is about as perfect as it gets, provided you have a lagoon view room.

**TR** *Do you ever dine in hotel restaurants?*

**NN** General policy – if you get in after 7pm then eat in the hotel and save the hassle of organising something more exciting… after that you eat out on the subsequent nights. I'm up for the hotel restaurant as a place of convenience, and sometimes they can be very good.

**TR** *Any extra-special places you have stayed?*

**NN** The Wawona Hotel in Yosemite National Park is very simple… the antidote to what we have been discussing… no TV… no telephone, no fluffy bathrobes… only signs about bears and saving water… no AC – no ventilation, you just open the window. Really basic and very special.

**TR** *Best experience in planning a trip?*

**NN** We once had an incredible travel agent in Sri Lanka who arranged the whole trip after we arrived and booked specific rooms in each place. Every single one of them was perfect.

## SPACE

The two things that matter when travelling – leg room on a plane and a room with a view in the hotel

# Nigel's

**HOTEL REQUESTS**

1 **KNOCK, KNOCK**
Please don't put me in a room with a noisy interconnecting door to another room, or near a lift

2 **RAINDROPS**
Please don't leave me the weather report for tomorrow saying that it will rain

3 **WOUND UP**
Please don't coil my charger cords and tie them in a knot

4 **GOODNIGHT**
Please no linen mat and slippers next to the bed

Bookings: +44 (0)20 7201 8070
masonroseprivate.com

# THE TAJ MAHAL PALACE, MUMBAI

—

*India's most impressive
and iconic hotel*

It sits in its full majesty overlooking the bay of Mumbai and directly opposite the Gateway of India – the monumental archway that travellers and traders first saw as they approached the city. The hotel with its vast tower and truly amazing Heritage Wing has welcomed princes and potentates, kings and rulers, plutocrats and presidents along with rock stars and artists throughout its great history. The main lobby is a hive of activity throughout the day and a great place to meet in the evening. Everybody who is anybody visiting this city will, at some point, pass through its portals.

The rooms and suites of the Heritage Wing have been beautifully and lovingly restored and lovers of the hotel have been flooding back to stay there. Its courtyard swimming pool is one of the most fashionable places to lunch and THE place for power breakfasts… and of course to relax and unwind after a long flight, a heavy day's shopping or a business meeting. The entrance to the Jiva Spa is hidden by luxuriant plants which provide shade as well as privacy. The Spa is the place for a reviving massage or facial… and it offers a state-of-the-art fitness centre with a special yoga programme.

But it is in its choice of restaurants and bars that this major city hotel is pre-eminent – eat Japanese, Indian, Mediterranean, Chinese, international – whatever you want, there is a restaurant or cafe serving it, while a must in the early evening is a cocktail in the Harbour Bar with its views. Later, head for the Starboard Bar for those wanting to taste Mumbai nightlife, complete with live music.

---

**HOTEL AT A GLANCE**

**ACCOMMODATION**
560 rooms and suites

**DINING**
8 restaurants and 2 bars

**RECREATION**
Spa, pool, art walk, Vedic astrology, private yacht cruises and fitness centre

**TRANSFERS**
Chhatrapati Shivaji International Airport 45mins by car

SIGNATURE EXPERIENCE

# BOOKS, BIJOUX AND BEAUTIFUL THINGS

The hotel's shopping arcade offers serious jewellery – antique and modern – then Nalanda, one of the best bookshops in the city, Burlington's the tailors who can make you a jacket, dress or shirt in 24 hours and Joy the shoe-shop for jewelled and inexpensive sandals.

66

Anyone who's anyone flocks to this Mumbai institution. Kings, princes, CEOs, all appreciate its gracious elegance and warm hospitality. You will too. Alabaster ceilings, onyx columns, silk carpets… it's no wonder it's called a Palace.

**Celeb magnet**

**Enigma** is one of the hottest nightclubs in town. Have the concierge set you up to queue-jump directly to the bar. DJ Akhtar gets the groove underway with a mix of Western and Bollywood music. The dance floor pulses under a mega chandelier illuminating the Bollywood stars that frequent this über-club. Get amongst it.

**Hindu sunset**

Take a boat out to **Elephanta Island Caves**, a UNESCO World Heritage site, for a taste of Hindu culture. Go late afternoon to see Mumbai from the water at sunset away of the mayhem of the streets. When you disembark drop into the Starboard Bar in the hotel for drinks. A refreshing buzz.

**Colonial clout**

A visit to the Prince of Wales Museum is an excellent respite from the clamour of the city, and a step back in time. There is an impressive collection of Hindu and Buddhist sculpture alongside miniature paintings, porcelain, weapons and stuffed animals. Make sure you get the audio guide and do 'Curator's Choice' to see the best bits. The boys will like the weaponry.

**Electrifying**

Think India, and think lush colourful fabrics. **Bombay Electric** is a palace of cool right across the road from the hotel. Clothing for women, men, kids, vintage, gifts… they have it all with lashings of local style. Cherry-picked fashion with a who's who clientele. It's the Barneys of Mumbai. Absolutely fabulous, sweetie.

# TAJ LAKE PALACE, UDAIPUR

—

*A shimmering fairytale on a lake*
*offers all the romance of Rajasthan*

Summoning up all the romance of the Rajputs, this exquisite pleasure palace floating on Lake Pichola is the stuff of dreams. Its white walls, battlements, turrets and arches gleam in the sunshine and glow by moonlight. Little wonder it is famed as the most romantic hotel on the planet.

Accessed by its own liveried launches, from the minute you arrive at its marble steps you feel that you literally are part of another world, another universe, away from the frenzy of everyday life… and yet within its walls everything that keeps you connected to everyday life is available – WiFi, DVDs and satellite TV!

However, ignore such intrusions when you can, and savour the scented gardens, the shaded courtyards, the dark pools and the gentle fountains. Enjoy the breezes high on the battlements while you sip a cocktail or surrender to a massage, savour the shadows of the evening and the glittering stars reflected in the lake… and know for a few minutes what the magic of being a Maharani must have been like. Absorb and remember the sensation, for memories are made of such moments. This is India at its most magical, its most seductive and its most unforgettable – in a shimmering white palace on the water.

---

**HOTEL AT A GLANCE**

**ACCOMMODATION**
83 rooms and suites

**DINING**
3 restaurants and bar

**RECREATION**
Spa including Jiva Spa boat, yoga
and meditation classes, outdoor
pool, heritage Champagne walks
and vintage car tours

**TRANSFERS**
Maharana Pratap Airport
45 to 60mins by car

+ 91 294 242 8800
tajhotels.com

SIGNATURE EXPERIENCE

# WATER THERAPY WITH A LUXURIOUS DIFFERENCE

Take to the lake on the Jiva Royal Spa Boat and be pampered with
a three-hour session of steaming, wrapping, exfoliating and massaging.
Simply heaven. Afterwards recline on cushions on deck as you survey
the numerous palaces bordering the lake while sipping a glass of
something bubbly.

66
—

A romantic dream palace of white marble floating in Lake Pichola. The real experience of feeling like royalty delivered on every level in total opulence. Breathtaking.

**Tigger**

Not the Winnie the Pooh variety, but the ones with big teeth and paws. **The Ranthambore National Park** is home to these gorgeous pussy cats, best seen with experts from a distance and not for patting. March – June is the best time to spot them. Also visit the Ganesh Temple at Ranthambore Fort, built about 1000 years ago.

**Royal spa**

The most indulgent spa experience has got to be the Soma, Nectar of the Gods at the **Jiva Spa**. Two therapists, aromatherapy massage, candle-lit ambience, rose petal bath, Champagne at sunset, and a floral blessing. Will that be all, Miss? That will be Your Majesty if you don't mind.

**History lesson**

When you're in a palace, it is kind of nice to know something about it. But so much more palatable when you have Champagne to lubricate the experience. Take the **Champagne heritage tour** of the hotel, but book privately so you can go at your own pace, and not dogged by irritating would-be historians.

**Curry favour**

Do you wish you could turn out a divine curry without pouring it out of a jar? **A private cooking lesson with Chef** will have you rustling up your own aromatic and utterly delicious curries. After your lesson why not take time to enjoy the Indian flavours for yourself with a private dining experience looking over the lake or palace. On your return home your neighbours at number 42 will be round to sample your cooking in the flash of a pan.

# PARK HYATT TOKYO

—

*Designed to thrill, a
star-studded place to stay*

Bill Murray and Scarlett Johansson might have starred
in 'Lost in Translation' but the Park Hyatt Tokyo stole the show.
It is not hard to see why as this sleek citadel is the height of design;
soaring bold architecture, tranquil modernist interiors, spellbinding
views of snow-peaked Mount Fuji and the throbbing metropolis
make this the most stylish place to stay.

The intimate Park Hyatt Tokyo cossets its guests in a very
singular manner; it swathes you in a special kind of luxurious care.
Rooms have the feel of expansive lofts; their exquisite style filled
with whimsical features such as rare water elm panelling, original
artwork and, from the windows, a dizzying panorama. Bathrooms are
vast with deliciously deep soaking tubs. A must-do is to take a dip in
the glass-enclosed pool on the 47th floor, preferably at dawn or dusk
as you feel as if you are swimming in the heavens. Whilst there check
out the spa, a truly relaxing urban oasis.

Dining is spectacular in every sense; contemporary Japanese
in the gorgeously crafted Kozue, classic brasserie style in Girandole and
for something truly special the New York Grill, where the world-
famous Wagyu beef is unbelievable. Post dinner enjoy the dazzling
city lights over cocktails and jazz at the bar or savour the gentle
magic of the bamboo garden softly lit by 'washi' paper lanterns.

---

**HOTEL AT A GLANCE**

**ACCOMMODATION**
178 rooms and suites

**DINING**
5 restaurants, 2 bars and
a patisserie

**RECREATION**
Spa and health club with
indoor pool and library

**TRANSFERS**
Narita International Airport
1hr 20mins by car

+ 81 3 5322 1234
tokyo.park.hyatt.com

---

SIGNATURE EXPERIENCE

# THE BUSINESS OF EATING, CATERING AND SHEER ENJOYMENT

An early morning visit to Tokyo's famed Tsukiji market is a must. This is where restaurateurs, hoteliers and the plain greedy come to buy that day's fare. There are acres of tuna, some the size of small islands, and stalls full of the most exotic fish and fruits of the ocean. Head for one of the local cafes to have an unforgettable repast of raw fish for breakfast.

"

———

Kinetic energy, techno cool and Zen
in one sushi roll of design decadence.
The swish of a silk kimono over sleek
patent leather as a breeze rustles through
bamboo fronds. Shy, bold, and seductive.

**Ladies who lunch**

Before you even arrive in Tokyo
you have probably heard of
the **Ginza** district. Sony and
Apple are iPad to shoulder pad
with Dior, Gucci and Hermès.
Rest your feet over lunch at
Alain Ducasse's **Beige** at the
top of the Chanel building.
An exclusive neighbourhood.

**Oenophile**

It's hard to drag yourself away
from the New York Bar at the
Park Hyatt, but for the wine
buff go to **Arossa**, a lovely
Australian wine bar and
restaurant. The surprise is that
it boasts 500+ vintages from
Australia and New Zealand,
ten of which are by the glass
daily. Nice drop, good on
ya mate!

**A tea of tranquillity**

If you are finding the sheer
energy of Tokyo whirring
around you dizzying and you
need to stop and breathe, take
a leaf out of my book and go
to **Hamarikyu Gardens**.
Dating from the 17th century,
it's a lush oasis of green in
which you can sip your green
tea from the traditional
teahouse and suck pine-
scented air into your lungs.

**Cool teens**

Do you have teens in tow
who are obsessed with
vampires and draining your
blood with a look? Take them
to **Tokyo Hipsters Club** and
suddenly you'll be the coolest
parent on the planet. Full of
über-jeans, custom sneakers
and t-shirts. And if the
weather is right head to the
rooftop cafe where the local
cool creatures of the night are
all sucking on a Coca-Cola.

# THE DATAI

—

## *Luxury hideaway sheltering among the riches of the rainforest*

So well hidden is this glorious hotel, both from the road and the beach below, that it comes as a stunning surprise when guests actually arrive. Hidden in a deep valley and surrounded by indigenous rainforest it offers the ultimate in luxurious seclusion – even though there are 110 rooms, a spa, four restaurants, a fitness centre and tennis courts.

It is a true example of how nature and modernity work seamlessly side by side and is an ideal destination for those seeking peace and quiet with glorious food, a little pampering and very little else. Of course should you want to exert yourself there are tennis courts, an 18-hole golf course nearby, a little light sailing and fishing, yoga and Pilates classes daily, mountain-biking; and if you are yearning for excitement, the Langkawi cable car will whisk you high over the rainforest, and reward you with magnificent views of the Andaman Sea.

But it is difficult to tear yourself away from the joys of the hotel – its restaurants serving both international and that great local melange of Indian/Malay and Thai food that helps make Malaysian cuisine as exotic as it is. And then there is the spa, a retreat within the jungle of just four treatment pavilions offering the best of Balinese and Ayurveda therapies. Spoil yourself with a two-hour ritual.

## HOTEL AT A GLANCE

**ACCOMMODATION**
110 rooms, suites and villas

**DINING**
4 restaurants and 2 bars

**RECREATION**
Spa, 2 pools, nearby golf, mountain
bikes, guided nature walks and
tours and culinary classes

**TRANSFERS**
Langkawi International Airport
30mins by car

SIGNATURE EXPERIENCE

# JUNGLE FORAY FOR A TRADITIONAL GOURMET DELIGHT

Head into the jungle – just 300 metres away actually – to a traditional
Malay wooden building, the Gulai House, for an authentic Indian
Malay meal accompanied by a cultural exploration of music and dance.

+ 60 4 959 2500
ghmhotels.com

*Tanya's travel secrets...*

66
—

Pure escapism in the most lush tropical rainforest on a powder beach lapped by azure waters. Day one and your city coil will immediately unravel leaving you tension-free and serene.

**Forest**

If you can tear yourself away from your busy schedule of relaxing, you must see the **Mangrove forest**. This ecological marvel between land and sea is only accessible by boat. Think Discovery Channel as you encounter exotic plants and animals in this natural habitat. Not a sofa in sight.

**Sans paparazzi**

Do you need total privacy? Book one of the **pool villas** which are all perfectly positioned to create a singular sensational abode. With your own plunge pool and daybed off your palatial digs, it's just the two of you, alone and out of camera lens range. Private paradise.

**Precious gem**

You must book in for the **Datai Jade Massage** which will dissolve any ounce of tension in your body. Two, yes, count them… two therapists bring the best of Japanese shiatsu, Balinese, Thai and Hawaiian lomi-lomi to create one stratospheric spa treatment. Pour yourself into bed or onto your daybed following the experience and sink into blissful sleep.

**Swing**

It don't mean a thing if you ain't got that swing, in the forest or on the golf course. Book time with the pro to take you round this **golf course** built within the 8,000-acre Gunung Mat Chin-Chang forest reserve. This course is all about thinking rather than power. Grab the right club and swing.

# TERENCE & VICKI

## ON TRAVEL

"
—

*We love new experiences, sights, people and of course, food.*

*Sir Terence and Vicki Conran are the tour-de-force couple whose work continues to set the pace of design.*

**TR** *How have you channelled your travel experiences into your Boundary Project in Shoreditch?*

**TC/VC** We have definitely funnelled our knowledge from our constant travels into this project. We have created a cheap and cheerful cafe called Albion on the ground floor with a bakery and its own small shop, ideal for breakfast. We have quite a grand restaurant and sexy bar in the basement with an excellent wine cellar. There are just 17 rooms of which five are suites. Finally the fantastic rooftop cafe, has an open log fire, comfortable chairs, and Welsh blankets for chilly nights or days, and of course cigars available.

**TR** *What's your idea of travel bliss?*

**TC/VC** A list of good restaurants, pre-planned and booked for lunch or dinner, and plenty of cash.

**TR** *Where do you go in the Far East?*

**TC/VC** We love the Park Hyatt Tokyo, it's very smart, serene and perfectly managed. The restaurant Kozue is wonderful, as is the buzzy bar and grill on the top floor with breathtaking views over the city. There is a marvellous swimming pool too. The Park Hyatt Shanghai is a remarkable hotel with many features quite unlike any other. The conference suites are particularly very unusual. The bathrooms are spectacular.

**TR** *Any special surprises about the food in the Far East?*

**TC/VC** The aesthetic pleasure of eating simple noodles served with such precision in exquisite bowls, boxes, pots, cups and glasses.

**TR** *Best place you have experienced recently?*

**TC/VC** Aman Bagh, Anwar Rajasthan. Set in a Moghul garden surrounded by ancient wild hills, this is a haven of luxury. Beautiful havelis, many with their own pool, and a very good kitchen garden providing the best salads in India. Lots of things to do, or you can do nothing, it's heavenly.

## MUSIC TO MY EARS
An iPod loaded up with all the music you've ever thought of wanting
▶

*Terence and Vicki's*

**CLASSIC TRAVEL TIPS**

1 **GLOBE TROTTER LUGGAGE**
Travel in elegant style with luggage that says it all

2 **BENTLEY**
Motor with grace and aplomb in an old Bentley

3 **BOOKS FROM JOHN SANDOE**
Buy a pile of hardback books recommended by the knowledgeable team at this timeless bookstore

# ONE&ONLY REETHI RAH

—

*One of the world's most luxurious getaways where pampering is an art form*

BEST FOR

HONEY-
MOONS

★★★★★

If you had a checklist for an island paradise, you would end up at One&Only Reethi Rah. Its name means 'beautiful island' and it certainly lives up to that with its verdant gardens, powdersoft sand, turquoise waters and a reef rich with coral and sea life.

This truly dreamy setting is home to 130 extremely private villas dotted all over the island – some on the beach, others built on stilts suspended above the ocean. As serene as their backdrop the interiors are in a chic contemporary Asian style. Number one priority is you, as each comes with a villa host who looks after you in the most charming and attentive way. If you can tear yourself away from snoozing on your daybed or the water villa's fabulous hammocks suspended over the sea there are dozens of diversions to entertain you. There are a staggering 12 beaches and for further exploration grab a bicycle or buggy.

Dishes from all corners of the globe are presented in the resort's restaurants or on your villa's private deck. From the über-cool beach bar Fanditha, sophisticated Tapasake set on stilts above the water teeming with colourful fish and the exquisitely designed Reethi Restaurant, dining is heavenly. For a quiet or active getaway, romance or spending time with the family One&Only Reethi Rah is a top recommendation.

---

**HOTEL AT A GLANCE**

**ACCOMMODATION**
130 villas

**DINING**
3 restaurants, bar, and 24hr
in-villa dining

**RECREATION**
Tennis academy, swimming pools,
watersports, PADI dive centre,
deep-sea Dhoni fishing, fitness
centre, spa, kids' club, beach
football and volleyball

**TRANSFERS**
Malé International Airport 75mins
by luxury private yacht

+ 960 664 8800
oneandonlyresorts.com

SIGNATURE EXPERIENCE

# A PERSONAL HAVEN OF WELLNESS AND RELAXATION

No stay is complete without experiencing the incredible One&Only Spa by ESPA, with over 100,000 square feet dedicated to the wellbeing journey. You will find not only individual treatment villas but swirling vitality pools, crystal steam rooms, lifestyle showers and relaxation suites. Devotees of yoga and meditation adore the calming environment of the open-air Chi Pavilion which extends out over the sea.

"

A gem set in sophistication. Paradise found, a desert island dream. You can't help but feel beautiful in a place where you can romance with your one and only love. Utterly divine.

**Dressed to kill**

Go to **Anya Hindmarch** for everything you need to look the part. Anya's sense of what is right for the season begins with an injection of sunshine and colour before you have even started a tan. Poolside or in the restaurant you'll look effortlessly elegant. As the Aussies would say…"Good on yer, Anya."

**Fish tank**

Finding Nemo will be a breeze when you dip one fin-clad foot into the 50-metre-visibility crystal-clear waters surrounding Reethi Rah. The only PADI National Geographic dive centre in the Maldives, and you can be qualified in a week! It's a veritable kaleidoscope of fish, turtles and manta rays gliding about gracefully waiting to strike a pose for your waterproof digital camera.

**Yoga followed by yoghurt**

Make the effort to get up for sunrise in the open-air Chi Pavilion for **private yoga** with the resident guru. Meditation or fat burning, it's all just what you need before slowly spooning yoghurt at breakfast in a state of total calm. Beats the rush hour.

**Romantic cocktail**

Take the Dhoni, a traditional sailing yacht; add chilled Champagne, gourmet canapés, and one gorgeous couple. Stir gently and voilà, you have your own sunset drinks on a **deserted island** all of your own. Comfy chairs, feet in the water, gentle breeze, and the hand of the one you love in yours. Unbeatable romance.

# SIX SENSES ZIGHY BAY

—

## *Sensual delight in a dramatic location*

Drama defines Six Senses' first resort in the Middle East. A mega-dramatic location on the edge of a peninsula, hidden by the high dark Hajar Mountains, bordered by the iridescent blue of the Arabian Sea and fringed by a cashmere-soft white beach. Arriving can be quite memorable too if you decide to leave your baggage in the capable hands of a driver while you hop onto a paraglider with the hotel's expert and descend by air to reception. Heart-stopping? Yes... but that applies to the views as you go down.

After that, you will probably have had enough excitement for a day or two and will just need to chill out in the sublime luxury of one of the pool villas – once ensconced in your holiday home, it is very difficult to tear yourself away even to visit the resort's renowned spa. But please do try and enjoy one of their rituals, which use only natural and organic ingredients in the oils and potions. Otherwise try a sunset cruise, while snorkellers will adore the crystal-clear waters.

However, this is a place for serious rest and relaxation and is an ideal romantic retreat... never more so than when Dining on the Edge, the restaurant set atop a mountain which is the place to watch the sun go down on Zighy Bay and count the stars as they come out at night.

## HOTEL AT A GLANCE

**ACCOMMODATION**
82 private villas

**DINING**
2 restaurants, bar, wine cellar
and deli

**RECREATION**
Spa, adventure experiences, dhow
cruises, snorkelling, jogging and
walking trails, mountain bikes,
beach volleyball, paragliding,
watersports and astronomy classes

**TRANSFERS**
Dubai Airport 1hrs 30mins by car

+ 968 26735 555
sixsenses.com

SIGNATURE EXPERIENCE

# THE MAGNIFICENCE
# OF THE SKY AT NIGHT

This is the place to go star-gazing. It doesn't get any better than
out here almost at the edge of land with vast midnight blue skies,
no lights to interfere and literally thousands of sparkling delights.
Lie back and count shooting stars as well as any number of
passing meteors.

66

—

Give way to your senses and naturally feel yourself slow down and unwind. Zighy Bay is the ultimate hideaway on a stunning stretch of beach. Wrapped in a cocoon of pampering in holistic heaven.

**Bond arrival**

Do you have a sense of adventure and derring-do? Why pull up in the driveway of the hotel like ordinary people when you can **paraglide** directly to the beach outside your villa from the top of Zighy Mountain? Yes! Really!… it's an absolute scream, literally. Fabulous dinner-party conversation piece.

**Secret staircase**

A one-hour 4X4 drive from the hotel will find you 1,200 metres above sea level at the **Sabatyn Plateau**. Explore the abandoned village of Sabatyn via the secret staircase. Full of ancient houses and stone towers, it's just incredible. Picnic on the mountain top and enjoy the most stunning views to Wadi Al Bih. Photographic inspiration and opportunity abound.

**On the edge**

There's nothing like a stunning view to add drama and romance to dinner. How about 300 metres up, beach and the resort below and sunset glowing over the sea? Don't worry, you are not teetering on a cliff – think large terrace, amazing food, and a stargazer to check out Lucy in the sky, or perhaps the Big Dipper?

**Go dhow**

Just the two of you or the whole family, on a dhow in the **Fjords of Musandam**. Your butler will arrange lunch on board. Older kids and teenagers will love the experience, the view and the snorkelling and kayaking. Imagine visiting what is known as the Norway of the Middle East in your own private dhow. Great fun.

# THE CHEDI MUSCAT

—

*The splendour of the desert
amid the traditions of Arabia*

BEST FOR

QUICK
WINTER SUN

★ ★ ★ ★ ★

With its dramatic location running from the beaches of the
Gulf of Oman and the vast blue expanse of the Indian Ocean in front,
to the wild backdrop of mountains and desert, the Chedi has all the
elements of an Arabian fantasy.

Within its environs are cool courtyards with fountains and
pools, carved archways and screens leading into magical gardens
scented with jasmine, a beautifully designed water garden, a state-of-
the-art spa and fitness centre, three swimming pools and restaurants
and cafes to tempt all palates. The rooms and suites are a magical
example of contemporary cool with neutral shades in natural
materials, all housed in traditional Omani-inspired buildings.

Best of all, the property is a mere 20 minutes from the
international airport and in even less time guests can be in the midst
of the hustle and bustle of the city's souks and markets. This is the
place to bargain and barter… but you must have time and patience.

After which, repair back to the tranquil acres of the hotel to
luxuriate in a beach cabana where cool drinks can be brought to you,
or be pampered in the Asian-inspired spa or simply relax by one of
the pools. Do make sure though that you divide your dining options
between the Arabian Courtyard for delicious Middle Eastern food
and the Beach Restaurant for spectacularly good seafood.

## HOTEL AT A GLANCE

**ACCOMMODATION**
159 rooms, suites and private villas

**DINING**
3 restaurants, bar lounge and
2 poolside cabanas

**RECREATION**
Spa, gym, swimming pools
(adults and children) and
flood-lit tennis courts

**TRANSFERS**
Seeb International Airport
(Muscat) 20mins by car

SIGNATURE EXPERIENCE

# EXPERIENCE THE PEACE OF THE WAVES AS THE SUN SETS OVER THE GULF

Watch the day slowly end, as the sun slips beneath the horizon and washes the gulf and the beach in a golden glow, while taking a sunset cruise. The best way to enjoy it is on a traditional dhow, which the concierge will organise.

+ 968 24 52 4400
ghmhotels.com

*Tanya's travel secrets...*

"

When winter's arctic chill is getting to you, this is the perfect place to thaw out in quiet luxury and guaranteed heat. Luxuriate poolside in the comfort knowledge that tomorrow's forecast is wall-to-wall sunshine.

**4x4**

Book a private off-road trip through the Hajar Mountains to Wadi Abyad and its famous water pools. There are nine- or four-hour trips – stipulate you only want the four hour version with sunset drinks. And ask the driver to take it gently; it can be a white-knuckle ride!

**Silver lining**

A full day trip via the oasis of Fanjah and Birkat Al Mauz to reach the amazing Nizwa and its very impressive 17th-century fort. Spend time at the souk for the amazing **Bedouin silver jewellery**. Fabulous with a white shirt, tan and your favourite jeans back in Blighty.

**Fast cat**

Do venture out to see Muscat, but do it quickly and not in the midday sun. Visit the **Sultan Qaboos Grand Mosque**. Be sure to check on the etiquette of what to wear. Crank the air conditioning, and plan on pool time when you get home.

**Retail therapy**

For the authentic local experience hit the **Muttrah Souk** sans jewellery and look for sandalwood and mother-of-pearl. Designerland is situated in the Qurum district with air-conditioned mall **Al Araimi**. Stop for a rich coffee at **Café Camilla**. Reflexology in the spa upon return.

# SONEVA KIRI
# BY SIX SENSES

—

*Taking eco chic to new heights,*
*this blissful island paradise is*
*the ultimate in barefoot luxury*

James Bond eat your heart out! Arriving at Soneva Kiri is a
very glamorous affair; first a private plane whisks you from Bangkok,
then a speedboat to the island of Koh Kood where your own personal
Mr or Ms Friday greets you and will be on hand throughout your stay.
    Such an entrance gives a glimpse of the untouched beauty
that awaits you; picture pristine white sands, crystal-clear waters
and lush tropical forests. A breathtaking backdrop for a resort so
groundbreaking it sets the benchmark for luxurious and eco-friendly
hotels. Everything is about style and sustainability; super-spacious
villas are in complete harmony with the setting; styled with a
contemporary colonial feel they come with panoramic water views,
private pool and a handy buggy to zip around the 100-acre estate.
For total guilt-free pleasure, book the pioneering Eco Villa which
spectacularly showcases the latest environmental innovations.
    How to spend your day is easy – the endless array of gorgeous
extras is enough to blur the senses. Be tempted by indulgent ice
cream and chocolate parlours; stargaze at the observatory, for kids
there's a cool Den and for you a sensational spa with out-of-this-
world treatments. You can jungle trek, snorkel on deserted islands or
simply relax in the sun. Come sunset check out the stunning bars and
restaurants; from authentic Thai cuisine to sublime fine dining each
is unique.

---

### HOTEL AT A GLANCE

**ACCOMMODATION**
29 private pool villas

**DINING**
5 restaurants and 3 bars

**RECREATION**
Spa, Kids' Den, outdoor cinema, watersports including PADI dive centre, tennis, fitness centre, jungle treks, astronomy and cooking classes

**TRANSFERS**
Bangkok airport 45mins by private plane and speedboat

+ 66 3961 9800
sixsenses.com

---

SIGNATURE EXPERIENCE

# THE SKY'S THE LIMIT

Innovative dining is big here; you can hop on a speedboat to one and relax on daybeds at another but the real high point is Treepod Dining. A steel and rattan cocoon is winched up 16ft into a eucalyptus tree; your waiter flies in Cirque du Soleil style on a zipline to serve simple Thai-inspired dishes. Not only fun but the view is fabulous too!

66

---

An island paradise in the Gulf of Siam that exudes tropical luxury. Wrapped in warm, genuine service. Soothed by balmy waters and gentle ocean breeze. Visually stunning with breathtaking views in accessible seclusion.

**Blissful back**

We could all use a little TLC for the back, and you've landed in just the right place. Book in for **Kati Vasti** in the spa. Kati is the lower back in Sanskrit. A ring of herbal paste is applied in a circle on your back holding warm oil in the middle for 30 minutes. Back massage and steam towels follow… ahh!

**Starry nights**

Can you believe Soneva Kiri has its own **observatory** to take in the spray of stars in the sky above? Astronomy lessons your kids will love. And more stars to be seen at **Cinema Paradiso**, the outdoor cinema. Classic movies complemented by cocktails and gourmet food. Popcorn and ice cream too!

**Art d'eco kids**

Boris Zeisser of 24H-architects has created the most incredible eco-friendly **Kids Den** out of local natural materials. At check-in your kids will get their personalised invite to this sting-ray-shaped camp of entertainment. While you chill out and regain your sanity, your little ones will be busy with iPods of music, cinema, painting and energy-burning activities.

**Scream**

We all scream for ice cream. And you will when you feast your eyes on El Bulli chef Jaume Esperalba's ice cream parlour **Soneva So Chilled**. There are 60 flavours of sorbet, gelato and ice cream for you to make your way through. You'll really scream when you discover it's right next door to **Ever Soneva Chocoholic**. Sweet dreams are made of this.

# JUMEIRAH BAB AL SHAMS

—

*Elegant desert retreat*
*in traditional style*

Driving through the Dubai desert surrounded by golden sand, you will begin to wonder whether the edifice you are nearing is a mirage. Relax, it's not – it is simply the favourite desert retreat of those who live, work and visit Dubai. A melange of Arabic styles with pools, archways, wind towers, pillars, palms and fountains throughout it quickly seduces the traveller's senses.

Rooms and suites feature cool contemporary muted shades interspersed with Bedouin rugs, brass tables and jewel-like lamps. The retreat is romantic and fairytale-like for couples and honeymooners and yet it is terrific fun for families. The children have their own Sinbad Kids' Club where they are entertained and cared for throughout the day so that grown-ups have a chance to relax and unwind by the pool or in the Satori Spa.

And although there is a fitness centre, the desert provides all the activity most of us require with guided camel rides across the sands – if you've never ridden a camel, try it. For although the beginning is startling when the beast stands up, after that it is surprisingly comfortable. Horseriding and 4x4 desert excursions as well as falconry displays are also on offer. And whatever you do, do not miss dinner at Al Hadheerah (one of the resorts' eight restaurants and bars) for a truly spectacular display of belly dancing, whirling dervishes and another falconry display!

### HOTEL AT A GLANCE

**ACCOMMODATION**
113 rooms and suites

**DINING**
3 restaurants, rooftop lounge,
pool bar and pizzeria

**RECREATION**
Spa, 3 pools, desert activities
including horse riding, camel rides,
4x4 trips, gym, archery centre,
croquet, petanque, kids' club

**TRANSFERS**
Dubai International Airport
45mins by car

+ 9714 8096100
jumeirah.com

SIGNATURE EXPERIENCE

# THE SENSATIONAL SOUND OF SILENCE

Ever wondered why travellers fall in love with the desert? It's not just its mystery, nor its size – it is its stillness. So, when nobody is watching take a walk on your own into the desert (you don't need to go far), sit and listen to its silence. So quiet you can almost hear it.

*Tanya's travel secrets...*

"

An air-conditioned Arabian fantasy
in the desert, close to Dubai but far
enough away to feel solitude and
peace. Inspiring serene sunsets that
will melt your stress away. You'll
feel like a princess.

**Have camel can travel**

Are you hankering to relive
SATC2? Grab your girlfriends
and choose your **camel**. Go all
the way and plan a completely
OTT Patricia-Field-worthy
outfit and climb aboard.
One hump or two?

**Arabian fairytale**

Prince! Grab your princess
and head next door to the
**Al Hadheerah Desert
Restaurant**. A recreation
of a traditional desert fort.
Live cooking stations,
wood-fired ovens, spit roasts;
the aromas will whet your
appetite. Get a henna tattoo
and dance the night away
to a live band.

**Cushy view**

There is nothing more serene
than a desert sunset. Especially
when you are poured post
spa into a sea of cushions in
the **Al Sarab Rooftop Lounge**.
Sipping on your G&T with
every fibre of your being in
a state of tranquillity.
Softly softly.

**Magic carpet ride**

Check out the **Blue Souq**,
which is also known as the
Central Market. Lovely vaulted
buildings in blue tiles. The
upper level has wonderful shops
full of silk and wool carpets
from Iran, Pakistan and India.
It's also a treasure trove of
silver jewellery and wearable
antiques. A whole new world.

# ONE&ONLY ROYAL MIRAGE

—

## *A palatial resort evoking the splendour and mystical spirit of old Arabia*

You are spoilt for choice at One&Only Royal Mirage as not one but three remarkable hotels are set in the sprawling grounds. Each is very distinctive in personality and style – The Palace, with its regal and grand aura; Arabian Court filled with the mystique of the Orient; and the exclusive Residence & Spa for a discreet opulence.

In the midst of hectic Dubai, this resort is like an oasis of calm. A wonderful place of intricate arches, domes and towers, interspersed by courtyards, acres of landscaped gardens, palm-shaded pools and cooling fountains. A kilometre stretch of beach, one of the best to be found, is the perfect playground for the many water activities. It is a dream spot for kids as they can ride camels, bellydance, water-ski and kayak while grown-ups can sneak off to the spa which boasts a slew of treatments including a traditional Hammam.

Then there is the cuisine. From Moroccan to Asian and Mediterranean to casual beachside seafood, eight world class restaurants feature a stunning array of different styles.

In all three hotels, guestrooms are spacious but if you are seeking unashamed self-indulgence choose the rooftop Prestige rooms in the Residence & Spa. These are divine with their private pool terrace complete with cushion-strewn gazebo and stunning views over the fragrant gardens to the Arabian Gulf beyond.

---

**HOTEL AT A GLANCE**

**ACCOMMODATION**
Arabian Court 172 rooms and suites
The Palace 235 rooms and suites
Residence & Spa 50 rooms, suites
and villa

**DINING**
8 restaurants, bars and nightclub

**RECREATION**
Health & Beauty Institute with
spa and Hammam, watersports,
swimming pools, kids' club, nearby
golf and desert trips

**TRANSFERS**
Dubai International Airport
30mins by car

+ 971 4 399 99 99
oneandonlyresorts.com

SIGNATURE EXPERIENCE

# HEIGHT OF DELIGHT

Make your way through the 2,000 lanterns and candles that light
the meandering paths to the Rooftop Lounge at The Arabian
Court. Mounds of embroidered cushions, the sky as your ceiling
and an undeniably chilled-out vibe make this the coolest place
to enjoy cocktails and oriental mezzes late into the night.

# Arabian nights await at this lavish palace in the Emirates. Far from the madding crowd, it's a true oasis, and the One and Only place to be in Dubai.

**Pampered puss**

Does the thought of getting dust on your Choos make you go Blanik? Don't go out during the day and self-combust in the heat, wait until the sun has gone down and make your way to the **Souk Madinat Jumeirah** which is a fabulous faux version of the real thing. Air-conditioning, narrow lanes, traditional architecture – all decorated with twinkling lights and crammed with treasures.

**Wild water**

Enjoy the thrill of jumping into the largest waterpark in the Middle East. **Aquaventure Waterpark** is overflowing with 42 fun-filled acres including Master Blasters, speedslide, rivers, rapids, Splashers children's play area and a private beach. Located at Atlantis, The Palm, Aquaventure is the ultimate fun day out for all the family.

**Star curry**

**Asha's** has the most fabulous contemporary Indian cuisine in Dubai. Asha Bhosle has 13,000 songs to her credit (the most recordings in the world), 1997 and 2001 MTV Viewers' Choice awards, The Freddie Mercury Award and a Filmfare Lifetime achievement award just to name a few. So you can imagine the dedication, finesse and attention to the cuisine in her gorgeous restaurant. In case you're wondering, this establishment does have an alcohol licence… Cheers.

**Back to the future**

It's Sunday night and you love 80s music? Go to the terrace at **Sho Cho** and secure yourself a strategic spot and put on your dancing shoes. They serve food if you need to munch, but the star attraction is the crazy crowd where tables become dance podiums. Go ahead… embarrass your kids. Everybody cut footloose!

# HENRY
## ON TRAVEL

*of travel is to*
*hat you like*
*at you don't…*
*do it.*

*The wonderful Henry Wyndham, Chairman of Sotheby's, is synonymous with fine art and record-breaking auctions.*

**TR** *How do you like to travel?*

**HW** Five-star bling, mega yachts and private planes are not my thing. I need to get as far away as possible to replenish and recharge. My idea of holiday hell is a safari…seen one lion, you've seen them all. Heaven is to get up late, read, listen to opera and rock and roll on my iPod, eat a club sandwich or a large plate of pasta, take a siesta and wrap up the day with some tennis or golf.

## SO MANY PLACES…

I have a huge file of places I want to visit before my toes curl up, you should too

**TR** *What are your favourite places?*

**HW** The Caribbean I adore – soft sand, turquoise water, but I am as yet to find my perfect spot. Perhaps you will find it for me? I don't go there for culture as that is what my day-to-day life is about. I go there to totally unwind and relax. India is my absolute favourite destination. I love the Indian people and I also love the British Colonial connection. I don't stay in palace hotels, but rather seek out the authentic experience so I can lap up the local culture.

**TR** *What makes a hotel special to you?*

**HW** An example would be The Carlyle in New York which, although it is a bit old-fashioned, I love because they always remember my name and say, "Hello Mr Wyndham". And the poached eggs and crispy bacon are spot on.

**TR** *Favourite restaurants?*

**HW** Restaurants serving nouvelle cuisine are not on my list. I am still in mourning for the loss of the amazing Gino's in New York, which was my daily haunt and favourite restaurant in the world. I love Rick Stein's in Padstow, am dead keen on Richard Carings Restaurants in London. Love Scotts, love Sheekys, and go to the Wolseley a bit too.

**TR** *What are your top travel tips?*

**HW** The Hebrides has the most incredible beaches you will find anywhere in the world.

*Henry's* **SNAPSHOTS OF HEAVEN**

**1 BEACHED**
Coll Island in the Hebrides has the best beach in the world. A horseshoe of white sand, lapped by crystal-clear water

**2 REAL FOOD**
I love a summer's walk back along the estuary enjoying an ice cream, following a simply delicious lunch at Rick Stein's

**3 GREAT RAIL JOURNEYS**
My favourite rail journey is along the sea to Bodmin Parkway. Gazing out the window on the Trans-Siberian, Blue Train or Orient Express is really the best way to see a country

# THE NAM HAI

—

*Hedonistic hideaway
on the South China Sea*

Possibly the most luxurious resort in the whole of Vietnam,
this all-villa property designed with space, light, service and privacy
in mind is the epitome of understated elegance. On a private stretch
of beach, which is covered with impossibly white, silky sand, you have
an unobstructed view across the blue of the South China Sea to the
misty Cham Islands, a short boat-ride away.

For those who wish to do nothing, this is the ideal place to
be; for beach babes, it couldn't be better with its kilometre-long
private beach; for sybarites there is an award-winning spa with every
type of wrap and massage available; for activity bunnies the Cham
Islands provide some of the best diving in south-east Asia; and for
culture vultures there are three Unesco Heritage Sites nearby.

It is worth persuading yourself to leave the hammock for a
visit to at least one of these – My Son deep in the jungle, a monument
to the area's Angkor heritage, Hué the former Imperial city and Hoi
Nan itself, an ancient trading post. The latter is awash with silk traders
and is the place to repair to for a bout of retail therapy.

After which, return to paradise on the coast at a resort where
your every need is catered for – delicious food at the two gourmet
restaurants, fabulous cocktails at the canopied bar and pure luxury
everywhere you turn.

Bookings: +44 (0)20 7201 8070
masonroseprivate.com

## HOTEL AT A GLANCE

**ACCOMMODATION**
60 villas and 40 pool
villa residences

**DINING**
2 restaurants and bar

**RECREATION**
Spa, 3 pools, health club, yoga
pavilion, tennis, golf, kids' club,
cookery school and library

**TRANSFERS**
DaNang International Airport
30mins by car

**SIGNATURE EXPERIENCE**

# THE DELICIOUS DELIGHT OF EVERLASTING ROMANCE

Hidden, glamorous, sensuous and oh-so-romantic, this is the almost ideal honeymoon haven… or the place to return to for all those important anniversaries. A place where you know you will be left alone and yet will still have everything you need. A place to remember, a place to celebrate.

+ 84 510 3940 000
ghmhotels.com

*Tanya's travel secrets...*

"

Sheer tranquillity on a stretch of amazing beach. A marriage of Vietnamese tradition and contemporary design. Add sensational cuisine, local history, and a spa to smooth the edges and you have the recipe for success.

**Immersion**

The Nam Hai offers the most wonderful experience for children called **Villa for Kids**. They can learn the Vietnamese language. They'll love running down the beach with the traditional kites they made themselves. And they even get to cook. Brilliant for young children and an immersion in Vietnamese culture.

**Chef**

With the plethora of cooking shows on TV, everyone loves the opportunity to master new skills in the kitchen. **Private cooking classes** will help you get to grips with the cuisine, and its layering of fresh delicate herbs. How about braised fish with turmeric, and Hué-style prawn and chicken pancakes? So delicious and such fun.

**Tailor**

The streets of Nam Hoi are paved with **silk** and lined with tailors. Come armed with pictures of your desired dress, jacket or shirt from your latest fashion magazines and let them work their magic. Go early in the week to allow for a fitting. Chic Unique, Yaly and Sarah's Boutique number among the better tailors. The only thing stopping you is your baggage allowance.

**Town life**

Nearby **Hôi An** historic centre has remained intact and is a UNESCO World Heritage site. Its narrow streets lined with 19th-century architecture were used as the set for the movie 'The Quiet American' starring Michael Caine. Go late so you can see all the coloured lanterns reflected in the river at night.

Africa

FRIC

# SHANTI MAURICE

—

## *Devoted to pleasure, peace and pure indulgence*

FAVOURITE
SPA
RESORT
★ ★ ★ ★ ★

Shanti Maurice is rather like a modern Garden of Eden. Tucked away in utter tranquillity on the unspoilt south coast of Mauritius, this intimately luxurious resort and world-class spa is the most soothing of escapes.

Acres of tropical landscaped gardens, a seemingly endless coral sand beach and breathtaking views of the surrounding green hills create an idyllic hideaway. Complementing this gorgeous setting are the spacious suites and villas, whose quiet elegance is both relaxing and supremely comfortable. With the beachfront villas you can practically plunge into the Indian Ocean from your door.

At the heart of this resort is a philosophy of wellbeing – and not just for the-grown ups, as they have a dedicated kids' club which offers everything from snorkelling and windsurfing to specially designed yoga, nature treks and close encounters with turtles. So while the children are off having fun, the adults can unwind in heaven at the peaceful spa.

Tailormade relaxation by day and a veritable feast of flavours by night. The superbly skilled chefs are masters at creating a tantalising blend of authentic specialities and international dishes as well as a wellness spa cuisine based on ancient Ayurvedic science.

Shanti Maurice is a place to ease your mind and body. You will come home looking and feeling brand new.

Bookings: +44 (0)20 7201 8070
masonroseprivate.com

## HOTEL AT A GLANCE

**ACCOMMODATION**
61 suites and villas

**DINING**
3 restaurants and 1 bar

**RECREATION**
Spa, yoga, watersports, tennis,
kids' club, cooking classes and
nearby golf

**TRANSFERS**
Sir Seewoosagur Ramgoolam
International Airport 40mins by car

+ 230 603 7200
shantimaurice.com

SIGNATURE EXPERIENCE

# FOR THE A TO Z OF RENEWED VITALITY

Nira Spa is the most blissful haven in which to experience what true wellbeing really means. This vast spa is the ultimate de-stress, with a treatment menu that covers everything from traditional Ayurveda to contemporary therapies and Watsu. Be sure to try the delicious Africology range, the aromatherapeutics and bespoke facial are divine. The setting is magical with lily ponds, an enchanting tea pavilion and beautiful gardens.

"

—

A playground of pleasure at the crossroads of Asia and Africa. An island that will surprise you with its lush green countryside, delectable food and genuine welcome. A jewel of rare brilliance and clarity.

**Tea-time**

We drink tea all the time, but have very little knowledge of how it ends up hanging from a string over our favourite mug. Pinkies up! Go to the **Bois Cheri Tea Estate** for a visit to the plantation, a brisk walk/run through the dusty museum and straight to the lodge for tea-tasting with a stunning view. A storm in a teacup.

**Saintly**

While you are on La Route du Thé, you will want to factor in lunch at the gorgeous **Le Saint Aubin**, a most beautiful plantation house that dates from 1819. Classic Mauritian cuisine made with the freshest ingredients direct from the garden. Order the special five-course menu and buy some rum before you leave. Divine.

**Love shack**

Heaven on the beach. Old rustic furniture, lanterns, anchors, fishermen's ropes… ubiquitous seashanti design for the **Fish and Rhum Shack**. But wait until you tuck into the flapping fresh lobsters and prawns with lashings of rum. Your sun-lounger neighbours will tell you the next day how fabulous your rendition of 'Roll Out the Barrel' was even though you have no recollection.

**Flipper**

Go faster than lightning and book a day trip on a catamaran or speedboat for dolphin-watching in **Tamarin Bay**. Sunblock, sunglasses, sun everything is essential for this day with dolphins in the wild up close. BBQ lunch onboard. Inspirational nature in action. It will make you flip.

# ROYAL MANSOUR MARRAKECH

—

*A magical Medina highlighting the beauty, elegance and grace of traditional Moroccan hospitality*

Conceived, designed and built as a traditional Medina complete with gardens, fountains, ornamental pools and cascades of blossom with separate residences – or riads – for each guest. This is taking the hotel concept to another stratosphere, where each guest has his own riad, each one has three floors including a totally private roof terrace, and each has its own discreet and completely attentive staff.

If privacy is the new luxury, total privacy is what we all crave… but with exceptional service and attention to detail. The décor throughout has been undertaken by Morocco's finest craft workers – whether in carving, weaving, painting or ceramics – and both the furniture and the rugs are exclusive to each of the 53 riads. This is a resort fit for the gods! The restaurants, under the consultancy of Yannick Alleno, include La Grande Table Marocaine offering traditional Moroccan haute cuisine, and La Grande Table Française offering French haute cuisine, both with a contemporary take. The wines are the finest from around the globe and there is an all-day-dining restaurant too.

One of the largest riads houses not only the largest spa in Marrakech, being 2500 square metres including 10 treatment rooms and three suites, but also the most luxurious – full of space, satins and scents with treatments redolent of traditional Moroccan therapies, and staff ready to pamper and cosset. This is a place to relax and refresh both mind and body.

---

**HOTEL AT A GLANCE**

**ACCOMMODATION**
53 individually designed riads

**DINING**
3 restaurants, bars and lounges

**RECREATION**
Spa with Hammams and Watsu
bath, library and nearby Medina

**TRANSFERS**
Marrakech Menara Airport
15mins by car

SIGNATURE EXPERIENCE

# STEAMY BLISS IN AN AWESOME MARBLED HAMMAM

Head for the spa and the Hammam where, seduced by the scent
of roses, a traditional beauty ingredient, in all the oils and unguents,
you will be steamed and scrubbed, massaged and nurtured… then
wrapped in hot towels before being led to a garden of total relaxation.

+ 212 (5) 29 80 80 80
royalmansour.ma

"

An exotic, delicious assault on the senses. Experience the vibrant colour, sounds and fragrances of the souk, or the rugged grandeur of the Atlas Mountains, and then return to your palatial oasis to contemplate.

**Treasure hunters**

Take a wrong turn looking for a Moroccan treasure and you might find yourself in a dusty alley being accosted by hustlers of the shopping variety. Instead take tea with **Laetitia Trouillet** who, as personal shopping consultant, will steer you in the right direction. Her tips for where to go for the best of Marrakech are simply the best.

**By appointment only**

**Akbar Delights** and **Moor** both sell the most exquisite linens, lanterns, kaftans, and babouches that will not permeate your home with the smell of camels.

**The soul of Marrakech**

**Atika** is the most delicious shoe shop this side of the Sahara. A riot of colour. Imagine… a pair of sublime suede loafers that look like Tod's in every shade of your wardrobe without breaking the bank.

**Don't be a souk**

Honking car horns, snake charmers and one-eyed hawkers grinning at you through two black teeth can be a bit too much. Go immediately with your driver to **Jardin Majorelle**. A gorgeous feast for the eyes of cobalt blue walls and lush plants, run by the Yves St Laurent foundation. Breathe in the pure oxygen those generous little ferns are pushing out.

# ONE&ONLY CAPE TOWN

—

## *An urban-chic waterfront resort with a big dash of African style*

As you enter One&Only Cape Town the visual drama is compelling. Your eyes are drawn to the three-storey picture window framing a breathtaking view of Table Mountain.

Equally arresting are the interiors – inspired by the rich culture of the land, they celebrate the dynamic vibrancy of Africa. Prominent South African artists were commissioned to create stunning contemporary works of art that are showcased throughout the resort. This design flair continues in the guestrooms. Not only are they the largest in the city but also the most stylish with their clean lines, rich indigenous woods and bright splashes of colour. The clever layout of the resort means you get to choose from rooms in the crescent-shaped Marina Rise or the more secluded Island Suites situated on one of the two lushly landscaped private islands surrounded by waterways. The other island is home to the One&Only Spa where the treatments will send you swooning into the depths of relaxation.

When it comes to chilling out this hotel has it spot on. The ultra-fashionable Vista Bar oozes glamour day or night and dining is spectacular. Linger at the world-class Nobu for mesmerising Japanese cuisine fused with local spices and divine South African seafood or visit Reuben's to savour the magic of one of South Africa's most beloved award-winning chefs, Reuben Riffel.

## HOTEL AT A GLANCE

**ACCOMMODATION**
131 rooms and suites

**DINING**
3 restaurants and bar

**RECREATION**
Spa, fitness centre, infinity pool,
KidsOnly Club, wine country
excursions and wildlife safaris

**TRANSFERS**
Cape Town International Airport
25mins by car

SIGNATURE EXPERIENCE

# JOURNEY THROUGH THE WINELANDS

Behind a tri-level floor-to-ceiling wall of glass and steel is The Wine Loft. This vast cellar is filled with over 5,000 bottles, from prestigious older vintages to up-and-coming South African boutique wines – it is an oenophile's delight. This is a spectacular venue for tasting sessions, private dining and viewing a seriously impressive collection of wine.

## Top 50

**La Colombe** restaurant is an impressive 11th in the world's top 50 restaurants. Under the watchful eye of Luke Dale Roberts, there is a simple elegance to this working wine farm in the Constantia valley. All locally sourced ingredients, an exciting mix of classic and contemporary French cuisine. consider it to be one of South Africa's best restaurants.

## Camp it up

In the über-trendy beachfront suburb of Camps Bay, **Paranga** is home to the gorgeous and glamorous… and that's just the staff. Stunning food and views along with a bar that boasts the most extensive Champagne list in South Africa. Book a driver.

## Style icon

You need **Olivia Davidson** on your arm to guide you through the fashion safari of Cape Town. Don't waste time, she will get you right to the heart of South Africa's designs and make you think about your wardrobe in a whole new way. A native of London and Paris, she'll make sure you don't go home looking like a lost cast member of 'The Lion King'.

## Cool hooves

Go to **Noordhoek** and take a glorious two-hours horse ride along the beach to Kommetjie. With the sea breeze blowing away all your cares, you marvel at the cranes, geese, and rare flamingo flocks. You may even spot some dolphins frolicking close to shore.

# LAURA
## ON TRAVEL

"

—

*They say your first tour,*
*like your first kiss, is special.*
*This is true for me.*

*Laura Morera is the Royal Ballet's Principal Dancer.*

**TR** *How did your first tour change your life?*

**LM** In 1995 I learned the legends of mountain trolls in Norway, discovered Copenhagen, admired Athens, strolled in Buenos Aires, sucked in the atmosphere in Israel, and drank coffee in Palermo. I worked hard, played harder, slept nothing, met my husband of today, and established an invaluable friendship with dancer Ricardo Cervera.

I ♥ TRAVEL!

I've shared my journeys with people I love and that is the key to any successful trip

**TR** *Any special memories of your travels for work?*

**LM** Oh, many, like dancing in an open-air theatre with the moon shining down on us and the Acropolis towering over us in Athens. Buying paper from a factory in Beijing for my wedding invitations. Dancing the night away with my friend Ricardo in a nightclub in St Petersburg. A charity performance in Kenya with giraffes and zebras around us. Coca-Cola at the top of a volcano, and sunrise with my husband in Bali.

**TR** *Tell me more about somewhere that has been very special to you?*

**LM** The Datai in Malaysia. Justin and I fell in love with the welcoming staff who did everything to accommodate our needs. It's a big hotel but it feels cosy and intimate. Just the right amount of luxury and seclusion for us and the beach is surrounded by mountains. The pool is huge. Make sure you get up for breakfast, it's well worth it, the perfect start to the day. The rooms are simple, with a feeling of understated elegance and the bathrooms are the type that make you go home and want to redecorate. After two visits we decided this was the place to get married. So with 30 guests the following year we tied the knot and had our perfect wedding.

## *Laura's* — EN POINTE ABOUT TRAVEL

1 MY GIFT TO YOU
Jijuden Guesthouse in Kyoto is my own personal secret that I am reluctant to share

2 EAT YOUR HEART OUT
My secret in Madrid is the Casa Lastra in the Lavapiés area of the city for its homemade quality food. Go with a good appetite and order fabada

# DELAIRE GRAFF ESTATE

—

*A visionary in wine, design, hospitality – and diamonds*

Laurence Graff, the world-famous diamantaire, had a dream which he has now realised by turning a winery on the edge of Stellenbosch into one of South Africa's leading wine and holiday destinations. In a very short space of time this all-suite hotel and spa has received numerous accolades – for design, for horticulture, for food and, of course, for wine.

The estate sits on the crest of a mountain pass between the country's two main wine-growing areas – Stellenbosch and Franschhoek. Here, Graff has assembled a superlative team of wine growers and makers, designers, landscape gardeners and chefs. The result – an elegant estate of 10 large and private lodges, each in its own space and for extra privacy hedged with the dense foliage of camellia and coffee jasmine. The main building houses a wine lounge and a glorious dining room designed by award-winning London designer David Collins.

The nearby spa offers a host of holistic therapies alongside a gym, swimming pool, Pilates studio and hair salon plus Indochine, a restaurant specialising in lighter, healthier cuisine. Throughout the lodges and spa is an awesome collection of contemporary art, chosen by Laurence Graff himself, while outside in the vast grounds, landscaped and designed by leading South African horticulturalist Keith Kirsten, are more than 300 indigenous plants.

And then there is the vineyard and its winery, already winning accolades and in pursuit of world-class excellence.

## HOTEL AT A GLANCE

**ACCOMMODATION**
10 lodges including
2 double lodges

**DINING**
Indochine Asian fusion restaurant

**RECREATION**
Spa, private cinema, infinity pool
and state-of-the-art gym

**TRANSFERS**
45 mins drive from
Cape Town airport

+27 21 885 8160
delaire.co.za

SIGNATURE EXPERIENCE

# PAMPER YOUR PALATE IN GREAT STYLE AND GREAT TASTE

One of the great advantages of staying on a wine estate is the proximity to the makers, the mixers and the teachers. In the early evening head for the Wine Lounge to savour (and drink) some of the estate's own wines under the watchful eye of the sommelier.

"

The Delaire Graff Estate manages to achieve the best of wine, cuisine, luxury accommodation, and cutting-edge design with quiet elegance. You are a personal guest in the home of friends of the most discerning and exquisite taste.

**Chocoholics unite**

With jaw-dropping views over the Simonsig Valley and Helshoogte mountains indulge in world-class cuisine by **Executive Chef Christiaan Campbell**. For dessert with a difference, succumb to a unique local 'wine and chocolate tasting' and experience sensational flavours like the iconic Delaire Shiraz paired with decadent dark chocolate. A tastebud match made in heaven.

**Up, up and away**

**Silvercross helicopters** are the ultimate way to explore the Cape Town wine lands and nature reserves. Charter a helicopter and go Shark-cage diving or viewing at Gansbaai, home of the Great White shark. Follow this by lunch at Grootbos, a five-star fynbos eco-reserve with great aerial whale watching en route. To finish, route through fantastic Cape mountains and enjoy the coastal scenery, before heading back to the hotel spa for a detox. This is the high life!

**Smart art**

Delaire is home to the most incredible artworks by South Africa's most sought-after artists. Laurence Graff's personal private collection is best experienced on a **personalised art tour**. Sculptures by world-famous sculptor Dylan Lewis are dotted across the estate. Admire the striking pieces by William Kentridge, Lionel Smit, Sydney Kumalo and Deborah Bell lining the walls of the estate's interior spaces. Up close and personal.

**Paradise found**

Privacy is the ultimate in modern luxury, and the **Owner's Lodge** is a secluded suite lovingly curated by David Collins, which balances creature comforts with cutting-edge design. Jo Malone's distinctive amenities are a refreshing start to the day, following sweet dreams between Egyptian cotton bed sheets. End the day with sundowners on your patio to the sound of a gentle evening breeze.

Americas

MER

Bookings: +44 (0)20 7201 8070
masonroseprivate.com

# CARLISLE BAY

—

## *The chicest beach retreat in the Caribbean's Leeward Islands*

White sand, a stunning curve of a bay and the warm blue waters of the Caribbean with dark green hills and rainforest as a backdrop – a perfect location for a quietly chic holiday. It's so smooth even the waves whisper so as not to disturb the solitude of this secluded bay on Antigua's unspoiled south coast.

Suites and apartments, designed by Mary Fox Linton, exude contemporary comfort and cool, with each having its own private terrace or balcony. Head to the Pavillion Bar for cocktails and live music. For food, head to East with its exciting pan-Asian cuisine, enjoy healthy grills and seafood at Indigo on the Beach or try a light lunch under the pergola by the pool… food and its excellence is one of the key hallmarks of CampbellGray Hotels.

Those looking for action not only have the beach and all its watersports activities but also a cluster of tennis courts, a swimming pool plus a fully equipped fitness centre. For the more indolent, the Blue spa offers pampering for all, while the screening room chooses all those independent arthouse films you promised to see and never have. Families are also catered for with movies to suit everyone. In fact, children of all ages, from seven to 70, are catered for at Carlisle Bay.

Bookings: +44 (0)20 7201 8070
masonroseprivate.com

## HOTEL AT A GLANCE

**ACCOMMODATION**
82 suites

**DINING**
2 restaurants and 3 bars

**RECREATION**
Spa, gym, watersports, tennis, yoga and Pilates, personal training, library, teenage activities, boat excursions, guided hikes, sailing, scuba diving, crèche and kids' club

**TRANSFERS**
V.C. Bird International Airport 30mins by car

+1 268 484 0000
carlisle-bay.com

SIGNATURE EXPERIENCE

# ROMANTIC RENDEZVOUS ON THE SEASHORE

The gentle lap of the waves, the shimmer of moonlight on the sea and the romance of a candlelit dinner for two on the jetty. Stars shining, wine cooling and food fit for the gods – in fact a feast for all the senses.

❝
—

Fabulously cool chic on the beach.
Go to sleep and wake up to the gentle
swish of the ocean on an island that
is paradise found. Iridescent waters
lapping impossibly white sand,
backed by lush rainforest.

**Blade runner**

You have only had a glimpse
of the terrain and emerald sea
on final approach, so get up in
the air again in a **helicopter**
and discover the spectacular
scenery of Antigua. You can
tour the whole island and take
in the volcano of Montserrat.
An exhilarating way to see it
all – from the air.

**Keep paddling**

Strengthen those shoulder,
back and arm muscles with
an eco **kayak adventure**.
An uninhabited island
paradise awaits, with
crystal-clear water to be
paddled about in. Snorkel
amongst the neon-striped
fish, collect shells, or just
float about in the warm
water. Your kids will love it.
Sunblock essential.

**Rainforest canopy**

So much fun and the most
unique jungle experience.
A 21-element **journey through
and above the rainforest**. A
series of zip lines, short trails
and suspension bridges, which
are topped off with a unique,
absolutely safe, 'Leap of Faith'
– a controlled 36-foot vertical
descent. Tree houses to rest
at midpoint. You Tarzan, me
terrified. Aaaaaaaaaah!

**Zen state**

Carlisle Bay is über-Caribbean
sleek, and what better place
to introduce yourself to the
joys of **yoga and Pilates**?
Measured careful exercise that
leaves you toned, and centred.
Time is on your side while on
holiday and a private lesson
in the garden will have you
hooked. Where's Sting when
you need him?

# HOTEL ST BARTH ISLE DE FRANCE

—

## *Mix glamour with charm at this perfect fusion in the Caribbean*

FAVOURITE

CARRIBEAN
RESORT

★★★★★

A small, charming and privately owned hotel sits on one of the prettiest beaches in St Barts – the Baie des Flamands – and with its pure white sand and pale turquoise clear sea, it is picture postcard perfect.

And while there are many attractions on the island – such as clubs, bars, cafes, terrific restaurants and boutiques to die for, it is very difficult to tear yourself away from this example of easy luxury. Here, nothing is too much trouble. Think Gallic style with Caribbean insouciance – whether you need a Daiquiri or a Citron Pressé, it will appear with a smile and a touch of grace.

This is the perfect place to do as little as possible – swim or float, take in some sun or sit in the shade with a book or three, and when it's time for lunch or dinner the freshest ingredients are prepared and served. Breakfast is ready when you are and sundowners are available long before the sun goes down.

Whether you stay on the beach or in one of the pretty garden suites and cottages you will enjoy perfect privacy. Should you want to indulge there is a Molton Brown spa with a plethora of treatments, and a boutique which will melt your credit card within seconds, so desirable is the merchandise.

## HOTEL AT A GLANCE

**ACCOMMODATION**
39 rooms, suites and villas

**DINING**
Restaurant and bar

**RECREATION**
Spa, gym, 2 pools
Nearby: watersports, sailing,
motorboats, windsurfing, jet-skiing,
deep sea fishing, diving and tennis

**TRANSFERS**
St Barths Airport 5mins by car
(following connecting flight
from Antigua)

+ 59 05 90 27 61 81
isle-de-france.com

# SOOTHE AND SMOOTH YOUR SUN AND SEA-KISSED SKIN

Even though you may be slathering sun-cream on your body all day long, it will still need extra care and attention after a day of sun, wind and sea… so take it along to the spa and organise a nourishing body wrap to remoisturise and pamper.

66
—

Someone has moved the South of France to the Caribbean – cheers; thanks alot. The most hair-raising landing strip arrival is worth it for an island dripping with cool chic and serious style.

**Rock & roll**

At **Eden Rock** make sure you have a table on the lower level for the best of the bay of St Jean. Order the mahi mahi which is simply prepared, fresh and delectable. You must break the 'no carbs' rule to sample the baked-on-site bread which is insanely delicious. Dress – resort chic and enjoy the romance of this wonderful setting.

**La table**

French Creole chef **Maya Beuzelin-Gurley** has been packing them in to what is one of the best restaurants in the Caribbean. Movie stars email their reservations, so make sure you've made yours before you hit the island. Elegant and comfortable with fresh fish, exotic daily specials, and Creole dishes. Too fabulous, go and be seen.

**Le fashion**

**Calypso Boutique** is easily one of the trendiest boutiques in St Barts. You will find it all here. Sunglasses, Marika Charles, Wren, I Love My Tee, Tes Rossi, all alongside the finest cashmere. Empty suitcase? Fill it here. Bring the beach home with you, and I don't mean sand in your knickers.

**Casa Nikki**

Just a short drive from its beachside locale lives the redesigned **Casa Nikki**. This is the too-cool-for-school place to shake your tanned booty after hours. It is where the yacht-hopping partygoers revel with its bumping sound system and endless bottle service. You can't get it better than this. Wear a handkerchief and order lots of Champagne.

# PARK HYATT BUENOS AIRES

—

## *Sex and sophistication in South America's smartest city*

Buenos Aires has to be one of the sexiest cities in the world…
and the Park Hyatt is THE place to stay. On the outside it has all
the grandeur and charm of its provenance as the Palacio Duhau while
on the inside it has all the cool of contemporary Argentina – large
spaces, vibrant colours and complete comfort. Best of all it is close
to wherever you want to be in this great city – shops, designers,
restaurants and galleries. Art, leather and jewellery are what to look
out for while you're there. The hotel even has its own gallery, the Paseo
de las Artes, which highlights the work of contemporary Argentinean
and South American painters and sculptors.

And while the delights of the hotel are seductive enough with
its four restaurants and bars, Ahin spa and spacious gardens, all of
Buenos Aires is waiting to tempt you. Go and be seduced, knowing
that you have this temple of tranquillity to return to. Tango is a must
– see a show and take a lesson – forget your inhibitions, this was once
described as the nearest thing to having sex standing up with your
clothes on. There are any number of tango shows, restaurants and
classes but make sure you head off to the San Telmo district on a
Sunday where the main square fills with arts and crafts during the day
and a huge tango milonga street party at night!

---

## HOTEL AT A GLANCE

**ACCOMMODATION**
165 rooms and suites

**DINING**
2 restaurants, salons and bar

**RECREATION**
Spa, indoor pool, fitness studio,
art collection and gallery

**TRANSFERS**
Ministro Pistarini International
Airport 45mins by car

SIGNATURE EXPERIENCE

# IN REMEMBRANCE
# OF THE GLORIOUS PAST

The Recoleta Cemetery, close to the hotel, is one of the
great cemeteries of the world, filled with vast marble and gold
mausoleums and tombstones. What a surprise it is to see how
modest (and yet always flower-filled) Evita's grave is…

+54 11 5171 1234
buenosaires.park.hyatt.com

*Tanya's travel secrets...*

"

―

# Parisian elegance in Latin America that can't be beaten. The tango speaks so eloquently to the spirit of Buenos Aires and its passionate people. Bohemia cool and totally hip.

### Tango

Victor, Tango, Bravo... no, we are not coming in to land. If you are coming to Buenos Aires, you must tango. **Mansion Dandy Royal** is a tango academy housed in the 1903 San Telmo mansion. Every Wednesday is La Shuesta to perfect your gancho, mordida and ochos. You've danced with Victor... OK, now Bravo! *Book through dehouche.com*

### Corker

Argentina screams New World wine, and **Terroir** will strike fear into any oenophile if they don't make a visit. Terroir is Alejandro's fantastic wine shop in Palermo where he is waiting to wow you with a private tasting of Argentina's finest wines. Don't miss it. I've popped my cork, case closed. *Book through dehouche.com*

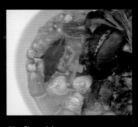

### Chef's table

Authentic travel is all about the unique experience. '**Puertas Cerradas**' is going to feature in your best of travel experiences for sure. It's dining in a chef's home with local cognoscenti, and glasses of fabulous local wine. Fresh ingredients, Chef decides what you eat. Cutting-edge gourmet. The unforgettable meal. *Book through dehouche.com*

### Science

Alejandro Diglio of the world-famous El Bulli is wowing the foodies at **Vineria de Gualterio Bolivar** with molecular gastronomy. Melt-in-your-mouth Patagonian lamb straight from the lab (kitchen), a provolone croquette, dark chocolate ice cream with mandarin orange reduction. Seventy wines by the glass. The last supper was never so good. *Book through dehouche.com*

# DAVID
## ON TRAVEL

"

—

*Listening to
my children's
chatter filled with
laughter and
curiosity is true
travel bliss.*

## David Giampaolo of Pi Capital is the most networked man in the City.

**TR** *Do you have favourite hotels?*

**DG** The usual suspects such as the Four Seasons, Ritz Carlton, Peninsula, and Mandarin Oriental. However I do look at new openings of independent hotels recommended by my friends; recent ones that come to mind are La Mamounia in Marrakech and Le Gray in Beirut.

**TR** *Where do you dine when travelling?*

**DG** When travelling on business I like to maximise use of the hotels I am in for quality and convenience. When I venture out I lean towards places that are family-owned and run, or those that are part of a reputable collection. Italian and Japanese cuisine are high on my list.

**TR** *What do you love or hate about travel?*

**DG** I love the excitement and adventure of seeing new places and meeting new people, or just visiting friends and loved ones who live abroad. I used to hate delays but I have mellowed and learned to live with them.

**TR** *City or beach?*

**DG** Both. I like Hôtel Costes in Paris, and also the Wynn in Las Vegas is a total blast. I also recently enjoyed the Six Senses in Oman and the Maldives. The big island in Hawaii is really wonderful and has some amazing resorts, but is a very long way from London.

**TR** *What do you consider to be reliable sources of travel information?*

**DG** In the main I trust recommendations from friends whom I know well enough to believe that their taste and views are similar to mine. And Mason Rose of course as their clientele are the kind of people who are as demanding as I am when it comes to honest advice.

### FAMILY TIES

Smaller and family-owned properties and restaurants recommended by friends whose tastes and views are reliable

## David's

**INVESTMENT IN TRAVEL**

**1 CAREFUL PLANNING**
When travelling, allow plenty of time to clear security, leaving you enough time to work and chill a bit in the first class lounge

**2 CONSISTENT FORECAST**
Staying with Four Seasons and flying British Airways I know that my expectations will be managed well

**3 VALUE-ADDED**
Hotels with a club are great, I particularly love the Ritz-Carlton's. Breakfast, early calls, meetings, evening drinks are all on tap moments from my room

Bookings: +44 (0)20 7201 8070
masonroseprivate.com

# HOTEL FASANO RIO DE JANEIRO

—

*Starck glamour on Rio's ritziest beach – where the stars come to play*

When Philippe Starck teamed up with the Fasano family, renowned throughout Brazil for their gastronomy and chic hospitality, the result was this hip and sexy boutique hotel. The setting, of course, could not be bettered with Two Brothers Mountain in the background and Ipanema Beach right in front. Indeed the hotel has its own private cabana on the beach from which it dispenses loungers, cold towels and shades.

Inside, the hotel is a paean to Starck's design philosophy with its use of glass and marble throughout, accented by billowing white curtains in the lobby and the surprise factor of a giant pekia tree-trunk masquerading as the reception desk. Colour accents are provided by Chinese yellow onyx lamps and aged red Argentinian brickwork – see this at its best in the Baretto Londra, Rio's most fashionable bar, with its Union Jacks and walls of LP covers of British rock legends.

The food of course is fantastic, which is only to be expected in view of Rogerio Fasano's dedication to all that is seriously delicious, whether you eat at the main restaurant Fasano al Mare, specialising in seafood, or want something lighter, in which case head for the rooftop bar. In fact this is literally the highpoint of the hotel with its infinity pool, heavenly cocktails and delicious light meals. Be here at sunset to discover what it is to be a true carioca.

## HOTEL AT A GLANCE

**ACCOMMODATION**
89 rooms and suites

**DINING**
Restaurant, bar and pool bar

**RECREATION**
Spa, infinity pool, steam room,
fitness centre and private
beach service

**TRANSFERS**
Rio de Janeiro-Galeão International
Airport 40mins by car; Santos
Dumont Domestic Airport 25mins
by car

+ 55 21 3202 4000
fasano.com.br

SIGNATURE EXPERIENCE

# INSTANT GLAMOUR EVERYWHERE – EVEN AT YOUR FEET

Every guest gets complimentary flip-flops from Brazil's hippest designer Oskar Metsavaht. Should you want to see more of his sports-chic designs, his flagship store is but a few minutes' walk from the hotel.

66
—

Rio pulsates with the rhythm of life and carnival. You can't fail to be intoxicated by Copacabana. I feel like the girl from Ipanema!

**Jungle fever**

The quick-fix way of getting some jungle action is to head to **Tijuca Forest** right in the middle of Rio. Tijuca is the world's largest urban forest consisting of some 32 square kilometres of Atlantic rainforest right in the heart of the city, featuring mountains, caves, streams and waterfalls – all easily accessible only a 20-minute drive from Fasano.

**Sweet treat**

Despite the name, **Clube Chocolate** sells everything but chocolate. Top international fashion designers share rails with the coolest creations from Brazil. This exclusive shop (complete with pet parrot) in fashion mall São Conrado is where well-heeled carioca women (and a few men) pick up their togs. Browse while sipping on Champagne from the in-house restaurant. Retail heaven.

**Le Gîte**

A 20-minute helicopter ride will find you landing atop a jungle-clad mountain. You're in the garden of **La Gîte**, a middle-of-nowhere amazing restaurant. Olivier the French chef and his Brazillian wife Valerie are about to wow you with a feast. Sit next to the waterfall while sipping on a caipirinha made from fresh limes from the tree next to you.

**A brazilian**

Brazilian mid-century furniture by designers like Sergio Rodriguez is all the rage. Head to **Rua Lavradio** in Lapa with vintage design expert Tatiana. The street is lined with antiques shops where you can pick up sought-after pieces like the Diz chair for a steal. When the evening comes, the street turns into a party as live samba bars are dotted among the boutiques.

Bookings: +44 (0)20 7201 8070
masonroseprivate.com

# CUIXMALA

—

## *One man's fantasy has become a paradise for all*

BEST FOR

**PRIVACY**

★★★★★

One of the world's finest luxury resorts located betwixt the jungle and the Pacific, Cuixmala was conceived as the private pleasure palace of financier Sir James Goldsmith. Known as much for his buccaneering financial ways as for the eco-warrior and serious conservationist he became, this estate is lasting tribute to his concern for nature.

Conservation was and remains a prime concern, which is why all 25,000 acres of Cuixmala are designated a biosphere reserve. It has its own wildlife sanctuary complete with freshwater crocodiles, zebra, antelope and a turtle hatchery, and three miles of the purest golden sandy beach. Just as much care has gone into the food served – all is organic and locally sourced, either grown in the resort's own gardens or from its nearby farm, while the ocean provides the rest.

While the exterior is wild and wonderful, the interior is exotic and exhilarating. Guests stay either in one of nine casitas of extraordinary size, fantastic colours and Mexican boho artefacts or in one of four casas of staggering opulence which seem to grow out of the jungle. Each of these latter come with its own staff and pool and everything a guest has ever thought of, but the crown jewel is La Loma, James's own private paradise. A Moorish – Mexican palace of quiet courtyards, tiled domes, fabulous furnishings and rooms you could fit a small county into.

## HOTEL AT A GLANCE

**ACCOMMODATION**
4 villas, 9 casitas

**DINING**
Restaurant and club house

**RECREATION**
3 private beaches, pool, snorkelling, kayaking, fishing, sailing, tennis, nature walks, mountain bikes, horse riding, massage treatments, nearby golf and surfing

**TRANSFERS**
Manzanillo International Airport 1hr 30mins, Puerto Vallarta International Airport 2hrs 30mins by car. Private airstrip on site

+ 52 (315) 351 0034
cuixmala.com

SIGNATURE EXPERIENCE

# NATURAL WONDERS EXPLORED AND ENJOYED IN TRUE OPULENCE

As the sun begins to greet a new day, head for the beach on horseback and bask in the pale gold light of the dawn. Return in the moonlight and watch the baby turtles hatch.

*Tanya's travel secrets...*

"

Eco-luxury in a compound of stunning beauty. A rare opportunity to experience the getaway of a family who appreciate a harmonious blend of nature and comfort coupled with authentic design.

**Jungle horses**

In the late afternoon, head down to the stables and **saddle up** for a spectacular ride through the terrain that surrounds this luxury resort. If you buck at the thought of a horse, mountain bikes are available. Communing with nature followed by cocktails at sunset. It's enough to make you whinny with delight.

**Christmas bar**

Barmen dressed as Santa? Actually no, rather a small town called **Barra de Navidad** which translated to English means 'The Bar of Christmas'. A sandbar in fact, about an hour away from Cuixmala and great for Mexican arts and crafts. A bar and Christmas – what a great combination. Let the retail festivities begin.

**Addicted to golf**

The **El Tamarindo Golf Club** is considered to be one of the most beautiful courses in the world. Located in an ecological preserve and designed by Robert Trent Jones Jr and David Fleming, it's a real masterpiece. The sea views are a total knockout. See you at tee time.

**Mexican fiesta**

The food is so fantastic at Cuixmala, you are going to miss it when you leave. So spend some time learning how to make some Mexican dishes with the chef in a **private cooking class**. Bring home some skills to go with the tan and the tequila. Host your own Mexican fiesta.

Bookings: +44 (0)20 7201 8070
masonroseprivate.com

# HACIENDA DE SAN ANTONIO

—

## *Supreme luxury in the shadow of the volcano*

The smaller, although older, sister of Cuixmala offers a totally different Mexican journey. A coffee plantation, organic farm and serious luxury hotel, it is possibly one of the grandest farmhouses you are ever likely to stay in. When Sir James Goldsmith first found it, he was determined it should be a true family home, and this is the style and ambience that welcomes guests.

Colourful and deeply comfortable, it pays homage not just to the landscape but also the arts and crafts of the country. The landscape of course is dominated by El Viejo – the old man – the slumbering giant of a volcano who sits, all passion spent, occasionally belching out bits of lava and smoke. The locals love and respect it – and you will too, especially if you take a hike to its lower slopes. The coffee plantation, a working ranch and the organic farm are close by and the hacienda's own gardens are as magnificent as any botanical garden you have visited.

The spirit of Mexico is everywhere in the hacienda from the rugs to the textiles, the carved wood and the ceramics. Each suite is individually designed and decorated with works by some of the country's leading craftspeople and artisans.

Bookings: +44 (0)20 7201 8070
masonroseprivate.com

## HOTEL AT A GLANCE

**ACCOMMODATION**
22 suites and 3 grand suites

**DINING**
Dining room, terrace, bar, pool
pavilion, club room, outdoor areas

**RECREATION**
Pool, tennis, horse riding, mountain
bikes, hiking, volcano excursion, bird
watching, picnics and local tours

**TRANSFERS**
Manzanillo International Airport 2hrs,
Guadalajara International Airport
2hrs 45mins, Colima Regional Airport
45mins all by car. Private airstrip on
site for charter flights.

+ 52 (312) 316 0300
haciendadesanantonio.com

SIGNATURE EXPERIENCE

# HEAD FOR THE HEIGHTS FOR A MEMORABLE EXPERIENCE

It has to be the volcano. It's not too energetic a walk but take a gentle
trek on its lower slopes to help you feel the heartbeat of the place,
not to mention to wonder at the landscape. Best done early in the
day before the sun gets too high.

*Tanya's travel secrets…*

66
—

A heavenly hacienda set in the most
beautiful ranch. The interior design
authentically reflects local origin in
great comfort and style. A fabulous
getaway to the real Mexico.

**Pueblo magico**

**Comala** is like a film set.
The look of old colonial Spain
– whitewashed houses, plaza
with gazebo bandstand. It's
famous for its handmade
wood furniture, food and live
mariachi bands. Why magic?
Go to the magic hill and watch
your car placed in neutral
roll uphill. And no… not
post Margarita.

**Saddle up**

You're at a hacienda, it
seems only appropriate that
the **El Jabali Ranch** is right
next door. Novice or expert,
there is a mount for everyone
of all ages and sizes. The
most wonderful way to see
this 5,000-acre working ranch.
Horses make you nervous?
Don't worry, hop on a
mountain bike and head
on out.

**Arts & Crafts**

**Tlaquepaque** is the decorative
arts capital of Mexico and you
won't be disappointed. Start
on Independencia pedestrian-
only street and take it from
there. Over 300 quaint shops,
galleries and boutiques all
housed in 18th-century
colonial mansions. It's
surprisingly cheap, so make
sure you wear flats. Drop into
the Quinta Don Jose boutique
hotel if you need to refuel.

**Bar skills**

If you want to perfect your
cocktail skills, book some
one-on-one time in the bar
to get a grip on your grappa.
They have a delectable
homemade mango grappa
which they use for their
magnificent Margaritas. Learn
how and make them at your
next summer BBQ. Olé!

Bookings: +44 (0)20 7201 8070
masonroseprivate.com

# ONE & ONLY PALMILLA

—

## *A fashionable hideaway with the finest location in all of Baja California*

One&Only Palmilla is one of the most spectacular resorts anywhere. For years it has attracted stars of the screen and the global jetset. It exudes glamour and that subtle kind of luxury that only the best can do.

The resort is perched on the tip of the Baja peninsula in Los Cabos, surrounded by coastline so privacy is assured. It also boasts a 27-hole Jack Nicklaus signature golf course, often voted among the best golf courses in America. Along the peninsula edge, single and three-storey 'casas' house the airy guestrooms. Each has a verandah or patio with a handy telescope to help spot the majestic grey whales offshore. Inside, the fabulous design blends the vibrant artistry of Mexico with sumptuous modernity and every contemporary amenity. Special touches are plentiful, from your welcoming pottery flask of tequila to the bedtime aromatherapy scents menu.

Sit back and luxuriate in the pampering spa treatment villas. Or jump feet first into the many aquatic adventures. The beach is one of the only swimmable ones in the area and sports lovers adore the deep-sea fishing, ocean snorkelling and diving. From poolside foot massages paired with ice pops to a personal butler on hand 24 hours a day, service is unparallelled yet unobtrusive.

Like everything here, dining is out of this world with a host of ultra-stylish venues and the cuisine of celebrated chefs, such as Michelin starred talent Jean-Georges Vongerichten who presents Market, his first outpost South of the Border.

---

## HOTEL AT A GLANCE

**ACCOMMODATION**
173 rooms and suites with 1 villa

**DINING**
4 restaurants and 1 bar

**RECREATION**
Private yacht, 2 swimming pools,
fitness centre, watersports,
KidsOnly Club, spa, yoga, golf
and desert exploration

**TRANSFERS**
San José del Cabo International
Airport 20mins by car

+ 52 624 146 7000
oneandonlyresorts.com

SIGNATURE EXPERIENCE

# IF YOU ARE IN THE MOOD TO SPLURGE

Look no further than the stunning Villa Cortez, for this one-of-a-kind masterpiece is an expansive four-bedroomed villa that has just about everything you could possibly want. Set on its own secluded beach, this gorgeous villa blends chic hacienda interiors with a relaxed coastal living vibe.

*Tanya's travel secrets...*

"

Taco yourself immediately to Los Cabos! Bel Air on sea as Hollywood makes its way south for the winter. You'll feel like a movie star too.

**Hummer adventure**

**Hummers** are the big Daddy of 4WDs ready to transport you from tranquillity to the big outdoors. Your escape will find you zooming across the amazing scenery of the East Cape, crossing the Tropic of Cancer and ending up on one of the most beautiful beaches in Baja. Great fun for the whole family.

**Exquisite equines**

Francisco J Barrena is the owner of the **Cuadra San Francisco** equestrian centre in Cabo San Lucas. Imagine attending riding school in Mexico? Come for one lesson or a series. Or maybe just a trail ride – or a carriage ride? How about the Full Moon ride? Yeehah!

**Whale of a time**

If you have escaped the winter in January through March, you are in town at just the right time for the most awesome natural spectacle, **whales** on their winter break. And no, it's not those large people by the pool, it's the swimming variety out at sea. It is the most awe-inspiring experience to see whales in action up close. Concierge will set you up with the right eco operator, water-proof camera a must. Splish splash.

**Artistic bent**

There is very little manufactured in Los Cabos that you might consider to take home – that is except for art. Book a driver to take you into San Jose del Cabo where you will find quite a number of galleries to browse. Everything from acrylic to textiles and sculpture. If you fancy the idea of painting yourself, lessons can be arranged with the **Marianela Art Gallery**. You get the picture.

Bookings: +44 (0)20 7201 8070
masonroseprivate.com

# MONTAGE BEVERLY HILLS

—

*Live like a movie star in this Hollywood pleasure dome*

Right in the heart of Beverly Hills this luxurious hotel offers elegance and exclusivity. Just half an hour from Los Angeles International Airport and just minutes from the retail heaven that is Rodeo Drive, and yet once inside its portals all is calm and tranquil.

Built in Spanish Colonial Revival style it is like a mini castle with its fountains and landscaped gardens, spacious rooms and grand public rooms. It also draws on those classic Californian colours of gold and sand, coral and cream to allow everything to reflect the light of the sun of America's golden state. And although the décor and architecture are an hommage to the city's history, the amenities are a tribute to all that is modern, comfortable, efficient and elegant.

The rooms and suites are spacious while the public rooms, bars and dining experiences are all the discerning guest requires. For instance, the new garden-side Scarpetta Beverly Hills, by acclaimed chef Scott Conant, delights with soulful Italian cuisine. It is as popular with locals as with guests with its manicured topiary gardens. The rooftop bar and grill has some of the best views of the Hollywood Hills by day as well as by night. It is here, too, that you get to relax by the pool after a tough morning's shopping. Also on offer is a Chef's Table, the ideal place to spoil yourself. However, as it only seats 12, it is best to make your table booking when making your reservation.

Bookings: +44 (0)20 7201 8070
masonroseprivate.com

**HOTEL AT A GLANCE**

**ACCOMMODATION**
201 rooms and suites

**DINING**
2 restaurants and lounge

**RECREATION**
Spa, beauty salon, fitness centre,
rooftop pool and private gardens

**TRANSFERS**
Los Angeles International
Airport 30mins by car, Bob Hope
International Airport 35mins by car

SIGNATURE EXPERIENCE

# SPACE AND GRACE IN A MOSAIC-DECORATED SPA

Spa Montage is a temple to wellbeing with a comprehensive menu
of massages, wraps, facials and rituals alongside an ever-rotating
choice of classes in yoga, Pilates, dance and aerobics. But for sheer
cosseting opt for the Anointing Ritual – which uses essence of
rose in the massage.

+ 1 310 860 7800
montagebeverlyhills.com

City of Angels where dreams are made and the legend of Hollywood is real. Front-row luxury seats for the greatest show on earth. Lights, cameras, action!

**Breakfast recovery**

Everyone is up at the crack of dawn being healthy in LA. Don't fret, you can go straight for red velvet pancakes at **Larchmont Bungalow Cafe**. They serve breakfast all day, and the freshly roasted coffee just wafts into your nostrils and lifts your eyelids.

**Ping pong**

Who knew it had become cool again? Susan Sarandon for one. **Spin Hollywood** is the LA version of the NYC original and the place to bat things about between cocktails. There's nothing like ping pong to break the ice on a date or when meeting up with new LA friends. Love all.

**Your close-up**

Want to celebrate the new you with photos that you'll love? **Michael Calas** manages to capture you through his lens in a way that is effortless and relaxed. His magic touch turns you into a star. Men and ladies, prepare for your cover shoot. In a snapshot, you're framed.

**Street cred**

In LA you drive, and your wheels say everything. Uh hmm, girlfriend! **Beverly Hills Rent a Car** is more Oscar de la, than Renta. Mercedes SL550? A Ferrari? Before you meet Jenny from the Block at The Ivy in yo hood, don't embarrass her at valet parking.

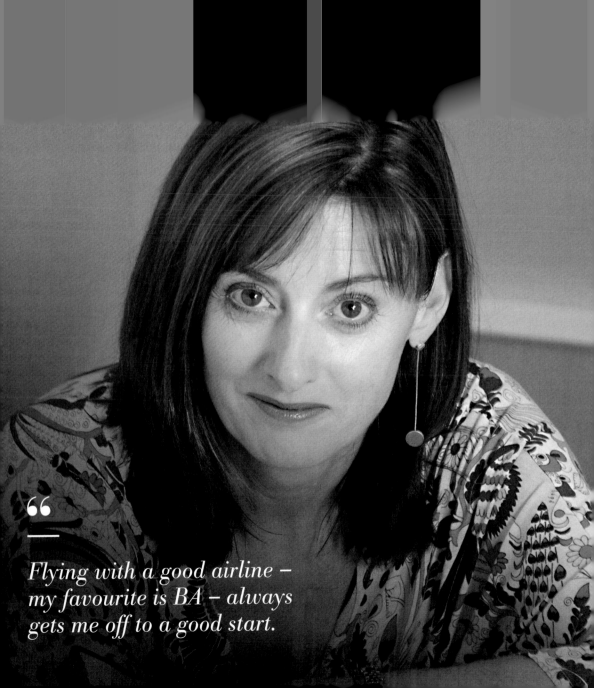

*Flying with a good airline –
my favourite is BA – always
gets me off to a good start.*

*The BAFTAs have been transformed into the glittering star-studded event that they are today by the amazing Amanda Berry.*

**TR** *Given your work with the film industry where do you stay in Hollywood?*

**AB** Sunset Marquis is my home from home in LA. Lovely staff for whom nothing is too much trouble, a warm welcome back every time, great location, a fabulous restaurant in a beautiful garden. The hotel prides itself on being low-key but is a favourite of British actors and musicians and with a recording studio in the basement you never know who you are going to bump into.

**TR** *Do you ever manage to get away for a weekend when you are working in London?*

**AB** I love a short break and like to head for Espléndido, Puerto de Sóller, Mallorca. It's a modern stylish hotel right on the water, great value with good-size rooms, and the breakfasts are fabulous. You open your curtains to a view of the sea and old trams rumbling past. Scandinavian-run and nice guests.

**TR** *And long-haul?*

**AB** We usually do long-haul trips at Christmas and favour South Africa, India and Australia.

**TR** *Any pet hates about hotels?*

**AB** My personal bête noire – lack of mirrors near sockets in the bedroom for drying my hair drives me nuts! Why do hotels believe that female guests want to dry their hair in a steamy bathroom?

## Amanda's
### STARRY RECOMMENDATIONS

**1 SEBASTIAN IN DEIA, MALLORCA**
A fantastic settting in a former stable in beautiful Deia that is a total must for foodies. As soon as you walk into the room you are immediately bathed in candle-lit romance and ambience

**2 THE MONKEY BAR, NYC**
Just like the red carpet at the BAFTAs, The Monkey Bar has a star-studded cast on any night with food to match. I love the menu, the banquettes and the relaxed but buzzy atmosphere

**3 SOHO HOUSE, LA**
Nick Jones has created the most fabulous club in LA, the views are quite frankly amazing and it is so stylish, both in its design and its members

### MOVIE MAGIC
Films I can watch over and over – The Insider, The Usual Suspects, Breakfast at Tiffany's, Slumdog Millionaire, Toy Story and Shakespeare in Love

# THE SETAI
# SOUTH BEACH

—

## *Slick, stylish and sassy*
## *on South Beach*

FAVOURITE
HIP
HOTEL
★★★★★

The hotel was originally built in the 1930s and is an exquisite mix of Art Deco and Asian. Perfectly restored under the rigorous eye of famed hotelier Adrian Zecha, the public rooms are achingly cool and sophisticated in a fusion of brick, bronze, wood and leather, while its sister building – a glass tower of 40 floors – is Miami to its core. Here, each suite or condo has vast windows or glass walls showcasing the shades of South Beach – blue skies, blue sea, bright lights – it's magical.

Guestrooms in the Art Deco building are a tad more restrained in the elegant lines and minimal touches that are truly Asian with teak walls and jade antiques brought from China. Black granite borders the floor and also provides the material for the large free-standing bath-tubs.

With its tropical gardens, three swimming pools, access to the beach, an ultra-fashionable bar and restaurant and private spa, it offers everything you might desire with all the fun and frenzy of Collins Avenue and South Beach just outside the door. But best of all it offers serenity and tranquillity; not to mention a great Martini once you are inside its giant doors.

Bookings: +44 (0)20 7201 8070
masonroseprivate.com

## HOTEL AT A GLANCE

**ACCOMMODATION**
130 rooms and suites, 1 penthouse

**DINING**
2 restaurants and bars with
alfresco dining

**RECREATION**
Spa, fitness centre, 3 pools,
yoga, personal trainers, nearby
watersports, golf, tennis and
deep-sea diving and private
yacht charters

**TRANSFERS**
Miami International Airport
25mins by car

+ 1 305 520 60 00
setai.com

SIGNATURE EXPERIENCE

# THE FEEL-GOOD FACTOR IN THERAPY HEAVEN

When you deserve some serious cosseting head for the spa and opt for the signature Jade Massage. It is totally hedonistic as two therapists set to work to soothe and smooth tired, aching and knotted muscles.

"

Miami Spice. Art Deco delicious with design cool on top. Bright sunshine and intensely blue sky. Nights gyrate to Cuban rhythms. Take a front-row seat at eye-candy central.

**Bin there done that**

Want to rub shoulders with some locals? Head to **Bin No. 18**, a family-run wine bar, for gourmet charcuterie and cheese platters in the European bistro style. Its industrial-chic décor is in keeping with its location in close proximity to the art scene of Miami. The cellar covers the spectrum of Old World and New, deliciously complementing the menu of chef/owner Alfred Patino. Barrels of style.

**Hippy hippy chic**

**Hip e.** is the boutique of the moment. No, not tie-dye and hemp fabric. Try Murano glass chandeliers, lacquer mirrors and cool brands like Tracy Reese, Vera Wang, Nicky Hilton, Vivienne Tam and Sworn Virgins. I especially love the complimentary Champagne or coffee and staff who treat you like a guest instead of a customer. Think the Vogue version of Woodstock and not a lava lamp in sight.

**Tip toe**

The **Miami City Ballet** was founded by one of America's greatest dancers, Edward Villella. As a patron you can attend class or rehearsal and see the stars up close in action at their headquarters just across the park from The Setai. How about the best seats in the house for a performance, or presenting a bouquet to the prima ballerina on stage at curtain call? It's all tutu much.

**Viva Versace**

The mansion is infamous, but it is an architectural design masterpiece so why not visit? The dining room is a visual spectacular presided over by **Barton G. Weiss**. Order Colorado rack of lamb and a bottle of Oregon Pinot Noir. You will be eating off and drinking out of Versace signature china and glassware. From Versace you expect O.T.T. and nothing less. You won't be disappointed.

Bookings: +44 (0)20 7201 8070
masonroseprivate.com

# THE MARK

—

*The quiet elegance of this Upper East Side location makes for a place to call your New York residence*

BEST

URBAN RETREAT

★★★★★

In the heart of the New York scene, The Mark Hotel has the most coveted residential address in all of Manhattan. Classic and chic with a timeless cachet, this stylish hotel has recently been transformed by the renowned French designer Jacques Grange. The exquisite new look effortlessly blends comfort with an avant-garde style that showcases specially created pieces by leading contemporary artists. The effect is a smart, 'au courant' mix of art and design.

Guestrooms are luxurious, serene retreats of pale soothing tones and are filled with the latest technologies. In fact so state-of-the-art is it, that the hotel has iButlers (a uniformed 'geek' squad) to help you if needed. The bathrooms, sheathed in black and white marble with the deepest tubs, are just pure glamour. This hotel is all about impeccable service and personal touches.

Everything at The Mark is as it should be for a landmark hotel. The in-house team are the best dressed anywhere with their Turnbull and Asser uniforms. Dining is under the guidance of the Michelin starred chef Jean-Georges Vongerichten whose input even extends to room service. If meeting up with friends then the fashionable The Mark Bar with its intriguing undulating 'cloud' bar is the place to be seen in. The Mark Hotel is not about style over substance; it is about a unique style with great substance.

## HOTEL AT A GLANCE

**ACCOMMODATION**
150 rooms and suites with
individually stocked bars

**DINING**
Gourmet restaurant and chic bar

**RECREATION**
Fitness centre by John Sitaras,
beauty salon and pet friendly
dining

**TRANSFERS**
JFK airport 60 mins by car,
La Guardia 30 mins by car

SIGNATURE EXPERIENCE

# CHAMPAGNE PAMPERING

Guests at the iconic Mark Hotel can spend an afternoon being
pampered by Frédéric Fekkai's personally selected staff of stylists and
beauty specialists. Enjoy a blow-dry, a make-up application by top
beauty brand Chantecaille, a manicure or pedicure, and a delicious
in-salon Champagne lunch from an innovative menu specially
crafted by Manhattan's pre-eminent chef, the award-winning
Jean-Georges.

+ 1 212 744 4300
themarkhotel.com

*Tanya's travel secrets...*

"

Take a hotel and add a liberal dash of hotel maestro James Sherwin and you really can't go wrong. Style, service, technology and comfort blend beautifully with the parfum scent of Frédéric Malle. Truly exquisite.

**Slim Calm Sexy**

So goes the title of Tara Stiles' book that expounds the virtues of yoga in your life. Instructor to Deepak Chokra, and with a husband who also teaches, so you are in good hands at **Strala Yoga**. Only $10 a class, with beginners at 9.30am on Sundays, and classes for all levels of experience. Set yourself on the road to a clear mind and fabulous body.

**Roar**

The special blend burgers with bacon, smoked gouda and caramelised onions at **The Lion** are insanely delicious. Or slide into one of the green leather banquettes below Warhols and Basquiats and order the lobster pasta. Or better still book the hidden private dining room upstairs for a group of friends and have everyone dip into the cheesecake in a jar.

**Roasted**

Are you over having filter coffee poured over old coffee by a surly diner waitress? Desperate for a proper brew? Go to **Third Rail**, one of the top ten coffee dens in New York. Owners Humberto and Rita will put the kick back in your day with a credibly creamy latte. Changing artwork and photography on the walls keep the caffeine-infused adrenalin pumping.

**Dazzling**

The Manhattan skyline must be seen from on high. The secret is to pre-book priority boarding tickets for a 6.00pm ride up the Rockefeller Center to **Top of the Rock**. The view is incredible and should be followed by a cocktail hour before taking up your orchestra aisle seats in the theatre district 10 minutes' walk away.

# THE PIERRE
## A TAJ HOTEL

—

*Location, location and location –*
*this is the best address in New York*

There cannot be a more glamorous location than this – on Fifth Avenue facing Central Park, with Tiffanys and FAO Schwarz almost next door, Bergdorf's two minutes' walk in one direction, Barneys the same distance in the other direction. While Carnegie Hall, MoMa and the Rockefeller Center are not much further.

Stylish, sophisticated and newly refurbished at a cost of $100 million plus, it has all the glitz and glamour that any East side habitué desires. Built in the 1930s to resemble a French château, it has always been a benchmark of elegance and calm, which it still retains in the midst of all the hip and funk of this great city. This explains why it has been in demand throughout the years to star in any number of movies and TV shows, and why it is still the choice of many stars, political leaders and financial captains as their home from home in New York.

It has also managed to evolve and change very discreetly. It was the first New York hotel to install radios and TVs, but now has Bose sound-systems, iPod docks and WiFi, all sitting unobtrusively in discreet array. It has also imported an outpost of London's most fashionable brasserie, Le Caprice, all cool black-and-white Bailey photographs and comfort food for grown-ups. It's the place to stay.

Bookings: +44 (0)20 7201 8070
masonroseprivate.com

## HOTEL AT A GLANCE

**ACCOMMODATION**
189 rooms including 49 suites

**DINING**
Restaurant, bar and lounge

**RECREATION**
Fitness centre

**TRANSFERS**
JFK Airport 45 to 60mins by car,
LaGuardia Airport 25 to 40mins
by car, Newark Airport 50 to
60mins by car

+ 1 212 838 8000
tajhotels.com

SIGNATURE EXPERIENCE

# LUXURY AND STYLE THAT KNOW NO BOUNDS IN THE HOTEL'S GRAND SUITES

Live like a princess or a potentate when you enjoy any of the hotel's Grand Suites. All are quite different in shape and size and offer between one and two bedrooms, and each has spectacular views over Manhattan. Decorated in lavish fabrics, rugs and marble, each has its own private dining room complete with a Murano glass chandelier. Take the Presidential Suite and you can have six bedrooms and exclusive use of the top floor.

"

—

New York pulses with excitement –
it truly never sleeps. Alicia Keys sang
"Big lights will inspire you", and they
do indeed. The Manhattan skyline
is a giant flickering neon that says
excitement 24/7.

**Cast party**

It's Monday night in New York and what to do? Jim Caruso presides over the great and not so great at **Birdland** with incredible dry wit and flair, at this open mike that attracts the crème de la crème of Broadway stars on their night off. It's brilliantly entertaining and one of New York's best kept secrets.

**Foodies**

Try **Il Buco** located in the East Village. Dining in an antique-filled restaurant with clued-in locals and celebrity chefs, is evidence of the sensational kitchen. The menu changes constantly and the patrons keep coming back for more. Savour being a New Yorker.

**Lovely locks**

Who tends to the tresses of the divine Tony/Oscar/CBE Catherine Zeta Jones? Liza with a Z? **John Barrett**, that's who; you'll find him working his magic at Bergdorf Goodman in a penthouse location overlooking Central Park that has all the vibe of a Vogue fashion shoot. His clients are the stars of film, TV, and Broadway and fashion. He'll make you look and feel like a star with a modern glamour and grace that is truly you. Shampoo with a view.

**Garden views**

You've done Central Park, now for something urban. Walk off brunch at Pastis with a stroll in **High line Park** located in the meatpacking district running from Gansevoort Street to 34th between 10th & 11th Avenues. Built on an old railway track above the city it offers fantastic views, spectacular architecture, and plenty of eye candy when the sun is shining.

**AUSTRALIA**

UST

# PARK HYATT SYDNEY

—

## *Über-luxury in Sydney's historical area of the Rocks*

See Sydney at its best from your own bedroom window – the Opera House, the Harbour Bridge and the water taxis and ferries that operate across the harbour throughout the day. This is a hotel filled with the light and space of the city in which it lives with walls of glass, clear contemporary design and the colours that epitomise sunshine. It's a hotel that exudes happiness within the historic environs of the Rocks district.

And although Sydney is a large city, almost everything a visitor needs or wishes to experience is within range. The Opera House a few minutes by water taxi, Circular Quay a short stroll away with its myriad cafes, bars and restaurants. The chichi shops boutiques and galleries of the Rocks almost surround you while the golden sands of Bondi are a mere 30 minutes away at the most. And for the rest of the time, savour the feast of indigenous art and culture that you will find in the Powerhouse Museum, the aquatic surprises at the Sydney Aquarium and the welcome of the locals. It's a paradise for foodies which begins in the hotel's harbour**kitchen**&bar which serves the best of locally sourced foods against the spectacular backdrop of the harbour, and which stretches to the many restaurants and cafes of the city as well as its great food markets. Those looking for that little bit of extra excitement can climb the bridge! Don't worry, there are expert guides… but not for you if vertigo is a problem. The views on the other hand are jaw-dropping.

Bookings: +44 (0)20 7201 8070
masonroseprivate.com

### HOTEL AT A GLANCE

**ACCOMMODATION**
155 rooms and suites

**DINING**
2 restaurants and 2 bars

**RECREATION**
Spa, fitness centre, rooftop terrace
with pool, private wharf

**TRANSFERS**
Sydney Kingsford Smith Airport
25mins by car

**SIGNATURE EXPERIENCE**

# A HEAVENLY WAY TO ENJOY THE HARBOUR LIGHTS

We all know that Sydney is glorious by day, but at night it is
intensely glamorous. In order to enjoy this side of it, take a cruise
around the harbour when all the lights are on – the shoreline
is spectacular.

+ 61 292 56 1465
sydney.park.hyatt.com

"

Consistently voted one of the world's favourite holiday destinations, Sydney is just spectacular. Laid-back Aussie style that belies its incredible cuisine and fashion trail-blazers. Down-under dynamite.

**Hair today gone tomorrow**

If you have been in the outback and swimming at Bondi, you might need a little attention to your locks. **Joh Bailey** is your man. Book in advance to see him at his salon in Double Bay, the Beverly Hills of Sydney. He even looked after Princess Diana when she was on tour down under.

**Beachside bliss**

As you turn off and head down the hill to Balmoral Beach you will be blessed with the most spectacular view through Sydney Harbour Heads. The **Bathers' Pavilion** sits at the bottom of this hillside of stunning homes with million-dollar views. Award-winning cuisine on the beach for lunch or dinner.

**Boutique boomerang**

You'll keep coming back for more at **Read's** in Woollahara in the stylish Eastern Suburbs. The best snapshot of Australian designers under one roof with over 50 represented on the hangers. You'll love Queen Street where the boutique is located; it just oozes with Aussie style.

**Bill's**

Ricotta hotcakes with honeycomb butter and banana? Corn fritters with roasted sweet tomatoes and crisp bacon? Creamy latte? Communal table with a slew of international magazines, or private tables for two. This breakfast joint is the DNA of the restaurants established by the now-famous **chef Bill Granger**. Don't miss it.

PA &

# ANANDA IN THE HIMALAYAS

## THE HEIGHT OF WELLBEING IN THE FOOTHILLS OF THE HIMALAYAS

The location itself is healing here at India's premier destination spa, high above the pilgrim town of Rishikesh, where the holy river Ganges flows through, and reputed to be the birthplace of yoga. Built in the grounds of the Maharajah of Tehri Garwal's summer palace, with most of the rooms and the spa itself in new buildings, and all with wonderful views of the mountains. The huge meeting hall within the palace is a great place for yoga when the weather is inclement – otherwise classes take place in the colonnaded Music Pavilion and at the Hillside Amphitheatre, open to the air and the views.

Indulge yourself in a multitude of therapies chosen from east and west, or put yourself into the hands of the Ayurvedic doctors who will prescribe a tailormade programme for you. The spa has a huge relaxation area, a pool and some of the most tranquil treatment rooms on earth. There is also a fitness centre with the very latest gym equipment. Add to this a series of visiting gurus, lectures and special programmes and you have a near-perfect spa.

---

**AT A GLANCE**

**ACCOMMODATION**
75 rooms and suites and 3 villas with private pools

**DINING**
Restaurant with treetop deck, pavilion and tea lounge

**RECREATION**
Rejuvenation treatments, outdoor pool, gym, yoga pavilions, billiard room, library, trekking, whitewater rafting, elephant safaris, golf

**TRANSFERS**
Dehdarun Jolly Grant Airport 1hr by car and 1hr flight from Delhi Domestic Airport

+ 91 1378 227500
anandaspa.com

"

Elevate your holistic approach to renewed energy by taking a spiritual journey to a Maharajah's palace estate. Fall into the arms of this divine retreat, and you'll eat, pray and love yourself to a brand-new you.

**Mind-blowing**

**The Ayurvedic treatment Shirodhara** is fabulous after a long journey and supports your valiant attempts to leave the stress of city life behind. Luke-warm herbal oil is poured in an even stream on to the forehead to pacify and revitalise the mind and the body. Benefits include intense rejuvenating and anti-ageing effects, improved memory and normalised sleep patterns. Clear head, clear mind.

**Empowerment**

Be empowered with **Reiki healing**. It's a gentle hands-on healing technique that promotes a deep level of relaxation and healing on a physical, mental, emotional and spiritual level. Reiki uses the universal life force energy to break up energy blockages within the body, stimulating the body's natural ability to heal itself. Reduces stress and anxiety and brings your body, mind, emotions and spirit into balance.

**Spring to life**

Give yourself up to the refreshing **Himalayan Spring Water Ritual**. Time is on your side, so being pampered for nearly three hours will not impact your schedule. The ancient wisdom of bathing and healing is applied via a foot ritual, lemongrass and ginger body scrub, hydro-aromatic bath, and a aromatherapy massage of orange and eucalyptus, topped off with an Ananda infusion. You're sparkling all over.

**Temple trek**

You'll begin to understand Shirley Maclaine when you trek to the **Kunjapuri Temple**. The snowcapped Himalayan Mountains jut majestically before you against the expanse of sky. Spa staff lead you on this 3–4 hour journey that is best experienced at sunrise or sunset when the light is truly incredible. You won't fall off the mountain, you'll feel like you can fly. Don't miss it.

# MATT
## ON TRAVEL

*"*

—

*Travel tips from the locals*
*is what it's all about.*

## Matt Roberts is the celebrated personal fitness trainer to the stars.

**TR** *Always busy with clients, how do you get away with your family?*

**MR** I like a low-key atmosphere, and hotels that are small with a chilled-out vibe. I hate en masse resorts with 4 pools and 600 people, drives me mad. We strike a balance between what is right for our six and eight-year old and what my wife and I want to do. It's not that tricky actually, as we prefer an authentic experience, not a kidsclub. The Chedi in Oman is a good example of this.

**TR** *Any special little gems from your travels?*

**MR** We found the most charming restaurant off the road between Amalfi and Pompeii. I can't remember the name but it was a little place sticking out over the sea on a rock with only six tables. No menu, you were served whatever came in that day, which for us was seabass. It was an amazing meal and totally authentic and very memorable.

**TR** *Do you like visiting cities?*

**MR** I adore Paris for its romance and go as often as I can with my wife. The Hôtel Costes is one of my favourites in the world. NYC is a fun place to go – chic, cool and happening, where I am more of a downtown than uptown man. And I think Barcelona is brilliant.

**TR** *Is there anywhere you go every year?*

**MR** The place I return to consistently year after year is Tuscany. I have rented various houses around the Florence and Luca area and I am always delighted to arrive and disappointed to leave. For me, the culture, the food and the pure style of Italy is compelling.

## Matt's
### FIT AND FABULOUS TIPS

**1 DO RUN RUN**
In NYC jog 50 blocks up to Central Park, around the Reservoir and back. A great way to get to know the city before breakfast

### QUICK GET-AWAY
Whenever you can fly from City Airport, it's quick and easy and more like flying from a private jet terminal

**2 GYM KIT**
Call the hotel in advance and find out what gym equipment they have and plan a workout programme with your own personal trainer before you go

**3 NUTRITION KNOW-HOW**
Get the hotel menus in advance and review with your nutritionist to plan your diet

# CHIVA-SOM

## A HAVEN OF LIFE AND A SOURCE OF GOOD HEALTH

One of the most famous destination spas in the world sits behind a high fence facing the beach at Hua Hin. Guests are here to detox, de-stress, lose weight or simply be kind to themselves – and for any or all of those reasons, you couldn't be in a better place.

Each visit begins with a wellness consultation when a programme is tailormade for each guest with a daily diary of treatments, consultations, lectures and fitness classes. Yet you are allowed to do as much or as little as you like. Almost every type of treatment is on offer from hydrotherapy to chakra balancing. A number of retreats are held with visiting experts and gurus throughout the year. Those wishing to improve their fitness levels are spoiled for choice with tai chi, Pilates, golf bio-mechanics, Thai boxing, aqua aerobics and tennis. Personal trainers will work out a special programme for you. There is an in-house Niranlada medi-spa for a spot of skin-rejuvenation, while an army of nutritionists, traditional Chinese medical therapists and holistic practitioners are on call.

**AT A GLANCE**

**ACCOMMODATION**
58 rooms and suites

**DINING**
2 restaurants

**RECREATION**
Medi-Spa, extensive wellness and spa therapies, fitness activities, yoga and tai chi pavilions, gym, golf

**TRANSFERS**
Bangkok Suvarnabhumi Airport 2hrs 30mins by car

+ 66 (0) 3253 6536
chivasom.com

“
—

Spa aficionados flock to this paradise in Thailand to be cradled in relaxation and rejuvenation. Set your own pace, re-centre, cleanse your mind and body, and leave glowing. Som enchanted Chiva.

**Cooked**

Have you gone to a spa to cleanse and detox and then come home to shepherd's pie and lashings of trifle? Join the **Spa Cuisine Cooking Class** to learn the secrets of Thai spa cuisine for yourself. You can continue with your health regime knowing how to cook with limited salt, fat and sugar whilst still making your taste buds burst with happiness.

**Computer knot**

Stress release therapy – a treatment developed in recent years by Chiva-Som's physiotherapy team, this treatment is specifically aimed at those who spend long hours desk-bound and working on computers. The treatment works on stressed musculoskeletal areas using myofascial relief technique, soft tissue release and upper body massage with superficial heat applied to the whole arm, increasing blood circulation and relieving tension.

**Let's face it**

Mi-en accupressure – a new treatment introduced in July 2010, this facial acupressure treatment is based on the classic Chinese medicine acu-points and is used to relax the muscles and tone the skin of the face, allowing a rejuvenated appearance to shine through. By stimulating the nerves and muscles, this treatment helps to detoxify, boost collagen production and enhance natural beauty.

**Zone out**

Sound bath therapy – Chiva-Som's specialist in music and meditation aims to restore the vibrational balance of the body. During emotional or physical stress, the vibrational harmony of the body is disturbed, so this treatment aims to bring you back into tune. Healing crystal and Tibetan bowls, a Chinese harp and other instruments immerse the body in a world of sound, creating profound relaxation.

# THE ORIGINAL F. X. MAYR & MORE HEALTH CENTRE

## A LAKESIDE RETREAT DEDICATED TO YOU, YOUR HEALTH AND WELLBEING

A plain wooden chalet sitting on the lakeside and surrounded by woods holds a magic all of its own and is known to connoisseurs across the globe. Its philosophy and regime hold strong to the original vision of Dr Xavier Mayr, on which the clinic has made its name. Each visit begins with a consultation with a doctor and an individual programme is prescribed, whether your visit is for de-stress, weight loss, fitness, allergies or general health. It is recommended that guests stay for a minimum of a week. The Mayr process believes that a healthy digestion is the key to good health, so many aspects of your treatment will be tuned to re-educating you on what to eat... and how to eat.

Also on offer are a number of treatments and therapies devoted to fitness and health – from the therapeutic effects of massage to Kneipp treatments. The centre also boasts a gym, sauna and indoor swimming pool. There are some great walks and hikes in the nearby woods, a lake to swim in, boat excursions and bicycles to help you explore the region.

### AT A GLANCE

**ACCOMMODATION**
57 rooms and 8 apartments

**DINING**
Restaurant

**RECREATION**
Extensive range of medical programmes including diet, health, detoxification and fitness, sauna with indoor pool, bikes, pedal boat on lake, skiing and ice-skating, nearby golf

**TRANSFERS**
Klagenfurt Airport 25mins by car;
Ljubljana Airport 1hr 30mins by car

+ 43 42 73 25 11 0
mayrandmore.at

"

—

# Ultimate discretion and expert medical attention that will leave you brimming with vitality and life.

BEST FOR

DETOX

★★★★★

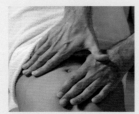

**Infused**

An exclusive offering that is a must on your schedule are the vitamin infusions. As you relax in a comfy leather armchair with footrest, the gentle team infuse directly to your vein vitamins recommended by your doctor during your initial consultation. Instant results coursing through your body boosting your vitality and immune system. Check the menu.

**Colonic**

The thought of this sends many people, especially men, running for the hills. But you will find the process at Mayr is very gentle, does not feel invasive, and is performed carefully at your own pace. The result is sensational and goes a long way towards helping the cleansing and healing process of your digestive system. Highly recommended.

**Seaweed scrub**

Dr Bolvari proposes that you book the Organic Pharmacy seaweed scrub treatment for the beginning and end of your stay. It helps with the detox process and leaves you positively glowing. It's absolutely a must. Follow with the 90-minute facial to zone out and leave looking gorgeous.

**Tips**

Go Ryanair from Stansted for nonstop flights; get a lounge pass online for airport comfort. Train from Liverpool Street to Stansted, but book a driver for when you come home. Pack t-shirts, swim and gym gear only, as dressing up is not required. Take good books or a stack of great DVDs to keep you entertained. Discuss specific rooms when booking to ensure most space and best view.

# in:spa RETREATS

## CHANGE YOUR LIFE, YOUR BODY, YOUR FITNESS LEVEL AND FEEL FANTASTIC

in:spa promises to make you look and feel amazing in just one week, which is probably why so many guests return year after year. In gorgeous sunny locations like Marrakech, the South of France and Andalusia, and in carefully selected exclusive properties, the in:spa team of friendly experts will transform your physical and mental wellbeing.

The expert team of massage therapists, nutritionists, chefs, yoga teachers, hiking guides and personal trainers ensure maximum benefits for every guest, such as weight-loss, improved fitness, greater flexibility, stress relief and a heightened sense of wellbeing.

in:spa retreats combine energising outdoor fitness activities and yoga, massage and gourmet healthy cuisine. The number of guests on every retreat is strictly limited, allowing everyone to enjoy personal nutritional consultations, daily yoga instruction in small 'same level' groups, daily fitness training, regular massages and individual care and attention. The one-to-one focus ensures that these luxury retreats are suitable for absolute beginners as well as the more experienced, of all ages.

### AT A GLANCE

**ACCOMMODATION**
A selection of private venues in gorgeous locations

**DESTINATIONS**
Andalusia, Marrakech and South of France

**DINING**
Full board and gourmet cleansing cuisine

**RECREATION**
Yoga, personal training, hiking, massage, nutritional advice

+44 (0)20 8968 0501
inspa-retreats.com

"

A complete transformation of your mental and physical wellbeing in stunning locations designed to inspire. Exercise that achieves results combined with the perfect balance of quiet reflection in expert professional care.

**Spring**

A beautiful converted monastery, set around a courtyard of formal gardens, and surrounded on all sides by rolling hills is the perfect place to refresh and rejuvenate your mind and body next spring. Enjoy the sunshine, relax by the magnificent pool after an invigorating hike through the countryside or work out with the expert trainers before a blissful restorative massage.

**Summer**

You'll wish you could spend a year in Provence when you check into the in:spa chateâu amid 200 hectares of vines, olive groves, forests and hills. You'll wash off the sweat of your hikes, yoga and workouts with luxurious L'Occitane toiletries. A dip in the pool? A game of tennis? Expert specialists maximise your health and fitness regime on the Côte d'Azur.

**Autumn**

If you want to up the exercise wattage but are not an iron man, then go for an in:spa intense programme. The same as a classic week but with a few more physical challenges and personal training that is a bit more demanding. Optional ideas like morning fun runs round out the programme, not your waistline.

**Winter**

Kick start your New Year's resolution in Morocco. The superb villa of Marrakech Liqama awaits you in the Palmerie. Imagine fresh juice and yoga as the sun rises behind the Atlas Mountains. Hiking and biking are combined with moments of tranquillity in the courtyards, canopied alcoves and tented terraces. Blissful booster shot.

# DESTINATION YOGA

## A HOLIDAY TO REST AND REFRESH MIND, BODY AND SOUL

Destination yoga is tailormade for those with a desire to improve, practise or simply learn yoga and the benefits it brings to mind and body. Beautiful and tranquil destinations are selected in places as diverse as Puglia in southern Italy, the island of Crete and India close to Bangalore. All take place in private houses or small hotels and all are chosen for both their comfort and the care that each guest receives not just from the yoga teachers but from the staff at each destination.

And while each week-long holiday differs slightly according to the practice of the teacher, each one offers at least two yoga sessions every day – one in the morning, and one in late afternoon. The teachers who accompany them are acclaimed as some of the best in the world. Classes also include meditation and pranayama techniques, while each location has its own swimming pool and lots of space to relax and do very little. The food is healthy and organic and you will almost definitely return home lighter and calmer.

**DESTINATIONS**
Greece, Morocco, Italy, Spain and India

**HIGHLIGHTS**
World's best yoga teachers, exclusive locations, suitable for all levels of experience, vegetarian and non-vegetarian options

+44 (0) 20 8968 0501
destinationyoga.co.uk

# FITSCAPE FITNESS HOLIDAYS

## GET FIT, HAVE FUN – THE GUIDING ELEMENTS OF FITSCAPE HOLIDAYS

If you are one of those people who is always promising yourself that you need to adjust your fitness levels and that you really must start on a proper regime… well, these holidays are your starting point. Here, in exclusive and extremely comfortable properties, you will work towards your fitness potential with experts and personal trainers. Not only will you lose weight – and that is a side effect, not the main point – but you will also return home energised, recharged and most important of all, motivated.

Training sessions take place each day and can include trekking, mountain-biking, circuit training, running, jogging and swimming alongside massage therapy, golf and tennis. However this is not a boot camp – you can work at your own pace under the supervision of the personal trainers and, while the week is challenging, it is designed to be fun. The food is delicious, healthy and plentiful. The holidays are designed to refresh and revitalise both your body and your mind.

### AT A GLANCE

**DESTINATIONS**
Italy, Spain, France and Morocco

**HIGHLIGHTS**
UK's top fitness instructors, general and sports-specific training, all levels of fitness, 7 night programmes, stylish venues, customised programmes with diverse activities

**NEW FOR 2011**
Fitness and skiing in the Italian Dolomites

+ 44 (0)20 8968 0501
fitscape.co.uk

# MOMENTUM ADVENTURE

## TAKE THE ROAD LESS TRAVELLED

If you've always longed for the great adventure, whether it's
fly-fishing in the remote Canadian wilderness, racing dune buggies
through the cactus forests of Baja California, or sleeping in custom-
made ice caves under the Northern Lights – then Momentum
Adventure can make the dream come true.

And while we all love great luxury travel, sometimes it's not
enough. Momentum Adventure creates unforgettable, tailormade
trips to the most dramatic, beautiful and wildest places on earth.
The company runs no more than a dozen trips per year, each of
them tailored to optimal seasonal timing and offering complete
security in dramatic environments – with a touch of luxury
and style.

---

**AT A GLANCE**

**DESTINATIONS**
South Pole, Arctic, Borneo,
Mongolia, Jordan, Yukon, Baja,
Kashmir, Lebanon, Japan, British
Columbia and St Moritz

**HIGHLIGHTS**
Itineraries led by the world's most
accomplished guides, tailormade
small expeditions, three different
categories of Sub-Zero, Wilderness,
Ski, all available for diverse ages,
bespoke exclusive trips

+ 44 (0) 1892 784646
momentumadventure.com

66
—

Whether you're after an adrenalin-fuelled adventure or a chance to explore virgin territories, Momentum's bespoke travel experiences are the last word in guided trips.

**Arctic adventure**

Experience peace and unbelievable natural beauty. Northern Lights, a snowmobile safari, manage your own team of dogs, how about a night in the exclusive ice caves? Warm up in the sauna and then take a dunk in the frozen lake. This is a level 2 for fitness which means most people will have no problem participating even as young as 14. A completely unique experience.

**Baja California**

On board state-of-the-art dune buggies you'll explore the 12th largest state in Mexico. The volcano fields and peaks of the Sierra de Baja California mountain range drop to the rugged coastline and beautiful beaches at the edge of the Pacific Ocean. The colour and terrain is spectacular. Share it with a friend, a lover, or your teenagers.

**Yukon**

A remote wilderness seen by very few people awaits in Canada's westernmost territory. Expert guide Jan Neuspiel, a specialist in rafting and climbing, will teach you survival skills from navigation to fishing for your dinner. Days on white water and nights under the stars by an open fire. The Great Outdoors will inspire and awe you.

**Corporate**

Whether you're looking for a dynamic team-building opportunity, unique incentive travel by way of reward or even innovative executive hospitality, Momentum Adventure takes a fresh, exciting approach to corporate journeys and events – guaranteed to deliver the very best results.

Villas

ILL

# UNIQUE PROPERTIES & EVENTS
—

*Chez moi, il mio castello, my home*

Whenever you wish, wherever you wish, the rental service of Unique Properties is entirely dedicated to individuals choosing to travel not only to favourite classic locations such as Italy, Africa, Greece and France, but also to more unusual destinations such as Brazil, India and Costa Rica.

We hold the keys to exceptional houses not normally available on the villa rental market. Our unrivalled company portfolio contains nearly a hundred properties in different countries with only three or four houses per destination, all of which have undergone our rigorous quality inspection focusing on key criteria such as charm, beauty, perfect service… representing a certain art de vivre.

In order to maintain a strong network of relationships throughout the world, our philosophy is based on an extreme discretion, and a well-thought-out concept of confidentiality for both clients and property owners.

Following numerous customer requests we are now also offering a tailormade service to organise your parties. We will be happy to assist you for any events from birthdays to anniversaries and weddings.

Personalised attention, care and availability are top priorities in assisting each of our clients.

Bookings: +44 (0)20 7201 8070
masonroseprivate.com

**FRANCE, CORSICA**

# VILLA IL MARE

A superb contemporary realisation located
in one of the most beautiful spots on the island!
The villa and lawns simply end up on a large
private sandy beach, long pool, tennis and the
most modern facilities are available in that
fully staffed six double bedrooms property.

**GREECE, ITHACA**

# AGHIOS A

There is no word to describe the beauty
of the gardens, or the views from Aghios A.
It is a real paradise on earth offering extremely
stylish interiors and excellent house staff.
The cherry on the cake is a Riva boat that
comes with the house, a perfect opportunity
to discover the coast and to have divine
lunches on board.

+ 44 (0)20 7788 7815
cedricreversade.com

SPAIN, IBIZA

# CASA BIANCA

Casa Bianca is a spectacular modern finca-style villa enjoying a unique location and breathtaking views over the sea. Sunset there is unforgettable. Many outdoor dining and sitting areas make it a unique and perfect place to entertain friends or simply relax with the family.

ITALY, NEAR CORTONA

# PALAZZO

Palazzo may be the only property today to offer simultaneously all the charm and refinement of Italy alongside the most modern amenities such as tennis, a heated pool, air conditioning and immaculate bathrooms. This is simply a dream house offering a lot of privacy and the most professional staff.

ITALY, CAPRI

# VILLA DEL ARCO

Villa del Arco, built at the end of the 18th
century by an old Caprese family, is situated
a few minutes from the Piazzeta and the
Quisisana Hotel. It went through a total
renovation for three years and now offers the
most exceptional facilities such as heated pool,
gym, Jacuzzi, air-conditioning… and a
breathtaking sea view. An alternative to any
five-star on the island!

PORTUGAL, TAVIRA

# LA QUINTA

This spectacular contemporary home lies in
18 acres of the natural reserve of Rio Formosa,
facing the sea and with direct access to a
fabulous sandy beach. La Quinta and its two
pools are surrounded by superb landscaped
gardens with many outdoor sitting and dining
areas. The staff have been in the house for
years and are extremely sweet and
professional.

ITALY, SICILY

# VILLA FIONA

Villa Fiona is one of the finest historic villas in Sicily, which now has been restored to offer the most modern facilities such as air-conditioning, WiFi, a large pool and tennis. Exotically planted gardens and fragrant citrus groves surround the villa, which is located a few kilometres from the beach and a short drive from the ancient, historic, delightful Siracusa. The property is ideal for a large family with its eight bedrooms, but also for a group of friends who would like to discover the area.

FRANCE, ST TROPEZ

# VILLA INFINITY

This fabulous new property is located in the gated residence of Les Parcs de St Tropez and enjoys spectacular panoramic, 180° sea views. Villa Infinity offers the latest technology such as an automatic cover for the pool which becomes a dance floor, air-conditioning, WiFi and anintegrated sound system. A fabulous villa to entertain friends in! Very stylish interiors with large suites and immaculate bathrooms. Infinity also enjoys superb reception rooms all facing the sea with huge terraces.

# TIM
## ON TRAVEL

> 66
> —
>
> *I'm not sure how much of a secret this great hotel is – but I'm very glad I'm in on it.*

*The Oscar, Tony, Grammy and Golden Globe award-winning lyricist, Sir Tim Rice's songs resonate around the world.*

**TR** *What travel destination inspires you?*

**STR** The Grand Hotel Europe has always provided the perfect base for me from which to explore the many historical sites of St Petersburg and the dodgy bars. It's minutes away from the Hermitage Museum and the Winter Palace Square. It's directly opposite the Philharmonic Society, and is situated on Nevsky Prospekt which is the central hub of the city. It is also around the corner from the Russian Museum and Park.

**TR** *Any fond memories?*

**STR** Cricket is my passion. I took my cricket team Heartaches CC to St. Petersburg to play two matches against Peter's Imperials and we played in the Russian Museum park. A sort of cricket pitch had been laid out for the first time in this beautiful park's history. Unfortunately, two yards too long, which was my excuse for failing to win either encounter. Plus there seemed to be a lot of Sri Lankans and Australians in the allegedly Russian team.

**TR** *What is special about the Pavarotti Suite where you always stay?*

**STR** Well, it's obvious that it's named after the celebrated Italian tenor who stayed there during his final tours in 2004. But what is really special for me is the antique grand piano which is the focal point of the room and the source of some relaxation for me, if not for the people in the nearby suites.

## MAKE WAVES

The Katina is a new luxury speedboat which was imported from Venice and provides an exclusive and unique way to explore the city

## Tim's NOTES ON TRAVEL

### 1 PERFECT SUITE
The Pavarotti Suite at the Grand Hotel Europe in St Petersburg is a personal favourite

### 2 PERFECT LOCATION
Explore the many historical sites of St Petersburg. The Russian Museum and Park are located around the corner from the Grand Hotel

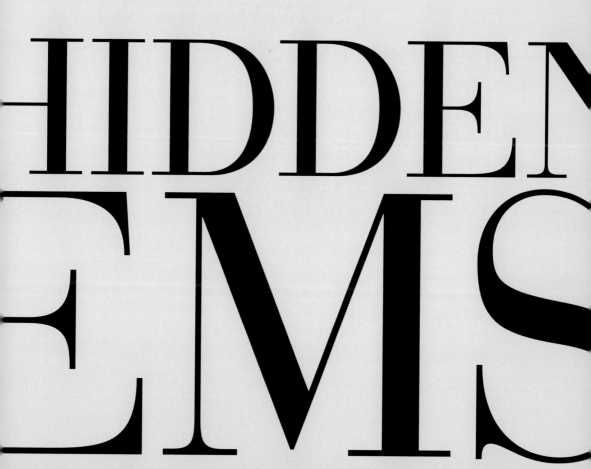

# HIDDEN GEMS

—

# HIDDEN GEMS ARE EXACTLY THAT – NOT IMMEDIATELY OBVIOUS AND SOMETIMES UNKNOWN. I FIND THEM ON MY TRAVELS OR MY FRIENDS SHARE THEIR BOUNTY WITH ME OVER LUNCH.

They come in all sorts of guises –
ranging from a B&B to a boutique
hotel or even a tree-house.

# THE OPPOSITE HOUSE

## AN UNCLUTTERED HAVEN OF CALM DESIGN

Encased in shimmering emerald glass, this gorgeous boutique hotel is Beijing's chicest hotspot. Singular interiors are a triumph of tradition meeting modern design; studio-style rooms are luxe in every detail; divinely delicious restaurants; and a classy cocktail bar, pulsing nightclub and the coolest stainless steel pool. The best of China is here.

### HOTEL AT A GLANCE

**ACCOMMODATION**
98 studios and penthouse

**DINING**
3 restaurants, lounge bar and nightclub

**RECREATION**
Indoor pool, treatment rooms, gym, complimentary minibar and WiFi

**TRANSFERS**
Beijing Capital International Airport 30mins by car

+ 86 10 641 76688
theoppositehouse.com

### TANYA'S TRAVEL SECRETS

**Imperial fashion**
Do you want to take something home that is authentic and local and that you can actually wear? **Red Phoenix** is the answer and home to designer Gu Lin. Beautiful silk and satin jackets with the most detailed and exquisite embroidery, including of course the phoenix. Divine for evening cocktails and one of a kind. Intimate luxury.

**Dazzling dinner**
**Mei Fu** was inspired by the Peking opera star Mei Lanfang (a man not a woman!). This glamorous restaurant has rooms filled with opera memorabilia; it simply oozes 1930s elegance. The menu is light and subtle, unlike the décor. A nice way to experience Peking opera without going to the theatre to see it. Note perfect.

# HOTEL BELLEVUE

## THE QUIET PLACE TO ENJOY THE HIGH LIFE

Perched high on a rock overlooking the beautiful bay of Miramare, this is the place to be when visiting Croatia's jewel – the heritage town of Dubrovnik. It is but a short walk to reach the walls that have fortified Dubrovnik for centuries but in tranquillity terms it is light years away. This is where you return to relax after a day's sailing, shopping or sightseeing. Here, you will be fed like a king and pampered like a queen in the hotel's Comfort Zone spa.

### HOTEL AT A GLANCE

**ACCOMMODATION**
91 rooms and suites

**DINING**
Restaurant, beach tavern and lounge bar

**RECREATION**
Spa and wellness centre, fitness centre, indoor pool and pebble beach

**TRANSFERS**
Dubrovnik Airport 30mins by car

+ 385 20 330 000
alh.hr

### TANYA'S TRAVEL SECRETS

**Girl guide**
So much nicer to shop with a driver to load your loot. And even better when they take you straight to **Maria Concept Store** jammed with exclusive designer clothes and accessories. Book in for reflexology and a manicure upon return. You'll glide into dinner in your new outfit.

**Revelling**
Feeling tanned and fabulous and in the mood to dance? In the Revelin Fortress you will find **Night Club Revelin**, which does exactly what it says on the tin. Dance all night and watch the sunrise over the old harbour – it's stunning. Night fever.

# ALMYRA

## A 21ST CENTURY REINVENTION OF CONTEMPORARY LUXE AND HOLISTIC UTOPIA

Styled by Karl Lagerfeld's interior designer this hip boutique resort oozes fashionable chic. Ultra-modern rooms are calming cocoons of white-on-white, the ultimate being the signature Kyma suites with their huge garden daybeds and roof terraces. The super-sleek spa is a delicious design haven. All is effortlessly in vogue, yet family-friendly too.

### HOTEL AT A GLANCE

**ACCOMMODATION**
189 rooms and suites

**DINING**
4 restaurants and lounge bar

**RECREATION**
Spa, watersports, tennis, fitness centre, indoor and outdoor pools, kids' club and Baby Go Lightly crèche

**TRANSFERS**
Paphos International Airport 10mins by car

+ 357 26 888 700
thanoshotels.com

### TANYA'S TRAVEL SECRETS

**Local flavour**
Take a drive up into the hills about 25km from Paphos to the village of Phyti. Ask for Maria at the **Phyti Tavern** and order the Stifado, which is slow-cooked beef with onions, red wine, bay leaves, and a dash of cinnamon. The meze here is a-meze-ing. Order local wine.

**Heat relief**
The hills are alive, thanks to Winston Churchill. Seriously, he ordered a reforestation programme of the **Troodos Mountains** which now provides the cool scents of pine, cedar and eucalyptus trees. Wonderful for walks. Take a picnic from the resort for a tranquil respite from summer heat.

# CHATEAU MCELY

## AN ARISTOCRATIC AND ROMANTIC RETREAT IN THE FOREST

The particular magic of this beautiful rural manor owes much to its charming owners. Restoring it was a labour of love, the result a pocket wonderland. There is truly special food, restorative walks deep into the forest, gorgeous rooms each with its own style and the divine Honey, Silk & Pearls Spa with its own unique aromatherapies.

### HOTEL AT A GLANCE

**ACCOMMODATION**
23 rooms and suites

**DINING**
Restaurant, patio and club

**RECREATION**
Spa, freshwater swimming lake, outdoor sauna, swimming pool, horse riding, cycling, children's playground, tennis and hiking

**TRANSFERS**
Prague Ruzyne Airport 1hr 30mins by car

+ 420 325 600 000
chateaumcely.com

### TANYA'S TRAVEL SECRETS

**Natural cosmetics**
Based on an original idea by Inez Cusumano and prepared in Jim Cusumano's **alchemist laboratory**, this pure natural line uses nine herbs and plants collected from the mystical St George forest. Roses, thyme, daisy and chamomile are transformed into face oil, masks and bath salts and are perfect for sensitive skin. Enchanting.

**Enchanting elixirs**
Discover your hidden scientist in the atmospheric **Alchymist Club** bar deep in the old cellars of the château. There are cocktails to bestow wealth, power, long life and sweet dreams, all developed to original secret recipes. The mysteries of science have never tasted so good.

# ADRÈRE AMELLAL

## A DIVINE DESERT DREAM OF TOTAL ORIGINALITY

Far from anywhere this spectacular eco-lodge is a breathtaking oasis of natural simplicity. The striking landscape of mountains, ancient olive and palm groves and bubbling springs harmonises perfectly with its traditional style. Rooms are authentically handcrafted; dining is beneath the stars or by candlelight, each night in a different venue. With no phones or electricity this is a true desert retreat.

### HOTEL AT A GLANCE

**ACCOMMODATION**
40 rooms

**DINING**
A new experience every evening

**RECREATION**
Natural spring pool, library, dune surfing, horse riding and jeep excursions

**TRANSFERS**
Cairo Airport 8hrs by car, Matrouh Airport 3.5hrs by car. Private jet arrangements possible

+ 202 2736 7879
adrereamellal.net

### TANYA'S TRAVEL SECRETS

**Silence is golden**
We rarely get the chance to stop and breathe, and there's no better way to do so than to take a trip out to the silence of the **desert**. A late-afternoon excursion to experience the sunset is a must. As you let the stillness sink into your bones, the vista of dunes will carry you away.

**Ancient civilisation**
A visit to the town of **Siwa** is a must to see the ruins of the **Shali Fortress** that dates from the 13th century. It's almost like a set from 'Star Wars' so take your camera. Walk around town and the marketplace to take in the local scene. You will find amazing fantastic silver jewellery and exquisitely embroidered garments.

# VILLA BELROSE

## QUIET ELEGANCE FAR FROM THE MADDING CROWD

In such a legendary destination you need stylish glamour and this villa residence is brimming with it. With pine trees and landscaped gardens all around, it has an exclusive hideaway feel. Rooms come with that special treat of a private terrace, ideal to sip rosé and enjoy the stupendous views over the bay.

### HOTEL AT A GLANCE

**ACCOMMODATION**
40 rooms and suites

**DINING**
Gourmet restaurant and poolside bar

**RECREATION**
Outdoor dining, beauty centre and heated outdoor pool

**TRANSFERS**
Nice Côte d'Azur Airport 1hr 10mins by car

+ 33 (0) 494 55 97 97
villabelrose.com

### TANYA'S TRAVEL SECRETS

**Beachcombers**
You want to do the beach and have little ones in tow? Then you might want to head to La Bouillabaisse with its sandy beach coupled with calmer shallower water. No kids? Then have Patrice find you the right table at **Le Club 55**. Order a goat's cheese salad, crudités, seabass, and a chilled bottle of the local Gassin Château Minuty rosé.

**Bardot memories**
Casual chic abounds at **L'Escale** where bare feet are not only acceptable but expected. The floor is sand, black-and-white photos of Bardot abound, and you'll find the seafood so fresh the fish are still flapping.

# SOHO HOUSE BERLIN

## RETRO-FUNK BANG IN THE MITTE

Style and chutzpah combined to turn an old Bauhaus department store turned Communist Party research centre into the hippest hotel in Berlin. Stark in places with concrete, aluminium and glass, lavish in others with velvet and chintz. With its rooftop pool, basement library, spa and cinema, plus wind-up gramophones, vast beds and a Damien Hirst in the lobby, why stay anywhere else?

### HOTEL AT A GLANCE

**ACCOMMODATION**
40 rooms

**DINING**
Restaurant and bars

**RECREATION**
Rooftop pool with terrace, spa, gym, private screening room and library

**TRANSFERS**
Tegel Airport 30mins by car

+ 49 30 40 50 44 0
sohohouseberlin.com

### TANYA'S TRAVEL SECRETS

**Best gourmet**
Special weekends in Berlin call for at least one über meal. Go to **Margaux** for the orgasmic experience of Michael Hoffmann's dishes of seduction and a stunning wine cellar. If you are vegetarian order the glazed winter vegetables with black Périgord truffles. Michael describes his food as 'cuisine avantgarde classique'.

**Suits me**
A classic overcoat silhouette? A smoking jacket reminiscent of Marlene Dietrich? Linen suits that say Cap Ferrat? Finest fabrics and expert tailoring evoke classic style and wave goodbye to brand proliferation. **Herr von Eden** will bring timeless elegance to your Berlin shopping experience. A wardrobe investment.

# GRANDHOTEL SCHLOSS BENSBERG

## A SCHLOSS WITH A VIEW, HOW CAN YOU GO WRONG?

Life at this magnificent baroque castle is on a grand scale. Originally built for a prince, it exudes old-world elegance and gracious luxury. The setting with its spectacular views of Cologne is the perfect backdrop for a feast of pleasures, none greater than the outstanding cuisine created by a world master.

### HOTEL AT A GLANCE

**ACCOMMODATION**
120 rooms and suites

**DINING**
3 restaurants

**RECREATION**
Spa, fitness centre, indoor pool and library

**TRANSFERS**
Cologne Bonn Airport 15mins by car

+ 49 (0) 2204 42888
schlossbensberg.com

### TANYA'S TRAVEL SECRETS

**Vendôme Dining**
**Chef Joachim Wissler** has created what is known as 'one of Germany's best restaurants', and it now boasts three Michelin stars. Enjoy his imaginative and refined dining experience, and ask the sommelier Romana to choose a wine from their impressive 900-strong selection. A timeless culinary experience.

**Caffeine fix**
The art of the coffee house was perfected in Vienna and brought here to Cologne in the guise of **Café Fromme**. If you are in need of a sugar rush to complement your coffee, the choice of chocolates, truffles and other delights is quite dizzying.

# SCHLOSSHOTEL LERBACH

## YOUR VERY OWN FAIRYTALE CASTLE

Nestled in the most beautiful parklands, this gorgeous manor hotel is positively dreamy. Romantic rooms designed in the English country style, a first-rate spa for that extra special pampering and fine dining from a gastronomic genius. Relaxing, charming and above all deliciously spoiling – what more could you want?

### HOTEL AT A GLANCE

**ACCOMMODATION**
52 rooms and suites

**DINING**
2 restaurants

**RECREATION**
Spa, fitness centre, indoor pool, cookery school and assorted customised activities including hot air ballooning

**TRANSFERS**
Cologne Bonn Airport 15mins by car

+ 49 (0) 2202 2040
schlosshotel-lerbach.com

### TANYA'S TRAVEL SECRETS

**Michelin star**
Want to be your own Masterchef and wow your friends with your next dinner party? **Nils Henkel** has been awarded three Michelin stars and will show you how in his amazing cooking school. Chop chop, book now, it's simply the most delicious experience.

**Fish gotta swim**
Imagine the gentle swish of the river, the breeze rustling through the trees andn you thigh-deep in water with **Rolf R Rennell** learning the skills of fly-fishing. Take a gourmet picnic to fuel your enthusiasm. You'll be surprised at how completely relaxed you feel. You're gonna fly.

# SEEHOTEL ÜBERFAHRT

## BAVARIAN PANORAMA WITH ALTITUDE

You could not wish for a more picture-perfect Alpine setting – a lake one side and mountains the other. Your own piece of the breathtaking panorama is guaranteed as all the rooms have a balcony or terrace. This spaciously stylish hotel is a wonderful getaway filled with welcoming Bavarian hospitality.

### HOTEL AT A GLANCE

**ACCOMMODATION**
188 guest rooms and suites

**DINING**
4 restaurants

**RECREATION**
Spa, fitness, kids' club, private beach, indoor and outdoor pools

**TRANSFERS**
Franz Josef Strauss International Airport, Munich 1hr 10mins by car

+ 49 (0) 8022 6690
seehotel-ueberfahrt.com

### TANYA'S TRAVEL SECRETS

**Baby me**
Are you the expectant couple who have one weekend of just the two of you before the screaming package arrives? Book the **Baby Moon** package with special spa treatments for Mum and Dad to be, coupled with gourmet food.

**Oom pah pah**
Think Bavaria, immediately think **beer and band**. More specifically, on the terrace in summer overlooking the lake. Work those biceps on a big beer stein, and get your laughing gear round a wurst. Not a Nancy in sight when you go oom pah pah.

# MYKONOS BLU GRECOTEL EXCLUSIVE RESORT

## SIMPLE SOPHISTICATION ON JET-SET ISLE

This is the coolest place on Mykonos, a super-luxury resort overlooking Psarou beach with the glittering white and blue of land and sea below you. Many of the island-style villas have their own private pool while the main infinity-edged pool hovers just above the sea. Soak up the sun from a private terrace, soak up the atmosphere at the Long Hours bar, soak up pampering oils at the Elixir Spa… and reward yourself at the Charisma jewellery boutique!

### HOTEL AT A GLANCE

**ACCOMMODATION**
100 bungalows and suites and 11 villas

**DINING**
2 restaurants and bar

**RECREATION**
Fitness gallery and spa, beach, infinity seawater pool, table tennis, nearby watersports, sailing and helicopter tours

**TRANSFERS**
Mykonos Airport 10mins by car, Mykonos Harbour 10mins by car

+ 30 22890 27900
mykonosblu.com

### TANYA'S TRAVEL SECRETS

**On trend**
Where does Sarah Jessica Parker shop on Mykonos? At **Soho Soho**, renowned for all things cool and fabulous. It's stylishly stacked with designer pieces, and the most seriously cool shop on the island. Not just for the ladies either, cross the street as Tom Hanks did for the menswear.

**Beach cool**
**Namos** is possibly one of the best beach restaurants on the planet. Theme music – The Stones. Staff straight off the catwalk. Order fried calamari, a Mojito, or a ice-cold bottle of Greek rosé. Sink back on your giant double sun-lounger and strike a pose. Tables become podiums after 5pm. Smashing.

# THE UPPER HOUSE

## AUTHENTICITY AND LUXURIOUS RESIDENTIAL CALM

High-rise and high style; this sensational boutique hotel is the talk of the town. There are endless pluses – fabulous central location, stunning contemporary Oriental design, a buzzy bar and the spectacular Café Gray Deluxe restaurant. Best of all are the unusually spacious rooms filled with smart touches and stupendous views over the harbour or hills of Hong Kong.

---

**HOTEL AT A GLANCE**

**ACCOMMODATION**
117 rooms and suites

**DINING**
Restaurant and bar

**RECREATION**
Secluded lawn, gym, hybrid cars, complimentary 'Maxi' bar, WiFi and iPod touch®

**TRANSFERS**
Hong Kong International Airport 30mins by car

+ 852 291 81 838
upperhouse.com

---

**TANYA'S TRAVEL SECRETS**

**Finding God**
Goods of Desire to be precise… three **G.O.D.** shops all feature classics of old colonial Hong Kong, with modern twists. Retro, exotic and a young edgy line called 'Delay no More'. Quite right too. Go now for cricket sweaters and antique furniture, my angel. Retail heaven.

**Aquatini panorama**
Join the hip crowd in this glam venue with the most spectacular view. Circular booths with strung beads and comfy sofas all add to the decadence. A voyeur's paradise of people-watching, and prices that don't sting the wallet. Drink lychee and champagne.

# THE CLIFF HOUSE HOTEL

## CLIFFHANGING LUXURY YOU NEVER WANT TO END

Perched on a cliff in a pretty fishing village, this boutique hideaway is a design stunner. Acres of glass make the most of jaw-dropping views across the bay; rooms are so stylish and comfortable you'll never want to leave. Tempting you out is a relaxing spa and the exceptional gourmet cuisine in the Michelin starred restaurant. A retreat for all seasons.

### HOTEL AT A GLANCE

**ACCOMMODATION**
39 rooms

**DINING**
Restaurant and bar

**RECREATION**
Spa, indoor swimming pool, gym, nearby golf and watersports can be arranged

**TRANSFERS**
Cork Airport or Waterford Airport 50mins by car

+ 353 (0) 24 87800
thecliffhousehotel.com

### TANYA'S TRAVEL SECRETS

**Romance afloat**
Take a sunset cruise on the bay with the one you love. With the sea air and the warm glow of the setting sun on your face, there's no better way to close out the day. Stars begin to sparkle and your mind drifts to the **Michelin dinner** that awaits at home.

**Horsing around**
If you are an equestrian or your kids are, the **Lake Tour Stables** has it all. Superb riding through the most idyllic countryside of mountain slopes, fabulous lakes and a beautiful unspoilt beach. Improve your skills in the arena or head out for a trek. The only thing you're saddled with is choice.

# INISH TURK BEG

## FRESH AND WILD IN THE ATLANTIC OCEAN

Be invigorated and inspired on a beautiful private island in Clew Bay, off the west coast of Ireland. Live in utter comfort in a range of island homes, all exquisitely catered with local produce and exceptional care. Surrounded by mind-boggling views in every direction, it is the place for a real lungful of life.

### HOTEL AT A GLANCE

**ACCOMMODATION**
15 rooms on the island, 4 rooms on the mainland

**DINING**
Dining room, BBQs, picnics

**RECREATION**
Watersports, sailing, fishing, horse riding, tennis, basketball court, target practice, indoor pool, games room, walking, crafts house, gym and nearby golf

**TRANSFERS**
Knock Airport 50mins by car, 10mins by helicopter

+ 353 87 657 3840
inishturkbeg.com

### TANYA'S TRAVEL SECRETS

**We are sailing**
New skills are great for the active traveller. Obtain your **sailing qualifications** from expert instructors who will take you out on Clew Bay to raise the sail. Pico, Feva, Dart and Vago are not the names of the island's pets but just some of the dinghies available to ply the bay.

**Whip crack away**
Duchess, Marcus and Jessie are all shoed up and ready to take on board the larger boned, meandering rider. Joey, Ger and Honey are lithe and ready for the experienced rider. The most wonderful way to see your way round this incredibly beautiful island. Bring a carrot, pat gently.

# KARMA KANDARA

## KARMA SUN LOUNGER TO LIE ON

Frazzled city people flock to Karma Kandara for its chilled-out escapism. It exudes an undeniably exotic vibe; from its dramatic cliff-top location right down to the super-cool beach club, this is zen heaven. To tempt you from your vast villa residence there is a magical spa and delectable dining experience coupled with the most amazing views in Bali, possibly the world.

### HOTEL AT A GLANCE

**ACCOMMODATION**
46 2, 3 and 4 bedroom luxury pool villas

**DINING**
Restaurant and rooftop bar

**RECREATION**
Private beach club, swimming pool, spa and kids' club

**TRANSFERS**
Bali Ngurah Rai International Airport 30mins by car

+ 62 361 848 2200
karmaresorts.com

### TANYA'S TRAVEL SECRETS

**Interior design**
**Tarita** is the place to visit for fantastic furniture design. They have spectacular pieces that will add style to any home. Founded by a Singaporean and an Italian, they will gladly ship anywhere in the world.

**Artful**
One of the upcoming districts in Bali is Petitinget where you will find **Biku**. A fabulous combination of antiques, restaurant, teashop, and bookstore all in one. An eclectic mix of now and the past, including a 150-year-old teak joglo from East Java. A whimsical unexpected urban and yet Balinese experience.

# IL PELLICANO

## RITZY RESORT LIVING ON THE MONTE ARGENTARIO

Small, elegant and exclusive, this is where the cognoscenti come when they want to get away from it all – or almost. For as well as every luxury on offer plus a host of activities from tennis to golf and a spa, there is also a fleet of Mercs to help you escape and explore the region, as well as a posse of boats to transport guests along the coast or to picnics on nearby magical isles.

### HOTEL AT A GLANCE

**ACCOMMODATION**
50 rooms and suites

**DINING**
2 restaurants and 2 bars

**RECREATION**
Health and beauty centre, heated saltwater pool, tennis, beach club, wine tasting, cooking courses and nearby golf

**TRANSFERS**
Rome Fiumicino International Airport 1hr 30mins

+ 39 0564 858 111
pellicanohotel.com

### TANYA'S TRAVEL SECRETS

**Modern wine**
Designed by the architect Renzo Piano, the ultra-modern **Rocca di Frassinello** is a refreshing departure from the ancient. Take a private tour of the winery before sampling premium Super-Tuscans like Le Sughere di Frassinello, Rocca di Frassinello and Poggio alla Guardia.

**Medieval**
**Capalbio** is a medieval 'Borgo' (hamlet) of ancient brick archways, stone walls, balconies spilling over with flowers, and tiny lanes. Be sure to see the Renaissance Palazzo Collacchioni and the majestic 'Rocca' (fortress). Stop for dinner at **Le Mura** with owners Roberta and Gerry, for a memorable dining experience.

# LA MADDALENA
# HOTEL & YACHT CLUB

## AN ENCHANTED ISLAND OF PINK AND WHITE SAND

With the spectacular beauty of an unspoilt archipelago all around it, this elegant new hotel and yacht club is a true pearl of the sea. Sailing is so incredible they held the Louis Vuitton Cup here. This ultra-stylish complex comes with a modern spa, restaurant, bar, acres of space for outdoor sports and a stunning marina.

### HOTEL AT A GLANCE

**ACCOMMODATION**
95 rooms and suites

**DINING**
1 restaurant and 1 bar

**RECREATION**
Marina, watersports, spa, gym, tennis, five-a-side football, shopping area and outdoor swimming pool

**TRANSFERS**
Olbia airport 30mins by car to Palau and from Palau to La Maddalena 15mins by ferryboat

+ 39 0789 794 273
lamaddalenahyc.com

### TANYA'S TRAVEL SECRETS

**Pink bubbles**
The Maddalena Archipelago is an area of pure natural beauty. Go by speedboat with driver and picnic to **Spiaggia Rosa** (the pink beach). It is one of the most breathtaking beaches in the world. Take pink Champagne, it seems only natural that you do.

**Independence Day**
Maddalena and Caprera Islands are linked by a road. **Giuseppe Garibaldi**, the famous Italian patriot and one of the fathers of independence, bought the island. Visit his house and memorial chapel. The island is stunning for its rock formations that anchor it in translucent water.

# BORGO SANTO PIETRO

## TUSCAN ROMANCE IN A JEWEL-BOX VILLA

This enchanting 13th-century villa has been so lovingly restored it feels more like a private home. Rooms radiate stylish Italian elegance; acres of glorious gardens are yours to explore; and you'll find a small but perfectly formed spa and out-of-this world Tuscan cuisine matched by a formidable wine cellar. Bliss in every exquisite detail.

### HOTEL AT A GLANCE

**ACCOMMODATION**
8 villa rooms and 3 garden suites

**DINING**
Restaurant and poolside bar

**RECREATION**
Tennis, spa, eco infinity pool, bikes, outdoor games, cooking lessons, wine tasting, nearby golf and kids' play area

**TRANSFERS**
Pisa Airport 1hr 45mins, Florence 1hr 10mins, Rome 2hrs 30mins, all by car

+ 39 0577 75 12 22
borgosantopietro.com

### TANYA'S TRAVEL SECRETS

**Opera under the stars**
In nearby Montesiepi you will find the Gothic abbey of **San Galgano**. In the summer the Accademia Chigiana of Siena stages opera in this roofless cathedral under the open sky. A romantic and moving experience you'll remember forever. They even have their very own 'sword in the stone'.

**Vegetarian hunting**
Always fancied the idea of hunting but don't want to kill any furry creatures? How about mushroom hunting? And in the autumn it's ripe for the picking. Rich wild mushroom risotto? Porcini on toast? The chef will be more than happy to cook the bounty of your forest pillaging. One side makes you smaller, and the other makes you taller…

# LE GRAY

## SEAMLESSLY STYLISH HOTEL FOR SOPHISTICATES

Cosmopolitan and hip, Beirut has for centuries been the choice of the cultured and savvy traveller, and now there is a hotel just made for him, Le Gray. From its location and décor – cool and contemporary but with all the cheer a guest requires – its rooftop restaurant Indigo with its views across the bright lights of the big city, its PureGray spa and fitness centre and its 500 pieces of contemporary art, it is the only place to stay.

### HOTEL AT A GLANCE

**ACCOMMODATION**
87 rooms and suites

**DINING**
Rooftop restaurant with terrace, café, bar and lounges

**RECREATION**
Spa, gym, personal trainers, rooftop pool and art collection

**TRANSFERS**
Beirut Rafic Hariri International Airport 15mins by car

+ 961 1 971 111
legray.com

### TANYA'S TRAVEL SECRETS

**Glamour**
Johnny and Sin Farah are your hosts at **Casablanca**, a traditional Lebanese house overlooking the seafront. Order the lobster which is so fresh its tail is waggling. The menu is East-West fusion, and fresh. The crowd is stylish and frenzied in this establishment that is The Ivy of Beirut.

**Showbiz**
The trendiest nightlife in Beirut is to be found at **Music Hall**, a converted cinema now a cabaret-style home to a cutting-edge music scene. With up to 12 acts performing each night, there is something for everyone. World music fusion with a glamour-packed audience.

# MAIA LUXURY RESORT & SPA

## A SOPHISTICATED BEACH PARADISE WITH A WHOLE LOT OF POLISH

Bespoke luxury and absolute relaxation are the order of the day at this heavenly hideaway. Amidst lush gardens and overlooking turquoise waters are deliciously sleek villas designed for lazing perfection – each with an infinity pool, thatched gazebo and dedicated butler. Five excellent chefs cater to your taste whims and the unbelievable spa transports you to a world of divine tranquillity.

### HOTEL AT A GLANCE

**ACCOMMODATION**
30 private villas with plunge pools

**DINING**
Restaurant and pool bar

**RECREATION**
Spa, fitness centre, beachfront pool, tailor-made programmes for children, free non-motorised watersports, scuba diving and deep sea fishing nearby

**TRANSFERS**
Mahé International Airport
25mins by car

+ 248 390 000
maia.com.sc

### TANYA'S TRAVEL SECRETS

**It's in the stars**
Gourmet, Strong, Refined, Sensual, Rebellious, Adventurous, Eternal and Trendy… what's your wine sign? Blind-taste six Grand Crus with the sommelier and find out. A wine concept developed by Philippe Raoux and Frédéric Brochet from Bordeaux on an island in the Seychelles? Grapevine your way to the cellar now.

**Castaway**
Imagine your own island for a whole afternoon? Gourmet picnic, just the two of you? Speedboat moored nearby? Your butler will arrange it all and make sure you aren't stranded overnight talking to a basketball in a cave. Honeymoon heaven.

# AMANDA
## ON TRAVEL

66

—

*I love the fact the world has become a smaller place… you can be anywhere within 24 hours.*

*Amanda Wakeley OBE, award-winning British fashion designer, shares her travel style.*

**TR** *Any special places off the beaten track that you love?*

**AW** There is this magnificent hotel in the Aravalli Hills in Udaipur called Devi Garh. It's minimal and yet luxurious design true to its original spirit. I vowed that I would one day go when I was in love; haven't managed that yet, but I did shoot a bridal campaign, which speaks for itself! Oh, and Mnemba Island off the coast of Zanzibar is true barefoot luxury. An extraordinary combination of African simplicity and cool luxury on the finest white sand beach. Magical isolation and sublime service.

**TR** *Where do you eat in these out-of-the-way places?*

**AW** When we are in Formentera, for true feet-in-the-sand dining we love Juan y Andrea where the seabass baked in salt crust is probably the best I have ever eaten. In the Swiss mountains after a long heli-ski descent we head for Café des Alpes in Orsières. Nothing tastes better than food you have really worked up an appetite for.

**TR** *Do you find packing a chore?*

**AW** I have it down to a fine art now in terms of knowing that I need to take my time to pack what I really need and nothing else. Short trips are a luxury as I don't have to take gym kit and laptop. I am a big believer in clothes you can dress up or down… I love jersey maxi dresses in the summer which look equally good with flats or heels.

## ESSENTIALS
Great service, immaculate cleanliness, and a good bed with the finest Egyptian cotton bedlinen are essential, not an option

*Amanda's* LUXE APPROACH TO TRAVELLING

1 **NO QUEUE**
Private jet is the ultimate luxury and the way to escape the nightmare of the airport. Leave when you want, and avoid being trafficked past shops in an attempt to get to a lounge

2 **SOFT TOUCH**
My featherlight cashmere blanket-size scarves so I'm cocooned in luxury even if I am stranded somewhere, or staving off aggressive plane and hotel room air-conditioning

3 **CRUNCH**
At Club 55 in St Tropez the freshest and best cruiteés platter presented on a chunk of cork bark and the Salade de Pampelonne

# LA RESIDENCE

## OPULENCE IN THE MIDST OF NATURAL BEAUTY

With the aura of a private château and every conceivable luxury, La Residence is the most glamorous place to stay in the Cape's gourmet mecca. You can wine-taste on horseback, dine on gastronomic sensations or laze by the pool taking in the magnificent vineyard vistas. Add in romantic suites crowned with bespoke grandeur and you have the ultimate winelands experience.

### HOTEL AT A GLANCE

**ACCOMMODATION**
11 luxury suites

**DINING**
Dining area

**RECREATION**
Infinity pool, spa and in-room beauty treatments, horseback wine tours, cheese tasting, carriage rides, trout fishing, hot air ballooning and nearby golf

**TRANSFERS**
Cape Town International Airport 50mins by car

+ 27 21 876 4100
laresidence.co.za

### TANYA'S TRAVEL SECRETS

**Local knowledge**
The Mont Rochelle Nature Reserve is just stunning. See it with localraconteur and all-round encyclopedia of knowledge **Professor Izak Rust**. Older kids and teens will love him, as will you. You'll emerge in touch with nature and with a new friend. Memorable.

**Chocoholics**
There's nothing like a delectable chocolate. Willy Wonka is not at home but **Huguenot** is. Take the 30-minute tour and then dive head first into a box of chocolates. Rehab not required, just buy supplies from the shop. No sharing.

# BIRKENHEAD HOUSE

## CLIFF-TOP MAGNIFICENCE OF STYLISH SEASIDE COMFORT

Dreaming of the perfect beach house? Then this petit-luxe coastal hotel is for you. Everything from its spectacular setting to its inviting ambience is just right. Interiors are fabulously eclectic, and the light, airy rooms sensationally individual. Book one at the front for spell-binding views of the beautiful coastline. Next door is a knock-out private villa.

### HOTEL AT A GLANCE

**ACCOMMODATION**
11 luxury rooms and adjacent villa

**DINING**
Choice of indoor and outdoor settings

**RECREATION**
2 swimming pools, 2 treatment rooms, small gym, boat trips, walking, whale-watching, shark diving, sea-kayaking, nearby golf and wine tours

**TRANSFERS**
Cape Town International Airport 1hr 15mins by car

+ 27 28 314 800
birkenheadhouse.com

### TANYA'S TRAVEL SECRETS

**Human kite**
If you have a head for adventure and dream of flying, take a **tandem paraglide** off Lion's Head. A bird's eye view with no previous experience outside the nest required. Your pilot will take pictures while you grip on tightly smiling through gritted teeth. Actually once you are underway you won't want to come down. Spread your wings and take flight.

**A whale of a time**
**Hermanus** is world-renowned as the best place for whale-watching. These gentle giants are often seen from the vantage point of Birkenhead House, so you have a front-row seat. If you want to get up close, take a boat trip around Dyer Island. A whale tale that will take your breath away.

# THE SAXON BOUTIQUE HOTEL, VILLAS AND SPA

## A HOTEL THAT IS PART OF HISTORY

A chic contemporary building hidden in tropical gardens provides a haven of tranquillity for travellers to Johannesburg. The hotel will be forever known as the place where Nelson Mandela stayed as he finalised his autobiography and has since been the choice of presidents, politicians, captains of industry and mega movie stars when they visit the city. Its interior is famous for its fine contemporary African art work. Stay here and be part of history.

### HOTEL AT A GLANCE

**ACCOMMODATION**
53 suites

**DINING**
Restaurant, terrace, bar and lounge

**RECREATION**
Saxon Spa and Studio with hydro facilities, fitness centre, 6 pools and private landscaped gardens

**TRANSFERS**
O.R. Tambo Airport (JHB International) 45mins by car; The Gautrain 15mins by train to Sandton Station then 5 mins to hotel by car

+ 27 11 292 6000
saxon.co.za

### TANYA'S TRAVEL SECRETS

**Fashionable Stanley**
If you want to find the epicentre of art and fashion in Jo'burg, **44 Stanley Avenue** is a good place to start, located in the Milpark district. From Indian antiques to handcrafted furniture and from the handmade African toys to Art Deco furniture and fabrics. Be sure to visit African Mosaique, the brainchild of Anna Getaneh a former international model. Oh Stanley, you shouldn't have!

**Freedom**
If you want to really understand South Africa today, there are two places to visit – **Constitution Hill**, the Old Fort Prison complex where Nelson Mandela was held, and the **Apartheid Museum**. Enlightening and renews your appreciation of what true freedom really means.

# SHAMBALA PRIVATE GAME RESERVE

## TAKE AN UNFORGETTABLE WALK ON THE WILD SIDE

See the big five – lion, leopard, rhino, buffalo and elephant – at close quarters during an early morning drive, or guided bush walk on this 12000 hectare wildlife sanctuary. Best of all take an elephant-back safari and get a new perspective on your surroundings from atop this great pachyderm. Sleep to the sound of the bush in one of eight luxury Zulu-style chalets. Savour the heartland of Africa.

### HOTEL AT A GLANCE

**ACCOMMODATION**
8 chalets

**DINING**
Dining area and bar

**RECREATION**
Game drives and walks, elephant back safaris, bush picnics, sunset cruises, star gazing and pool

**TRANSFERS**
O.R. Tambo Airport (JHB International) 2hrs 30mins by car, Lanseria Airport 2hrs by car

+ 27 11 292 6030
shambalagamereserve.co.za

### TANYA'S TRAVEL SECRETS

**Inspirational**
It is impossible to think of South Africa and not say Nelson Mandela. At Shambala they have created a private residence known as 'The Nelson Mandela Centre for Reconciliation'. It is a place of tranquillity and peace which is a true reflection of everything Madiba believes in.

**Slowly**
Winding down from the city takes time. A first evening cruise on the **Steyn Dam** will help set the pace. You, drink in hand, the African bush, birdlife rush hour, and the sun burning into the horizon. Feel your stress dissipate, your tension melt, and your furrowed brow relax.

# ROYAL MALEWANE

## THE BIG FIVE – SPLENDOUR, PRIVACY, SERVICE ATMOSPHERE, SPA

The magic of this celebrated safari lodge is all-embracing. Suites have an outrageously extravagant colonial feel; vast canopied beds covered in crisp white linens, Victorian baths, open fireplaces and a plunge pool on your balcony. Dining is deliciously sumptuous, the spa one of the most stylish anywhere and all around is the thrill of the unadulterated wild kingdom of Africa.

### HOTEL AT A GLANCE

**ACCOMMODATION**
6 luxury suites and 2 ultra-luxury suites each with 2 bedrooms; all with private plunge pool

**DINING**
Several locations from dining area to Bedouin tents and bomas

**RECREATION**
Game viewing, horse riding safaris, wildlife rehabilitation centre, hot air ballooning & spa with heated lap pool

**TRANSFERS**
KMIA (Nelspruit) Airport 2hrs by car or 25mins by private plane; Eastgate Airport 45mins by car

+ 27 15 793 0150
royalmalewane.com

### TANYA'S TRAVEL SECRETS

**Star track**
In the world of rangers and trackers it doesn't get better than **Juan Pinto and Wilson Masiya**. Their qualifications, specialist knowledge and certified skills mean you get the best safari experience available in a vehicle or on land. Wildlife up close with the best.

**Cushy cuisine**
How about dinner in a Bedouin tent filled with Persian cushions and lit by lanterns? Add dinner prepared by **John Jackson**, awarded the Blazon by the Chaine des Rôtisseurs. Sip your after-dinner liqueur under the stars. It's a recipe for romance.

# GRAN HOTEL LA FLORIDA BARCELONA

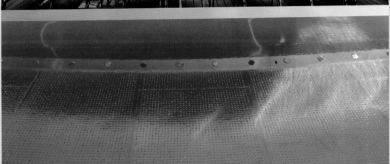

## FAR FROM THE MADDING CROWD

High above the city this luxurious retreat not only provides spectacular views of the city, the Mediterranean and the Pyrenees, but is a mere 15 minutes from all the fun and action of the Catalonian capital. It's where discerning guests find respite and tranquillity in its renowned restaurant, cosy bars and Zen Zone spa.

### HOTEL AT A GLANCE

**ACCOMMODATION**
70 rooms and suites

**DINING**
Restaurant, bar and lounge

**RECREATION**
Spa, Jacuzzi, indoor and outdoor pools, fitness centre and sun terraces

**TRANSFERS**
El Prat Barcelona Airport 25 to 30mins by car

+ 34 93 259 30 00
hotellaflorida.com

### TANYA'S TRAVEL SECRETS

**Sweet tooth**
Aussies Christopher King and Tommy Tang have cornered the market in designer candy with **Papabubble**. Their sweet treasures are made right in front of you. Suck on the adult-styled slightly naughty lollipops and check out the amazing window display. It's fabulous… Sugar Babes watch out.

**Catalan cuisine**
Albert Adria, brother of famous El Bulli chef Ferran, runs **Inopia**, an unpretentious restaurant serving fantastic Catalan cuisine. Try the pinchos, which is skewers of tender lamb, salt cod, ham croquettes, and anything fried such as anchovies and potato. Lip-smackingly sensational.

**WINTER
FAMILY
FAVOURITE**
★★★★★

# CHALET HOTEL HORNBERG

## CHALET SKI
## THE BLACK RUN,
## DARLING?

Warm homely comfort, impeccable
service and three generations of
charming family owners make this
cosy chalet a divine Alpine escape.
Its fabulous location means you
can ski right up to your door; and
for relaxing après-ski head to the
amazing saunas and steam bath.
In summer the mountains are
gorgeous for picnics.

**HOTEL AT A GLANCE**

**ACCOMMODATION**
35 rooms and suites

**DINING**
Restaurant and bar

**RECREATION**
Wellness, indoor pool, freshwater
pond for swimming, kids' areas,
mountain bikes, tennis and hiking

**TRANSFERS**
Geneva Airport 2hrs by car

+ 41 33 748 66 88
hotel-hornberg.ch

**TANYA'S TRAVEL SECRETS**

**Swiss treats**
For the most tantalising raclette
and fondues head to the 'Huttli'.
Built in 1726, this adorable old
wooden cottage has been converted
to a den of delicious temptations.
The best thing is it is just in front
of the hotel. You will love it.

**Dinner with a view**
Wow! You will be stunned by the
view from the exquisite Restaurant
Sonnenhof. Wonderful wooden
beams abound in this traditional
mountain restaurant where, for
a change, the food is as good as
the view.

# THE DYLAN AMSTERDAM

## A GORGEOUS SECRET JEWEL IN THE HEART OF THE CITY

Picture canal houses around a manicured courtyard, add in a large dash of style and you have The Dylan. Situated in Amsterdam's trendy 'Nine Streets' district this polished urban haven is the chicest place to stay. Rooms are design heaven, the restaurant Michelin-starred, the bar ultra-fashionable and the hidden garden a treasure.

### HOTEL AT A GLANCE

**ACCOMMODATION**
40 rooms and suites

**DINING**
Restaurant, bar, lounge and long gallery

**RECREATION**
Bike rental, private boat tours, fitness centre, in-room massages, garden and nearby museums

**TRANSFERS**
Amsterdam Schiphol Airport 25mins by car

+ 31 (0) 20 530 2010
dylanamsterdam.com

### TANYA'S TRAVEL SECRETS

**Legacy**
Let's be Frank, **Anne's house** is as ubiquitous a tourist attraction in Amsterdam as Big Ben is in London. But it holds its place in history and you need to see it once to appreciate what happened. The Secret? Book tickets online and go at opening time to avoid crowds.

**Buono**
Good food, clean and fair is the motto at **Bussia,** a desirable gem of an Italian restaurant that is one of the finest in Amsterdam. Step through the red door and be prepared to linger over wild duck with figs, octupus crostini, and 30 Barolo wines to choose from. Bellissimo!

# AMBERLEY CASTLE

## ROMANCE, HISTORY AND LUXURIOUS COMFORT IN ROLLING COUNTRYSIDE

There is nothing quite like staying in a castle; regal grandeur is very spoiling. At Amberley you will be entranced by rooms with richly bedecked four-poster beds and original features. The cuisine is a gastronomic delight; and for a truly unique dinner the über-chic thatched tree-house Mistletoe Lodge is a must. A perfect place to stay for Glorious Goodwood.

### HOTEL AT A GLANCE

**ACCOMMODATION**
19 rooms and suites

**DINING**
Restaurant

**RECREATION**
Tennis court, croquet lawn, 18-hole professional putting course, tree-house with restaurant, gardens and lakes

**TRANSFERS**
Central London 1hr 45mins by car; London Gatwick Airport 40mins by car; helipad on site

+ 44 (0)1798 831992
amberleycastle.co.uk

### TANYA'S TRAVEL SECRETS

**Speed**
This does not involve a commuter bus and Sandra Bullock, but rather Goodwood and its fabulous Festival of Speed. Go to see a plethora of amazing cars and motorbikes from over 100 years of motor racing. Brmmm brmmm.

**Honeymoon**
The word honeymoon is purported to have come from the ancient practice of newlyweds drinking a glass of mead to increase fertility. Go to **Lurgashall Winery** to experience mead first-hand along with wine made from hand-gathered elderflowers and rose petals! Surprisingly delicious… who knew what was brewing in West Sussex!

# BUCKLAND MANOR

## A HIDEAWAY OF TIMELESS CHARM AND RELAXING COUNTRY STYLE

Like the most hospitable private house this mellow old manor envelops you with welcoming warmth. Cosy rooms cocoon you in comfort; there are roaring log fires to read papers by and quintessentially English gardens to laze in. The chef's imaginative menus make the most of all the wonderful local produce and breakfast is definitely something to be lingered over. The perfect getaway.

---

### HOTEL AT A GLANCE

**ACCOMMODATION**
13 rooms

**DINING**
Restaurant

**RECREATION**
Tennis court, croquet, putting green, horse riding, biking, fishing, walking and nearby excursions

**TRANSFERS**
Central London 2hrs 30mins by car; Birmingham International Airport 50mins by car; helipad on site

+ 44 (0)1386 852626
bucklandmanor.co.uk

---

### TANYA'S TRAVEL SECRETS

**Gardening leave**
**Hidcote** has to be one of England's truly great gardens. Take a delightful wander along the herbaceous borders of the garden rooms which make up this Arts and Crafts-style masterpiece. Whatever the season there is always a vibrant display of colour from spring bulbs to autumn's red border.

**Merchants**
**Edward Sheldon** have been wine merchants in the historic market town of Shipston-on-Stour since 1842. Supplier to the area's most affluent country houses, they have recently opened their original 18th century wine cellars to private visits. You're guaranteed to leave with a bottle or two in the car.

# HOTEL TRESANTON

## WHERE THE ENGLISH RIVIERA MEETS CAPE COD

This renovated yacht club overlooking Falmouth Bay changed the idea of seaside hotels forever when Olga Polizzi brought her inimitable style to bear on one of England's most beautiful coastlines. Simple and chic, it is the last word in comfort with great beds, huge sofas and armchairs you never wish to leave. Outside the entire Cornish coast awaits – enjoy the walks or take a ferry ride to nearby ports, bays and villages. Return to delicious locally-sourced food, or an evening in the private cinema.

### HOTEL AT A GLANCE

**ACCOMMODATION**
29 rooms

**DINING**
Restaurant and bar

**RECREATION**
Sailing, windsurfing, fishing, beach, bridge weeks, nearby golf, horse riding, marine life and bird watching, walks and local garden visits

**TRANSFERS**
Central London 5hrs by car, Newquay Airport 45mins by car, St Austell Train Station 35mins by car

+ 44 (0)1326 270055
tresanton.com

### TANYA'S TRAVEL SECRETS

**True love**
Channel Grace Kelly and Bing Crosby in 'High Society' and board the **Pinuccia**, the most beautiful yacht in St Mawes Harbour. The hopeless romantic can sail the bay with the sea breeze in their hair and love in their heart. Guaranteed proposal acceptances boarding now.

**Musicality**
Go for the chamber music concerts in the **St Mawes Methodist Chapel**. Saturday includes a special dinner and world-renowned musicians. Debussy and Dover sole? Fauré and foie gras? It's homage to the senses with a side of luxury accommodation. Book early!

# HOTEL ENDSLEIGH

## LUXURY LODGE ON THE EDGE OF DARTMOOR

Adjacent to one of the most romantic and wild areas of the country, this former shooting lodge has been sympathetically and beautifully restored by hotelier Olga Polizzi. While the house, with just 16 rooms, is inviting and comfortable, it is the 108 acres of garden and woodland which are the real star. Designed by Humphry Repton they are full of surprises, grottoes, follies and magnificent plants. Grab a map and a picnic and spend the day exploring.

---

**HOTEL AT A GLANCE**

---

**ACCOMMODATION**
16 rooms

**DINING**
Restaurant

**RECREATION**
Fishing, walking, horse riding, game and clay pigeon shooting and in-room beauty treatments

**TRANSFERS**
Central London 3hrs 30mins by car, Plymouth Airport 45mins by car, Exeter and Newquay Airports 1hr by car

+ 44 (0)1822 870000
hotelendsleigh.com

**TANYA'S TRAVEL SECRETS**

**Market**
The farmer's variety. **Pannier Market** in Tavistock is a veritable treasure trove of fresh produce. A wonderful experience for mixing it up with the locals and stocking up with tasty supplies to take home to your larder. You'll be brewed, pickled, baked and smoked with delight.

**Exclusive fish**
The hotel is a member of the **Endsleigh Fishing Club** which means access to the best eight miles of salmon and sea trout fishing in England. With the ghillie showing you how to hook the bounty you'll be thrilled and flapping. Big fish, little fish, where's my lox?

# DEAN STREET TOWNHOUSE

## COSY GEORGIAN ELEGANCE IN THE BUZZ OF SOHO

Oozing a very English-chic style, this boutique bolthole is a seriously hip hangout. Fabulous art on the walls, hardwood floors, mellow panelling and comfy vintage armchairs make for a relaxed upbeat mood. Deeply comfortable rooms are spread over four floors and vary from tiny to bigger. Top marks go to the excellent British cooking in the all-day dining room.

### HOTEL AT A GLANCE

**ACCOMMODATION**
39 rooms

**DINING**
Restaurant and bar

**RECREATION**
Nearby Cowshed spa, shopping, theatres, museums and galleries

**TRANSFERS**
London Heathrow 30 to 45mins by car, 1hr by tube

+ 44 (0)20 7434 1775
deanstreettownhouse.com

### TANYA'S TRAVEL SECRETS

**Caring about you**
If you only have to remember one name for a restaurant in London, it's **Richard Caring**. His restaurant stable includes The Ivy, Caprice, Scotts and Cecconis synonymous with simply great food, comfort, elegance and sublime service. The crowd is the who's who of entertainment, media, business, fashion and royalty. Guaranteed dining success.

**Glee**
Is your TV guilty pleasure **Glee**? Attend a private class at the world-famous Pineapple Studios. Sing or dance with a professional, or just watch them in action. Followed by pre-theatre dinner, then best seats in the house at a West End production and drinks with cast members.

# THE HEMPEL

## ONE IS VERY LUCKY TO HAVE A GARDEN IN CENTRAL LONDON

With its sleek-chic aesthetic this design icon is the coolest boutique hotel in town. From the hip new art gallery to the sexy chilled-out vibe of the restaurant and bar, everything is on trend. Rooms are ultra-stylish – the most sublime has to be the Lioness Den; and the icing on the cake the perfect Zen Garden.

### HOTEL AT A GLANCE

**ACCOMMODATION**
50 rooms, suites and apartments

**DINING**
Restaurant and bar

**RECREATION**
Garden and outdoor terrace and art gallery

**TRANSFERS**
London Heathrow 40mins by car/20mins via Heathrow Express Train (Paddington Station)

+ 44 (0)20 7289 9000
the-hempel.co.uk

### TANYA'S TRAVEL SECRETS

**It's electric**
Since the movie 'Notting Hill' was released tourists have been pouring in like a flood. Avoid them and a book a two-seater sofa at the **Electric Cinema**. This is the only place to watch a movie in London with its state-of-the-art technology and cushy to boot. Sip Ruinart and nibble on canapés. Is that Harvey Weinstein over there?

**Hey Mr DJ**
Do your kids think you are totally uncool? Spin them out and get yourself to the Ministry of Sound for the one-day Superclub DJ course. Exit with street cred and skills. Put the record on! Record? Try disc, Dad...!

# BALFOUR CASTLE

## EMBRACE THE SPORTING LIFE ON THIS WILD ISLAND HIDEAWAY

A magical castle right in the heart of Orkney with turrets and towers, history and heritage, which will cocoon and cosset you while offering experiences to remember. Ride or hike across the island, spot grey or common seals, or take part in one of the best wildfowl shoots in the country. Later relax with a treatment from Heaven and feast on local foods. Available for exclusive hire only.

### HOTEL AT A GLANCE

**ACCOMMODATION**
9 rooms

**DINING**
Morning room, lunch conservatory, dinner dining room

**RECREATION**
Wildfowling, clay shooting, tennis, trout fishing, paintballing, horse riding, cooking lessons, bird watching, walking, billiard room, archery and private cinema

**TRANSFERS**
Kirkwall Airport, 10mins taxi, 5 mins in boat

+ 44 (0)1856 711 282
balfourcastle.co.uk

### TANYA'S TRAVEL SECRETS

**Exclusive shoot**
In wildfowling circles, Balfour, Shapinsay and Orkney are spoken of in reverential tones. Located on the migration route from Arctic breeding grounds, the situation is ideal. Add expert local knowledge, and you're bang on target for the best shoot followed by wee drams and conversation by the fireside in complete luxury.

**Heaven**
Dannii Minogue and Michelle Pfeiffer swear by Deborah Mitchell's all-natural organic skin and body treatments. A gorgeous blissfully quiet room is set aside at Balfour for treatments using Deborah's amazing products. Try the heavenly lymph drain massage; you can lose up to 4lbs while feeling totally relaxed.

# YNYSHIR HALL

## A HOME OF ROYAL HERITAGE IN STUNNING COUNTRYSIDE

Stresses and strains melt away at this cosseting haven. Surrounded by an awe-inspiring landscape of majestic mountains, serene gardens and the famed Dyfi estuary, it is hard to imagine a more relaxing spot. Add in a super-talented chef whose Michelin-starred cuisine will have you drooling, fabulously eclectic rooms inspired by famous artists and personalised wellbeing treatments. Total bliss.

### HOTEL AT A GLANCE

**ACCOMMODATION**
9 rooms and suites

**DINING**
1 restaurant and bar

**RECREATION**
Wellbeing therapies, walking, nature reserve, wild food tours with chef, croquet, nearby golf, pony treks, clay pigeon shooting, quad biking and fishing

**TRANSFERS**
Central London 4hrs 40mins by car; Manchester International Airport 1hr 30mins by car; helipad on site

+ 44 (0)1654 781209
ynyshirhall.co.uk

### TANYA'S TRAVEL SECRETS

**Musical inspiration**
Take a walk in **Cwm Einion 'Artists' Valley'** to experience what inspired Robert Plant to write 'Stairway to Heaven'. Listen to it on your iPod in a warm bath when you return.

**Townies**
If you need a change of pace, the university town of **Aberystwyth** is only seven miles away. With a Norman castle and cliff railway with panoramic view, it's a great diversion for townies young and old. Drop into the **Mecca Coffee Shop** for your caffeine fix.

# THORNBURY CASTLE

## A REAL ROYAL RETREAT

Kings and queens have stayed here, barons have behaved badly while lords and ladies have lived, loved and possibly flirted outrageously within these walls. This is the only Tudor castle turned luxury hotel. Henry VIII and Anne Boleyn are reputed to have slept here – you can too, if you book the Duke's Bedchamber. In fact all rooms are bedchambers with four-posters, rich rugs, fires and every comfort. The food is sublime, the gardens exquisite, the welcome fit for a king… and queen. It is also the most romantic location for a wedding or honeymoon!

### HOTEL AT A GLANCE

**ACCOMMODATION**
26 rooms

**DINING**
Restaurant

**RECREATION**
Vineyard, gardens, croquet, archery, clay pigeon shooting, falconry, fishing, quad biking and in-room beauty treatments

**TRANSFERS**
Central London 1hr 30mins by car, Bristol International Airport 30mins by car; helipad on site

+ 44 (0)1454 281182
thornburycastle.co.uk

### TANYA'S TRAVEL SECRETS

**The final furlong**
You are right on the doorstep of one of Britain's most famous racecourses. The highlight of the season is of course the Cheltenham Gold Cup in March. Booking corporate hospitality is essential to secure access to the members' lawn. It's a real winner. Place your bets.

**British wine**
The **Three Choirs Vineyard** Estate Reserve Siegerrebe 2006 won the Gore Brown Trophy for best wine in 2008. Definitely worth a visit to experience the winery for a tasting. Stop for lunch in the restaurant and order Chef Darren Leonard's twice-baked goats' cheese soufflé.

# STON EASTON PARK

## A STATELY HOME MORE THAN A HOTEL

A glorious Grade I listed building, this Palladian mansion is as grand as grand hotels get with its antiques, classical art, old-style service, roaring log fires, four-poster beds and free-standing baths. Just a few miles from Bath, one of Britain's favourite cities, and Wells, the smallest in the country, it is the place to stay when visiting or exploring the West Country. Its 36 acres of classic parkland, designed by Repton but restored by the renowned Penelope Hobhouse, are simply breathtaking.

### HOTEL AT A GLANCE

**ACCOMMODATION**
22 rooms

**DINING**
Restaurant

**RECREATION**
In-room beauty treatments, tennis, billiard room, garden tours, croquet, river cruises in vintage launch, nearby golf, hot air ballooning and country pursuits

**TRANSFERS**
Central London 2hrs 50mins by car, Bristol International Airport 20mins by car; helipad on site

+ 44 (0)1761 241631
stoneaston.co.uk

### TANYA'S TRAVEL SECRETS

**Witch way?**
To **Wookey Hole** of course! Just outside the town of Wells are caves that have been inhabited for 700 years. The Witch's Parlour is a must see, as is the light show designed by Peter Gabriel's lighting man Patrick Watkinson. Spooky sensation.

**Evensong**
**Wells Cathedral** has a choral tradition that stretches back over 800 years. Wells Cathedral Choir consists of 18 boys and 18 girl choristers and 12 men. The combined power of their soaring voices in this historical building of ecclesiastical majesty is awe-inspiring.

# BABINGTON HOUSE

## METRO CHIC AND COUNTRY HOUSE COOL

This is the house we all wish our friends had in the country – welcoming, warm and comfortable, where we can behave just as if we were home. It serves the food we love, when we want it, it has a special Little House for our children to play in and a Cowshed Spa in which we can play. It has a cinema and acres of gardens and grounds, which is why it is so difficult to leave.

### HOTEL AT A GLANCE

**ACCOMMODATION**
32 rooms

**DINING**
Restaurants and bar

**RECREATION**
Spa, crèche, billiards, indoor and outdoor pools, gym, steam room, sauna, aroma rooms, cinema, tennis courts, cricket pitch, croquet lawn and five-a-side football

**TRANSFERS**
London Heathrow 1hr and 30mins by car

+ 44 (0) 1373 812266
babingtonhouse.com

### TANYA'S TRAVEL SECRETS

**Time out**
Are you a frazzled parent who needs to breathe just for a moment? Check your little ones into Little House and have them entertained all day while you moo contentedly in the **Cowshed** and drift off to sleep. Inventive, fun staff so your kids will love it. Superb sanity check.

**It's a gas**
Dragging yourself out of bed at the crack of dawn will all be worth it once you begin to soar in a **hot air balloon** over the stunning countryside. An intermittent hiss as your pilot glides you over the trees and fields. Romance aloft.

# THE SAMLING

## A FAIRYTALE COUNTRY COTTAGE

With breathtaking vistas all around, this charming hotel is the coolest getaway. Choose from rooms in the main house or divine stone cottages; each crammed with luxurious touches and intriguing features. The innovative Michelin-starred cuisine is heaven on a plate and the delightful hot tub in the garden is the perfect spot for a glass of Champagne overlooking Lake Windermere.

### HOTEL AT A GLANCE

**ACCOMMODATION**
11 boutique rooms

**DINING**
Restaurant

**RECREATION**
Croquet, hot air ballooning, sheep herding, clay and laser pigeon shooting, archery, picnics in the vast grounds and hot tub

**TRANSFERS**
Central London 5hrs by car
Carlisle Airport 1hr by car
Helipad on site

+ 44 (0)1539 431922
thesamlinghotel.co.uk

### TANYA'S TRAVEL SECRETS

**Take a hike**
**Wainwright** first visited the Lake District in 1930 but it was not until 1952 that he commenced work on his famous walking guides. Be sure to take one of his hikes; he knew every nook and cranny of the area intimately. Follow his instructions for scenic grandeur.

**Aerial views**
If you have a sense of adventure and really want to see it all, take a **tandem paraglide** flight. You'll soar like a bird over the spectacular landscape with an experienced pilot doing the driving. It's an exhilarating experience not to be missed.

# FOUR SEASONS CARMELO

## TRANQUILLITY AMID THE TREES

One of South America's best-kept secrets is this charming resort on the banks of the Rio de la Plata. Hidden by great swathes of pine and eucalyptus trees, it is the ideal place to come for total rest and relaxation. The beaches on the river, one of the widest in the world, are soft and sandy and the water silky; the food is local, delicious and healthy; while the nearby wineries are a revelation. If you're looking for action there is a championship golf course, horse riding in the hills or bicycling along the river bank.

### HOTEL AT A GLANCE

**ACCOMMODATION**
44 rooms and suites

**DINING**
2 restaurants and 2 lounges

**RECREATION**
Spa, golf, swimming pool, bikes, horse riding trails and tennis

**TRANSFERS**
Carmelo International Airport 10mins by car

+ 598 (4542) 9000
fourseasons.com/carmelo

### TANYA'S TRAVEL SECRETS

**Grape news**
**Irutia Bodega** is one of the country's oldest wineries and perfect for a private tasting visit. Tannat is to Uruguay as Malbec is to Argentina. With comparisons to the Medoc Entre-Deux-Mer region of France, oenophiles will be delighted with the prize-winning varieties. Only 15 minutes from the resort.

**Detour**
Don't fly from Buenos Aires, take the leisurely route and stop at **Colonia del Sacramento**. Founded by the Portuguese in the 17th century, it's all cobbled streets and colonial buildings steeped in history. Don't miss the artists' workshops and antique shops. A charming detour en route to the resort.

# PLAYA VIK JOSÉ IGNACIO

## THE ULTIMATE BEACH RETREAT

Just outside the village of Faro José Ignacio, overlooking the sands and wild waves of the South Atlantic, sits this near-perfect hideaway. Its unrivalled location, with nothing but sea and sky around it, has attracted visitors from all over the world and its sense of isolation has brought respite to the tired, the stressed and the overworked. This is where you come to swim, dive, surf or do nothing at all, but mostly where you want to watch the sunset, described as being the best on the planet.

### HOTEL AT A GLANCE

**ACCOMMODATION**
6 casas

**DINING**
Dining room with terrace and BBQ

**RECREATION**
Wine cellar, games room, gym, pool, spa, beach, boogie boarding, boat trips, whale-watching and art

**TRANSFERS**
Punta del Este Airport 30mins by car, Montevideo Airport 1hr 30mins by car

+ 598 94 605 212/314
vikretreats.com

### TANYA'S TRAVEL SECRETS

**Gastronomy**
In the village of Garzon the villagers still travel by horse and cart. In the leafy village square is the gastronomically spectacular **Restaurant Garzon**. Francis Mallmann's intimate dining room overlooks the village and herb garden. The open-plan kitchen and wood-fired stove deliver food that will make your taste buds sing. *Book through dehouche.com*

**Whale tail**
Jose Ignacio is great even in the winter months. Nature lovers – note this is one of the best places to experience the migration of the **Southern Right Whale**. They can be seen from shore, but book a boat trip to get a close-up view of a tail breaking the surface. *Book through dehouche.com*

**MY FAVOURITE HIDDEN GEM**
★★★★★

# DUNTON HOT SPRINGS

## 'BUTCH CASSIDY AND THE SUNDANCE KID' MEETS RALPH LAUREN

Saddle up and head to the Colorado Rockies for the ultimate wilderness retreat. Stay in restored hand-hewn log cabins filled with gorgeous character; dine deliciously 'en famille' in an authentic saloon and bathe in mineral-rich springs inside or outdoors. This former ghost town complete with chapel has all the credentials for a unique adventure experience.

### HOTEL AT A GLANCE

**ACCOMMODATION**
12 cabins (2 to 8 people)

**DINING**
Saloon and bar

**RECREATION**
Cross-country and heli-skiing, snow shoeing, horse riding, hiking, fly fishing, river rafting, mountain biking, hot springs, library and spa

**TRANSFERS**
Cortez Airport 1hr by car

+ 1 970 882 4800
duntonhotsprings.com

### TANYA'S TRAVEL SECRETS

**Summer lens**
The scenery is so stunning, how can you capture it and take it home other than in your mind? With an expert photographer you'll take to the trails and be shown how to see it all through a different lens. Train your eye and master your camera. Frame your memories.

**Powder hounds**
Dunton Hot Springs sits a mere 15 minutes from probably the best heli-skiing on the globe. Luxury miners' cabins lie in the valley below three 14000-foot peaks. Six runs a day over two days should have you hollering with delight. The ultimate experience for the avid skier.

# SOHO HOUSE NEW YORK

## DOWNTOWN COOL, UPTOWN CHIC

Small in size, just 24 rooms, but these are no ordinary rooms – they are designated playpen, playroom, playhouse and playground depending on size. You get the picture. Add the rooftop pool, the screening room and library, the Cowshed spa, the Swarovski chandeliers and the hippest clientele. The Meatpacking District is high on the 'where to stay' list in the city and this is the designated spot.

### HOTEL AT A GLANCE

**ACCOMMODATION**
24 rooms

**DINING**
Restaurant, rooftop dining terrace and bars

**RECREATION**
Spa with steam rooms, rooftop pool, gym, private screening room, library and games room

**TRANSFERS**
JFK Airport 1hr by car, Newark Airport 30mins to 1hr by car

+ 1 212 627 9800
sohohouseny.com

### TANYA'S TRAVEL SECRETS

**Spot on**
Been to market? Stayed at home? I'm sure you found a suitable rest room. Go to **Spotted Pig** where April Bloomfield is serving smoked haddock chowder which you should eat at a stool in the window while watching the world go by. Go on, be a piggy and get spotted.

**Fashion junkie**
Avant-garde fashionistas gird your plastic and go to **Kirna Zabete**. Some like it haute, and this boutique has it all. A lucite ceiling and lavender floor speak to the collection of jewellery, accessories and amazing clothes. Get your fix, you'll be giddy with choices.

# ADDRESS BOOK

**EUROPE**

**14**

### HOTEL AMIGO

Rue de l'Amigo 1-3
Brussels 1000, Belgium
+32 (0)254 74747
roccofortecollection.com

**Marianne Gray**
38/40 rue des Chapeliers, Brussels
+32 22 511 00 01

**Comic Strip Museum**
20 rue des Sables, Brussels
+32 2 219 1980

**Aux Armes de Bruxelles**
13 rue des Bouchers, Brussels
+32 2 511 5550

**Linda van Waeseberghe**
Style Consult BVBA
Rue Antoine Dansaertstraat,
93 B12, 1000, Brussels
+32 475 84 17 54
lindavanwaesberge.be

**18**

### EXCELSIOR HOTEL & SPA AND VILLA AGAVE

Frana Supila 1220000
Dubrovnik, Croatia
+385 (0)20 430 830
alh.hr

**Kamenice**
Gunduliceva Poljana 8
Dubrovnik, Croatia
+385 (0)20 323 682
alh.hr

**The Museum of Modern Art**
Put Frana Supila 23
Dubrovnik, Croatia
+385 20 426 590

**Ronchi Hat Factory**
Lucarica 2
Dubrovnik, Croatia
+385 20 323 699

**22**

### ANASSA

Baths of Aphrodite Road
8830 Polis, Cyprus
+357 26 888 000
thanoshotels.com

**Chrysorroiatissa Winery**
Panagia, Cyprus
+357 26 722 457
(40 km north-east of Pafos, turn
right before Stroumbi village)

**Mystery Family Tavern**
Polis Chrysochous, Cyprus
+357 26 322 509
+357 99 434 044

**26**

### THE AUGUSTINE

Letenska 12/33
Prague 1 – 118 00
Czech Republic
+42 (0) 266 11 22 33
roccofortecollection.com

**Manesova**
Třebízského 4
120 00 Prague
+42 (0) 222 724 581

**Beltissimo**
Na Prikope 22 (Slovansky dum)
New Town, Prague 1
+42 (0) 222 211 646

**Kampa Park**
8b Na Kampe
Prague 11800
+42 (0) 296 826 102

**Lobkowicz Palace**
Nelahozeves Castle 1
277 51 Nelahozeves
Czech Republic
+42 (0) 315 709 111
lobkowiczevents.cz

**30**

### CHÂTEAU DE BAGNOLS

69620 Bagnols, France
+33 4 74 71 40 00
chateaudebagnols.co.uk

**Pérouges town**
Rue des Rondes,
01800 Pérouges, France
+33 (0) 4 74 61 01 58
perouges.org

**Lyon Antique Quarter**
Lyon, France

**Maison de la Danse**
8 Avenue Jean Mermoz
69008 Lyon, France
+33 (0) 4 72 78 18 18

**Paul Bocuse**
40 rue de la Plage
Collonges-au-Mont-d'Or
Pont de Collonges
Lyon, France
+33 (0) 4 72 42 90 90

**36**

### HÔTEL LE BRISTOL

112 rue du Faubourg
Saint Honoré
75008 Paris, France
+33 (0) 1 53 43 43 00
lebristolparis.com

**Brasserie de l'Île St-Louis**
55 quai de Bourbon
75004 Paris, France
+33 (0) 1 43 54 02 59

**Pierre Hermé – Macarons & Chocolats**
4 rue Cambon
75001 Paris, France
+33 (0)1 58 62 43 17

**Sabbia Rose**
71-73 rue des Saints-Pères
75006 Paris, France
+33 (0) 1 45 48 88 37

**Cire Trudon**
78 rue de Seine
75006 Paris, France
+33 (0) 1 43 26 46 50

**40**

### GRAND-HÔTEL DU CAP-FERRAT

71 bd du Général de Gaulle
06230 Saint-Jean-Cap-Ferrat
France
+33 (0) 4 93 76 50 50
ghcf.fr

**Villa Ephrussi de Rothschild**
06230 Saint-Jean Cap Ferrat
France
+33 4 93 01 33 09

**Paloma Beach Club**
Route de Sainte-Hospice
06230 Saint-Jean-Cap-Ferrat
France
+33 4 93 01 64 71

**44**

### BEAUVALLON PRIVÉ

Boulevard des Collines
Beauvallon-Grimaud
83120 Ste-Maxime, France
+33 (0) 4 94 55 78 88
lebeauvallon.com

**Hotel Sube**
15 quai de Suffren
Saint-Tropez, France
+33 (0) 4 94 97 30 04

**Sandales Tropéziennes**
16 rue G. Clemenceau
83990 Saint-Tropez, France
+33 04 94 97 19 55
rondini.fr

**Sportmer Speed Boats**
Route des Salins
83990 Saint-Tropez, France
+33(0)494 97 32 33
sportmer.com

**Ferme La Douceur**
Quartier La Rouillere
83350 Ramatuelle, France
+33 (0)4 94 79 24 95
fermeladouceur.com

**48**

**LA COLOMBE D'OR**

1 place Général de Gaulle
06570 St Paul de Vence, France
+33 (0) 4 93 32 80 02
la-colombe-dor.com

**La Petite Cave de St Paul**
47 rue Grande
06570 St Paul de Vence, France
+33 (0) 4 93 32 59 54

**Fondation Maeght**
623 chemin des Gardettes
06570 St Paul de Vence, France
+33 (0) 4 93 32 81 63
fondation-maeght.com

**La Verrerie de Biot**
5 chemin Combes
06410 Biot, France
+33 (0) 4 93 65 03 00
verreriebiot.com

**La Petite Maison**
Restaurant La Petite Maison,
11 rue Saint François de Paule
06300 Nice, France
+33 (0) 4 93 85 71 53
lapetitemaison-nice.com

**52**

**HOTEL DE ROME**

Behrenstrasse 37
10117 Berlin, Germany
+49 30 4 60 60 90
roccofortecollection.com

**Berlinomat**
Frankfurter Allee 89
Friedrichshain
10247 Berlin, Germany
+49 30 420 81 445

**Bar Jeder Vernunft**
Schaperstrasse 24
10719 Berlin, Germany
+49 30 883 15 82

**Bonanza Coffee Heroes**
Oderberger Strasse 35
Berlin, Germany

**Prater**
Kastanienallee 7-9
Prenzlauer Berg
14050 Berlin, Germany
+49 30 448 5688

**58**

**AMIRANDES GRECOTEL EXCLUSIVE RESORT**

P.O. Box 106 Gouves
711 10 Heraklion, Crete
+30 28970 41103
amirandes.com

**Agreco Farm**
Adelianos Kampos
Adele Village
GR 74 100 Rethymnon, Crete
+30 283 10 721 29

**Boutari Fantaxometocho Winery**
70100 Skalani, Iraklion
+30 281 073 1617

**62**

**VILLA SAN MICHELE**

Via Doccia 4
50014 Fiesole
Florence, Italy
+39 055 5678 200
villasanmichele.com

**NewTours**
Via Pietro Toselli 73
Florence, Italy
+39 055 328 9741

**Teatro del Sale**
Via dei Maci 111
Florence, Italy
+39 055 200 1492

**Loretta Caponi**
Via delle Belle Donne 28
Florence, Italy
+39 055 211 074

**Angela Caputi**
Borgo SS. Apostoli 44/46
Florence, Italy
+39 055 292 993

**66**

**GRAND HOTEL A VILLA FELTRINELLI**

Via Rimembranza 38-40
25084 Gargnano, Italy
+39 0365 798 000
villafeltrinelli.com

**Locanda San Vigilio**
Punta San Vigilio 37016
Garda, Italy
+39 045 725 6688

**Fondazione Arena di Verona**
Via Roma 7/d
37121 Verona, Italy

**70**

**HOTEL DE RUSSIE**

Via del Babuino 9
00187 Rome, Italy
+39 06 328881
roccofortecollection.com

**Scuola Gladiatori**
Via Morsasco 9
00166 Rome, Italy
+39 340 464 4078

**Caffè della Pace**
Via della Pace 3/7
Rome, Italy
+39 06 686 1216
caffedellapace.it

**Castel Romano Designer Outlet**
Via del Ponte di Piscina Cupa 64
00128 Rome, Italy
+39 06 505 0050
mcarthurglen.com

**74**

**FORTE VILLAGE RESORT**

Km 39
6 Santa Margherita di Pula
09010 Sardinia, Italy
+39 070 92171
fortevillageresort.com

**80**

**VERDURA GOLF SPA & RESORT**

SS 115 KM 131
92019 Sciacca (AG), Italy
+39 0925 998 180
roccofortecollection.com

**M.A.T.E.S.**
Vicolo Storto
3 Caltabellotta, Italy
+39 0925 952 327

**Planeta Winery**
Contrada Ulmo
92017 Sambuca di Sicilia (AG)
Italy
+39 0925 1955460
planeta.it

**Bar Barbagianni**
P.za Eroe Dei Due Mondi 8
58015 Orbetello (GR)
barbarbagianni.it

**84**

**GRAND HOTEL TIMEO**

Via Teatro Greco 59
98039 Taormina
Sicily, Italy
+39 0942 627 0200
grandhoteltimeo.com

**Bam Bar**
45 Via di Giovanni
Taormina, Italy

**88**

**CASTEL MONASTERO**

Colonna del Grillo
Località Monastero
d'Ombrone n. 19
53019 Castelnuovo Berardenga
Siena, Italy
+39 0577 570001
castelmonastero.com

**The Mall**
Via Europa 8
Leccio, Reggello 50060
Florence, Italy
+39 05 8657775

**Palio di Siena**
siena@ilpalio.org
ilpalio.org

**92**

**HOTEL CIPRIANI**

Giudecca 10
30133 Venice, Italy
+39 041 520 7744
hotelcipriani.com

**Harry's Bar**
Calle Vallaresso 1323
30124 Venice, Italy
+39 (0) 41 528 5777

**Locanda Cipriani**
Torcello
30012 Venice, Italy
+39 (0) 41 730 150

**Hotel Gritti Palace**
Campo Santa Maria del Giglio
30124 Venice, Italy
+39 (0) 41 794 611

**Osteria La Zucca**
Sestiere Santa Croce 1762
30135 Venice, Italy
+39 (0) 41 524 1570

**HÔTEL DE PARIS**
Place du Casino
98000 Monaco
+377 9806 3000
hoteldeparismontecarlo.com

**Society Club**
Metropole Monaco
17 avenue des Spélugues
98000 Monaco
+37793252501
tomford.com

**Jimmy'z Nightclub**
Sporting Club
26 avenue Princesse Grace
98000 Monaco
+377 98 06 70 68
jimmyzmontecarlo.com

**Heli Air Monaco**
Heliport de Monaco
98000 Monaco
+377 92 050 050
heliairmonaco.com

**Monte Carlo Beach Club**
Avenue Princesse Grace
06190 Roquebrune Cap-Martin
+33 493 286 666
jimmyzmontecarlo.com

**HOTEL ASTORIA**
Ul. Bolshaya Morskaya 39
St Petersburg
190000 Russia
+7 812 494 5757
roccofortecollection.com

**Marinsky Theatre**
1 Theatre Square
St Petersburg, Russia
+7 (812) 114 1211

**Tania Illingworth**
Russian Travel Consultant
68 Ashley Gardens
London SW1P 1QG
United Kingdom
+44 (0) 20 7834 5630
+44 (0)7855 434 733
tania.illingworth@gmail.com
rctours.com

**The Onegin**
11 Italianskaya Ulitsa
St Petersburg, Russia
+7 812 570 0058

**HOTEL VILLA MAGNA**
Paseo de la Castellana 22
Madrid 28046, Spain
+34 915 871 234
hotelvillamagna.com

**Casa de América**
2 Paseo de Recoletos
Madrid, Spain
+34 91 595 4800

**Museo del Traje**
2 Avenida Juan de Herrera
Madrid, Spain
+34 91 549 7150

**Las Bailarinas**
Calle Piamonte 19
Madrid, Spain
+34 91 319 9069

**Mercado de Fuencarral**
Calle Fuencarral 45
Madrid, Spain
+34 91 521 4152

**HOTEL PUENTE ROMANO**
Bulevar Principe Alfonso von
Hohenlohe, s/n
29602 Marbella, Spain
+34 952 82 0900
puenteromano.com

**Boutique K2**
Estacion 1
Esquina Pasaje
(Plaza de los Naranjos)
29600 Marbella, Spain
+34 952 858 469

**Picasso Museum**
Calle San Agustin 8
29015 Malaga, Spain
+34 952 602 731

**On the Quay Restaurant**
14 Queensway Quay
Gibraltar
+350 200 43731

**MARBELLA CLUB HOTEL**
Bulevar Principe Alfonso von
Hohenlohe, s/n
29602 Marbella, Spain
+34 952 8222 211
marbellaclub.com

**Polo House Marbella**
Bulevard Principe Alfonso
Von Hohenlohe
29600 Marbella, Spain
+34 952 900 380
polohouse.net

**Babylonia Palace**
Ctra. de Istan – Km 0,8
29600 Marbella
+34 952 82 88 61
oliviavalere.com

**Ascari Race Resort**
Carretera Ronda
Campillos, Km 30,5
29400 Ronda
Malaga, Spain
+34 952 18 71 71
ascari.net

**GSTAAD PALACE**
Palacestrasse 28
3780 Gstaad, Switzerland
+41 33 748 50 00
palace.ch

**Lorenz Bach**
Hauptstrasse 2
3780 Gstaad, Switzerland
+41 26 9258050

**Café du Cerf**
Le Village
1659 Rougemont
Vaud, Switzerland
+41 0 26 925 81 23

**BAUR AU LAC**
Talstrasse 1
8001 Zurich, Switzerland
+41 44 220 50 20
bauraulac.ch

**0815/2**
Kreuzstrasse 26
Zurich, Switzerland
+41 44 242 0815

**Kunsthaus**
Heimplatz 1
Zurich, Switzerland
+41 44 253 84 84

**Trois Pommes**
Storchengasse 6
Zurich, Switzerland
+41 44 211 0621

**Fraumünster**
Fraumünsterstrasse
Zurich, Switzerland

**PERA PALACE**
Meşrutiyet Caddesi No: 52
Tepebaşi 34430
Istanbul, Turkey
+90 212 377 40 00
perapalace.com

**Sortie**
141 Muallim Naci Caddesi
Kurucesme
Istanbul, Turkey
+90 212 327 85 85
sortie.com.tr

**Sunset Grill & Bar**
Adnan Saygun Caddesi
Yol Sokak No 2, Ulus Parki
Ulus Istanbul, Turkey
+90 212 287 03 57/58
sunsetgrillbar.com

**Cagaloglu Hamami**
Cagaloglu
Istanbul, Turkey
+90 212 522 24 24
cagalogluhamami.com.tr

**THE ROYAL CRESCENT HOTEL**
16 Royal Crescent
Bath BA1 2LS
United Kingdom
+44 (0) 1225 823333
royalcrescent.co.uk

**Little Theatre**
St Michael's Place
Bath BA1 1SF
United Kingdom
+44 (0) 1225 330817

**The Egg Theatre**
Sawclose
Bath BA1 1ET
United Kingdom
+44 (0) 1225 823409/448844

**Demuths Vegetarian Restaurant**
2 North Parade Passage –
off Abbey Green
Bath BA1 1NX
United Kingdom
+44 (0) 1225 446059

**Topping & Company Booksellers**
The Paragon
Bath BA1 5LS
United Kingdom
+44 (0) 1225 428111

## 136

### LOWER SLAUGHTER MANOR

Lower Slaughter
Gloucestershire GL54 2HP
United Kingdom
+44 (0)1451 820456
lowerslaughter.co.uk

**Cheltenham Festivals**
109 Bath Road
Cheltenham
Gloucestershire GL53 7LS
United Kingdom
+44 (0) 1242 774400
cheltenhamfestivals.com

**Sudeley Castle**
Winchcombe
Gloucestershire GL54 5JD
United Kingdom
+44 (0) 1242 602308

**Openroad Classic Car Hire**
+44 (0) 845 0705142

**Daylesford Organic**
Daylesford
Near Kingham
Gloucestershire GL56 0YG
United Kingdom
+44 (0) 1608 731700

## 140

### CLARIDGE'S

Brook Street
Mayfair
London W1K 4HR
United Kingdom
+44 (0) 20 7629 8860
claridges.co.uk

**Berry Bros & Rudd**
3 St James's Street
London SW1A 1EG
United Kingdom
+44 (0) 800 280 2440

**Hyde Park Stables**
63 Bathurst Mews
London W2 2SB
United Kingdom
+44 (0) 20 7723 2813

**The Wallace Collection**
Hertford House
Manchester Square
London W1U 3BN
United Kingdom
+44 (0) 20 7563 9500

**Tower of London**
London EC3N 4AB
United Kingdom
+44 (0) 20 3166 6226

## 146

### ST JAMES'S HOTEL AND CLUB

7-8 Park Place
St James's
London SW1A 1LS
United Kingdom
+44 (0) 7316 1600
stjameshotelandclub.com

**Royal Opera House**
Bow Street
London WC2E 9DD
United Kingdom
+44 (0) 20 7240 1200

**London School of Photography**
77 Oxford Street
London W1D 2ES
United Kingdom
+44 (0) 20 7659 2085

**St James's Park, London**
London SW1A 2BJ
United Kingdom
+44 (0)20 7930 1793

**The River Café**
Thames Wharf
Rainville Road
London W6 9HA
United Kingdom
+44 (0) 20 7386 4200
rivercafe.co.uk

## 150

### THE BERKELEY

Wilton Place
Knightsbridge
London SW1X 7RL
United Kingdom
+44 (0) 20 7235 6000
the-berkeley.co.uk

**Annee de Mamiel**
Acupuncturist
Sloane Square
9a Wilbraham Place
London SW1X 9AE
United Kingdom
+44 (0) 20 7730 7928
demamiel.com

**Regent's Park Open Air Theatre**
The Ironworks
Inner Circle Regents Park
London NW1 4NR
United Kingdom
+44 (0) 844 826 4242

**Neville's**
5 Pont Street
Belgravia
London SW1X 9EJ
United Kingdom
+44 (0) 20 7235 3654

**The Grenadier**
18 Wilton Row
London SW1X 7NR
United Kingdom
+44 (0) 20 7235 3074

## 154

### THE CONNAUGHT

Carlos Place
Mayfair
London W1K 2AL
United Kingdom
+44 (0) 20 7499 7070
the-connaught.co.uk

**Petersham Nurseries**
Church Lane, off Petersham Road
Petersham, Richmond
Surrey TW10 7AG
United Kingdom
+44 (0) 20 8940 5230

**Harrods**
87-135 Brompton Road
Knightsbridge
London SW1X 7XL
United Kingdom
+44 (0) 20 7730 1234

**Anya Hindmarch**
Bespoke
15-17 Pont Street
London SW1X 9EH
United Kingdom
+44 (0) 20 7838 9177

**Nuttall**
2 Pond Place
London SW3 6QJ
United Kingdom
+44 (0) 20 7584 8989

## 158

### CLIVEDEN

Taplow
Berkshire SL6 0JF
United Kingdom
+44 (0)1628 668561
clivedenhouse.co.uk

**Burnham Beeches Golf Club**
Burnham
Buckinghamshire SL1 8EG
United Kingdom
+44 (0)128 661448
bbgc.co.uk

**Cool Hooves Polo**
c/o Royal County of Berkshire
Polo Club
North St Winkfield
Berkshire SL4 4TH
United Kingdom
+44 (0) 1344 891 558
coolhoovespolo.co.uk

## 162

### SHARROW BAY

Lake Ullswater
Penrith
Cumbria CA10 2LZ
United Kingdom
+44 (0)1768 486 301
sharrowbay.co.uk

**The World of Beatrix Potter**
Bowness-on-Windermere
Cumbria LA23 3BX
United Kingdom
+44 (0) 844 504 1233
hop-skip-jump.com

**Go Ape! Whinlatter**
Whinlatter Forest Park
Whinlatter Pass
Braithwaite, Keswick
Cumbria CA12 5TW
United Kingdom
+44 (0) 845 643 9215
goape.co.uk

**The Bond Museum**
Southey Hill Trading Estate
Keswick, Cumbria CA12 5NR
United Kingdom
+44 (0) 1768 775 007
thebondmuseum.com

**The Punchbowl Inn**
Crosthwaite, Lyth Valley
Cumbria LA8 8HR
United Kingdom
+44 (0) 1539 568237
the-punchbowl.co.uk

## 168

### VON ESSEN FAMILY SET

**Fowey Hall**
Hanson Drive, Fowey
Cornwall PL23 1ET
United Kingdom
+44 (0)1726 833866
foweyhallhotel.co.uk

**Moonfleet Manor**
Fleet, Nr Weymouth
Dorset DT3 4ED
United Kingdom
+44 (0)1305 786948
moonfleetmanor.co.uk

**The Elms**
Stockton Road,
Abberley, Worcester
Worcestershire WR6 6AT
United Kingdom
+44 (0)1299 896666
theelmshotel.co.uk

**The Ickworth**
Horringer
Bury St Edmunds
Suffolk IP29 5QE
United Kingdom
+44 (0)1284 735 350
ickworthhotel.co.uk

**Woolley Grange**
Bradford-on-Avon
Wiltshire BA15 1TX
United Kingdom
+44 (0)1225 864705
woolleygrangehotel.co.uk

## ASIA

**174**

### PARK HYATT BEIJING

2 Jianguomenwai Street
Chaoyang District
Beijing, China 100022
+86 10 8567 1234
beijing.park.hyatt.com

**Paloma Sanchez**
Shop A115, Nali Patio
81 Sanlitun Bei Lu
Chaoyang District
Beijing, China
+86 10 6501 2706

**Star Gallery**
2 Jiuxiangiao Road
Chaoyang District
Beijing, China
+86 10 8456 0591

**The Lan Club**
Chaoyang
Beijing, China
+86 10 5109 6012/13

**Badaling Wall**
Yanqing
Beijing, China

**178**

### THE PULI HOTEL AND SPA

1 ChangDe Road
200040 Shanghai, China
+86 21 3203 9999
thepuli.com

**The Villa**
No. 1 Taojiang Lu
Shanghai, China
+86 21 6466 9322

**Fu 1088**
Changning District
Shanghai, China
+86 21 5239 7878

**Franck Provost**
1/F Hong Fang Zi
35 Shanxi Nan Lu, China
+86 21 6267 5171

**Chinatown**
471 Zhapu Road
Nr Wujin Road
Hongku, China
+86 21 6307 7607

**182**

### RAMBAGH PALACE

Bhawani Singh Road
Jaipur
Rajasthan, India
+91 141 221 1919
tajhotels.com

**Gem Palace**
M.I. Rd
Jaipur, India
+91 (0) 141 236 3061

**Hot Pink**
Narain Niwas Palace
Marain Singh Rd
Jaipur, India
+91 (0) 141 510 8932

**Dr Vinod Shastri**
Chandi Chowk
(behind Tripoli Gate)
Jaipur, India
+91 (0) 141 261 3338

**Niros**
M.I. Rd
Jaipur, India
+91 (0) 141 237 4493

**186**

### UMAID BHAWAN PALACE JODHPUR

Near Circuit House
Umaid Bhawan Palace
Jodhpur, India
+91 291 251 0101
tajhotels.com

**Bishnoi Safari**
Mr Deepak & Dhanraj
H. No. 1, Sir Pratap Coloney
Airport Road , Ratanada
Jodhpur 342001 (Raj.), India
+91 93147 21655
bishnoivillagesafari.com

**Bhangarh**
Jaipur
Rajasthan, India

**Girdikot & Sardar Market**
Jodhpur
Rajasthan, India

**Pushkar Camel Fair**
Rajasthan, India
pushkarcamelfair.com

**192**

### THE TAJ MAHAL PALACE, MUMBAI

Apollo Bunder
Mumbai 400001, India
+91 226 665 3366
tajhotels.com

**Enigma**
Juhu Tara Road
Juhu Beach City
Mumbai, India
+91 (0) 22 6693 3000

**Bombay Electric**
1 Reay House
Best Marg
Mumbai, India
+91 (0) 22 2287 6276

**Prince of Wales Museum**
159-161 M.G. Road
Shahid Bhagat Singh Marg
Kala Ghoda, Fort, Bombay
Maharashtra 400 023, India
+91 (0)22 2844484
bombaymuseum.org

**Elephanta Island Caves**
Raj Bandargaon
Mumbai, Maharashtra, India

**196**

### TAJ LAKE PALACE, UDAIPUR

Post Box No. 5
Udaipur
Rajasthan 313001, India
+91 294 242 8800
tajhotels.com

**Ranthambore National Park**
SH 6, Sawai Madhopur,
Rajasthan 322001, India
+91 120 4052615 99
ranthamborenationalpark.org

**200**

### PARK HYATT TOKYO

3-7-1-2, Nishi-Shinjuku
Shinjuku-ku
Tokyo 163-1055, Japan
+81 3 5322 1234
tokyo.park.hyatt.com

**Ginza**
Chuo-ku
Tokyo, Japan

**Beige**
Chanel Ginza Building
3-5-3 Ginza
Chuo-ku
Tokyo 104-0061, Japan
+81 3 5159 5500

**Arossa**
1-26-22 Shoto
Shibuya-ku
Tokyo, Japan
+81 3 3469 0125

**Hamarikyu Gardens**
1-2-1 Hamarikyu Teien
Chuo-ku
Tokyo, Japan
+81 3 3541 0200

**Tokyo Hipsters Club**
6-16-23 Jingumae
Shibuya-ku
Tokyo, Japan

**204**

### THE DATAI

Jalan Teluk Datai
07000 Pulau Langkawi
Kedah Darul Aman, Malaysia
+60 4 959 2500
ghmhotels.com

**210**

### ONE&ONLY REETHI RAH

North Malé Atoll, Maldives
+960 664 8800
oneandonlyresorts.com

**Anya Hindmarch**
One&Only Reethi Rah
North Malé Atoll, Maldives
+960 664 8800

**214**

### SIX SENSES ZIGHY BAY

Zighy Bay
Musandam Peninsula
Sultanate of Oman
+968 26735 555
sixsenses.com

218

## THE CHEDI MUSCAT

PO Box 964
PC 133
Al Khuwair, Muscat
Sultanate of Oman
+968 24 52 4400
ghmhotels.com

**Nizwa**
Ad Dakhiliyah Region, Oman

**Sultan Qaboos Grand Mosque**
Salalah, Oman

**Souk Muttrah**
near Muscat, Oman

222

## SONEVA KIRI
## BY SIX SENSES

110 Moo 4, Koh Kood Sub-District
Koh Kood District
Trat 23000
Thailand
+66 (0) 3961 9800
+66 (08) 1345 2791
sixsenses.com

226

## JUMEIRAH BAB AL SHAMS

P.O. Box 8168
Dubai, United Arab Emirates
+9714 8096100
jumeirah.com

**Blue Souq**
Sharjah, Sharjah
United Arab Emirates
+97 15472-6710

230

## ONE&ONLY ROYAL
## MIRAGE

Jumeirah Beach
PO Box 37252
Dubai, UAE
+971 4 399 9999
oneandonlyresorts.com

**Souk Madinat**
Madinat Jumeirah
Dubai, UAE
+971 4 366 8888

**Aquaventure Water Park**
The Palm, Jumeirah, Dubai
The Palm Islands
United Arab Emirates
+971 4 426 0000
atlantisthepalm.com

**Asha's**
Pyramids
Wafi City
Dubai, UAE
+971 4 324 4100

**Sho Cho**
Dubai Marine Beach Resort & Spa
Jumeirah
Dubai, UAE
+971 4 346 111

236

## THE NAM HAI

Hamlet 1
Dien Duong Village
Dien Ban District
Quang Nam, Vietnam
+84 510 3940 000
ghmhotels.com

**Hôi An**
Quang Nam, Vietnam

**Chic Unique tailor Hoi An**
62 Phan Boi Chau Street
Hoi An Ancient Town

## AFRICA

242

## SHANTI MAURICE

Rivière des Galets
Chemin Grenier, Mauritius
+230 603 7200
shantimaurice.com

246

## ROYAL MANSOUR
## MARRAKECH

Rue Abou Abbas El Sebti
40 000 Marrakech
+212 (5) 29 80 80 80
royalmansour.ma

**Laetitia Trouillet**
+212 (0) 661 477 228

**Akbar Delights**
42 rue de la Liberté
Apartment 47
1st Floor
Marrakech, Morocco
+212 (0) 671 66 1307
By appointment only

**Moor**
7 rue des Anciens Marrakchis
Marrakech, Morocco
+212 (0) 671 66 1307

**Atika**
Guéliz
34 rue de la Liberté
Marrakech, Morocco
+212 (0) 24 43 6409

**Jardin Majorelle**
Marrakech, Morocco
+212 (0) 5 24 43 6409

250

## ONE&ONLY CAPE TOWN

Victoria & Alfred Waterfront
Cape Town 8001, South Africa
+27 21 431 5888
oneandonlyresorts.com

**Sleepy Hollow Horse Riding**
Sleepy Hollow Lane
Noordhoek, South Africa
+27 21 789 2341
sleepyhollowhorseriding.co.za

**Olivia Davidson**
+27 72 411 8079

**La Colombe**
Constantia Uitsig
Spaanschemat River Rd
Constantia 7800, South Africa
+27 (0) 21 794 2390

**Paranga**
Shop No. 1
The Promenade
Victoria Road, Camps Bay
Cape Town, South Africa
+27 21 438 0404

256

## DELAIRE GRAFF ESTATE

P.O. Box 3058
Stellenbosch 7602
South Africa
+27 21 885 8160
delaire.co.za

**Sivercross Helicopter**
Cape Town International Airport
South Africa
+27 21 934 2556
silvercross.co.za

## AMERICAS

262

## CARLISLE BAY

Old Road
St Mary's
Antigua, West Indies
+1 268 484 0000
carlisle-bay.com

**Caribbean Helicopters**
PO Box 170
Jolly Harbour
Antigua, West Indies
+1 268 460 5900
caribbeanhelicopters.com

266

## HOTEL ST-BARTH
## ISLE DE FRANCE

Baie des Flamands
BP 612
97098 Saint-Barthélemy
French West Indies
+59 05 90 27 61 81
isle-de-france.com

**On the Rocks**
Eden Rock Hotel
Baie de St Jean
FWI -97133
St Barths
French West Indies
+59 05 90 29 79 97

**Maya's Restaurant**
B.P. 197
Gustavia
+59 05 90 27 75 73

**Calypso**
Route de Saline
Saint Jean 9713
+59 05 90 27 78 39

**Casa Nikki – St Barths**
Gustavia Harbor
St Barths, French West Indies
+59 0 590 27 63 77

270

## PARK HYATT
## BUENOS AIRES

1661 Alvear Avenue
Buenos Aires, Argentina
+54 11 5171 1234
buenosaires.park.hyatt.com

**Mansion Dandy Royal**
922 Peidras
Buenos Aires
+54 11 4361 3537

All other secrets book
through Dehouche
Dehouche SA
Leblon
Rio de Janeiro, Brazil
+55 21 251 23895 (Rio)
+44 (0) 871 284 7770 (UK)
dehouche.com

HOTEL FASANO
RIO DE JANEIRO

Avenida Vieira Souto 80
Rio de Janeiro, Brazil
+55 21 3202 4000
fasano.com.br

Book through Dehouche
Dehouche SA
Leblon
Rio de Janeiro, Brazil
+55 21 251 23895 (Rio)
+44 (0) 871 284 7770 (UK)
dehouche.com

Rua Lavradio in Lapa
Rio de Janeiro, Brasil

Clube Chocolate
Estrada da Gávea 899 store 202
São Conrado Fashion Mall
São Conrado
+55 (0)21 3322 3733

Parque Nacional da Tijuca
Rio de Janeiro, Brazil

CUIXMALA

Km 46.2 Carretera Melaque –
Puerto Vallarta
La Huerta, Jalisco
Mexico CP 48850
+52 (315) 351 0034
cuixmala.com

El Tamarindo Golf Club
Km 7.5 Carretera
Barra de Navidad-Puerto Vallarta
Jalisco C.P. 48970
Mexico
+52 315 351 503

Barra de Navidad
Jalisco, Mexico

HACIENDA DE SAN
ANTONIO

Domicilio Conocido S/N
San Antonio, Comala
Colima, Mexico CP 28463
+52 (312) 316 0300
haciendadesanantonio.com

Tlaquepaque
Jalisco, Mexico

El Jabali Ranch
Hacienda de San Antonio
Domicilio Conocido S/N
San Antonio, Comala
Colima, Mexico CP 28463
+52 (312) 316 0300
haciendadesanantonio.com

Comala
Colima, Mexico

ONE&ONLY PALMILLA

Km 7.5 Carretera Transpeninsular
San José del Cabo
BCS CP 23400 Mexico
+52 624 146 7000
oneandonlyresorts.com

Hummer Adventure
Terramar Destinations
San José del Cabo
BCS, Mexico
USA +(314) 754 88 08
Cabo +(624) 142 92 15
terramardestinations.com

Cuadra San Francisco
Cabo Real – between Cabo San
Lucas and San Jose del Cabo
Mexico
+52 624 144 0160

Whale Watching
Blue Adventures
Marina Cabo San Lucas
Mexico
(Bookings through hotel concierge)

Marianela Art Gallery
Obregon and Morelos
San Jose del Cabo
Baja, Mexico
+52 624 161 5069

MONTAGE BEVERLY HILLS

225 North Canon Drive
Beverly Hills, CA
90210, USA
+1 310 860 7800
montagebeverlyhills.com

Larchmont Bungalow
107 North Larchmont Boulevard
(between Beverly Boulvard
& First Street)
Los Angeles, CA, USA
+1 323 461 1528

Spin Hollywood
Mondrian Hotel
8440 W. Sunset Boulevard
(at Oliver Drive)
Hollywood
Los Angeles, CA, USA
+1 323 848 6000

Michael Calas Photography
1124 N Vista Street
West Hollywood, CA, USA
+1 213 804 3116
michaelcalasphotography.com

Beverly Hills Rent a Car
9732 Little Santa Monica Blvd
Beverly Hills, CA, USA
+1 310 274 6969

THE SETAI SOUTH BEACH

2001 Collins Avenue
Miami Beach, FL
33139, USA
+1 305 520 60 00
setai.com

BIN No.18
1800 Biscane Blvd
Miami, FL
33132, USA
+1 786 235 7575

Hip.e
359 Miracle Mile
Coral Gables, FL, USA
+1 305 445-3693

Miami City Ballet
2200 Liberty Avenue
Miami Beach, FL
33139, USA
+1 305 929 7010 Box Office

Versace Mansion
1116 Ocean Drive
Miami Beach, FL
33139, USA
+1 305 576 8003

THE MARK

Madison Avenue
77th Street
New York, NY
10075, USA
+1 212 744 4300
themarkhotel.com

Strala Yoga
623 Broadway, 4th floor
New York, NY
10012, USA
+1 917 488 7195
stralayoga.com

The Lion
62 West 9th Street
New York, NY, USA
+1 212 353 8400
thelionnyc.com

Third Rail Coffee
240 Sullivan St
New York, NY
10012, USA
+1 (555) 555 5555
thirdrailcoffee.com

Top of the Rock
Rockefeller Center
30 Rockefeller Plz # M50
New York, NY
10112-0005, USA
+1 (212) 698-2000
topoftherocknyc.com

THE PIERRE

2 East 61st Street
New York, NY
10065, USA
+1 212 838 8000
tajhotels.com

Birdland
315 West 44th Street
New York, NY
10036-5402, USA
+1 212 581 3080

Il Buco
47 Bond Street
New York, NY
10012-2450, USA
+1 212 533 1932

John Barrett Salon
754 Fifth Avenue
9th Floor
New York, NY
10019, USA
+1 212 872 2700

## AUSTRALASIA

**312**

### PARK HYATT SYDNEY

7 Hickson Road
The Rocks, Sydney, NSW
Australia
+61 292 56 1465
sydney.park.hyatt.com

**Joh Bailey**
7 Knox Street
Double Bay, Australia
NSW 2028
+61 (02) 9363 0731

**Bathers' Pavilion**
The Esplanade
Balmoral, Australia
NSW 2088
+61 (02) 9969 5050

**Reads**
130 Queen Street
Woolahara, Australia
NSW 2025
+61 (02) 9328 1036

**Bill's**
433 Liverpool Street
Darlinghurst
NSW 2010
+61 (02) 9360 9631

## SPA & ADVENTURE

**318**

### ANANDA IN THE HIMALAYAS

The Palace Estate
Narendra Nagar
Tehri-Garhwal
Uttarakhand – 249175
India
+91 1378 227500
anandaspa.com

**322**

### CHIVA-SOM

73/4 Petchkasem Road
Hua Hin
Prachaub Khirikhar
77110 Thailand
+66 (0) 3253 6536
chivasom.com

**324**

### THE ORIGINAL F.X. MAYR & MORE HEALTH CENTRE

Golfstrasse 2
9082 Maria Wörth-Dellach
Austria
+43 42 73 25 11 0
mayrandmore.at

**326**

### IN:SPA RETREATS

Studio 8
160 Barlby Road
London W10 6BD
United Kingdom
+44 (0)20 8968 0501
inspa-retreats.com

**328**

### DESTINATION YOGA

Studio 8
160 Barlby Road
London W10 6BD
United Kingdom
+44 (0)20 8968 0501
destinationyoga.co.uk

**329**

### FITSCAPE FITNESS HOLIDAYS

Studio 8
160 Barlby Road
London W10 6BD
United Kingdom
+44 (0)20 8968 0501
fitscape.co.uk

**330**

### MOMENTUM ADVENTURE

The Barn
Faircrouch Lane, Wadhurst
East Sussex TN5 6PT
United Kingdom
+44 (0) 1892 784646
momentumadventure.com

## VILLAS

**336**

### UNIQUE PROPERTIES & EVENTS

27 Old Gloucester Street
London WC1N 3XX
United Kingdom
+44 (0)20 7788 7815
cedricreversade.com

## HIDDEN GEMS

**346**

### THE OPPOSITE HOUSE

The Village, Building 1
No. 11 Sanlitun Road
Chaoyang District
Beijing, China 100027
+86 10 641 76688
theoppositehouse.com

**Red Phoenix**
30 Sanlitun Beilu
Chaoyang
Beijing, China
+86 10 6416 4423

**Mei Fu**
24 Daxiangfeng Hutong
Xicheng
Beijing, China
+86 10 6612 6847

**347**

### HOTEL BELLEVUE

Pera Cingrije 7
20000 Dubrovnik, Croatia
+385 20 330 000
alh.hr

**Maria**
SV Dominika bb 20 000
Dubrovnik, Croatia
+385 (0) 20 321 330
maria-dubrovnik.hr

**Night Club Revelin**
Dubrovnik, Croatia
+385 (0) 20 322 164
revelinclub-dubrovnik.com

**348**

### ALMYRA

Poseidonos Avenue
PO Box 60136
8042 Paphos, Cyprus
+357 26 888 700
thanoshotels.com

**Phyti Village Tavern**
Phyti
Paphos District
+357 2673 2540

**349**

### CHÂTEAU MCELY

Mcely 61
289 36 Mcely
Czech Republic
+420 325 600 000
chateaumcely.com

**350**

### ADRÈRE AMELLAL

Siwa Oasis, Egypt
+202 2736 7879
adrereamellal.net

**351**

### VILLA BELROSE

La Grande Bastide
Boulevard des Crêtes
83580 Gassin/St Tropez
France
+33 (0) 494 55 97 97
villabelrose.com

**La Bouillabaisse**
St Tropez , France
+33 4 94 97 54 00
saint-tropezhotel.com

**Le Club 55**
Plage de Pampelonne
Ramatuelle, France
+33 4 94 55 55 55
club55.fr

**L'Escale**
9 Quai Jean Jaurès
St Tropez , France
+33 4 94 97 00 63
joseph-saint-tropez.com

**352**

### SOHO HOUSE BERLIN

Torstrasse 1
10119 Berlin
Germany
+49 30 40 50 44 0
sohohouseberlin.com

**Margaux**
Unter den Linden 78/Eingang
Wilhelmstraße
10117 Berlin, Germany
+49 30 2265 2611
margaux-berlin.de

**Herr von Eden**
14 Alte Schönhauserstrasse
Mitte
Berlin 10119, Germany
+49 30 2404 8682
herrvoneden.com

**353**

### GRANDHOTEL SCHLOSS BENSBERG

Kadettenstrasse
51429 Bergisch Gladbach
Germany
+49 (0) 2204 42888
schlossbensberg.com

**Café Fromme**
122 Breite Strasse
Cologne 50667, Germany
+49 221 257 6157

**354**

**SCHLOSSHOTEL LERBACH**

Lerbacher Weg
51465 Bergisch Gladbach
Germany
+49 (0) 2202 2040
schlosshotel-lerbach.com

**355**

**SEEHOTEL ÜBERFAHRT**

Überfahrtstrasse 10
83700 Rottach-Egern
Germany
+49 (0) 8022 6690
seehotel-ueberfahrt.com

**356**

**MYKONOS BLU GRECOTEL
EXCLUSIVE RESORT**

Psarou
GR-846 00
Mykonos
+30 22890 27900
mykonosblu.com

**Soho Soho**
81 Matoyanni
Mykonos
+30 22890 26 760

**Namos**
Psarou, 84600
Mykonos
+30 22890 24180

**357**

**THE UPPER HOUSE**

Pacific Place
88 Queensway
Hong Kong
+852 291 81 838
upperhouse.com

**G.O.D.**
48 Hollywood Road
Central, Hong Kong
+852 2805 1876
god.com.hk

**Aqua Spirit**
30th floor
One Peking Road
Tsimshatsui, Hong Kong
+852 3427 2288
aqua.com.hk

**358**

**THE CLIFF HOUSE HOTEL**

Ardmore
Co. Waterford, Ireland
+353 (0) 24 87800
thecliffhousehotel.com

**Lake Tour Stables**
Carrigavantry
Tramore, Ireland
+353 (0) 51 381 958

**359**

**INISH TURK BEG**

Clew Bay
Kilmeena, Westport
Co. Mayo, Ireland
+353 87 657 3840
inishturkbeg.com

**360**

**KARMA KANDARA**

Jalan Villa Kandara
Banjar Wijaya Kusuma
Ungasan, Bali 80362
+62 361 848 2200
karmaresorts.com

**Tarita**
JL. Bypass Ngurah Rai No. 910
Denpasar Selatan
+62 361 724566
tarita.com

**Biku**
JL Raya Petitenget No. 888
Seminyak
Kerobokan
+62 361 8570888
bikubali.com

**361**

**IL PELLICANO**

Località Sbarcatello
58018 Porto Ercole
Grosseto, Italy
+39 0564 858 111
pellicanohotel.com

**Rocca di Frassinello**
Loc. Giuncarico
Comune di Gavorrano
(Grosseto), Italy
+39 0577 742903
castellare.it

**Le Mura**
Via Magenta 7
Capalbio 58011, Italy
+39 0564 896692

**362**

**LA MADDALENA HOTEL
& YACHT CLUB**

Piazza Faravelli – Località Moneta
07024
Isola La Maddalena
Sardinia, Italy
+39 0789 794 273
lamaddalenahyc.com

**363**

**BORGO SANTO PIETRO**

Loc. Palazzetto 110
53012 Chuisdino (Si), Italy
+39 0577 75 12 22
borgosantopietro.com

**San Galgano**
53012 Chiusdino Sienna
Tuscany, Italy
sangalgano.org

**364**

**LE GRAY**

Martyrs' Square
Beirut Central District
Lebanon
+961 1 971 111
legray.com

**Casablanca**
Ain el Mreisseh, Corniche
Beirut, Lebanon
+961 1 369 334

**Music Hall**
Starco Building
Downtown Beirut, Lebanon

**365**

**MAIA LUXURY RESORT
& SPA**

Anse Louis
P.O. Box 722
Mahé, Seychelles
+248 390 000
maia.com.sc

**368**

**LA RESIDENCE**

Elandskloof Private Road
Elandskloof Farm
Franschhoek
South Africa
+27 21 876 4100
laresidence.co.za

**The Mont Rochelle Nature
Reserve**
+27 21 876 3603

**Huguenot Chocolate Factory**
62 Huguenot Rd (Main Rd)
Franschhoek
+27(0)21 876 4096
huguenotchocolates.com

**369**

**BIRKENHEAD HOUSE**

7th Avenue Voelklip Hermanus
Cape Town
South Africa
+27 28 314 800
birkenheadhouse.com

**Tandem Paraglide and
Whale Watching**
+27 (0) 21 762 2441

**370**

**THE SAXON BOUTIQUE
HOTEL, VILLAS AND SPA**

36 Saxon Road
Sandhurst
Johannesburg
South Africa
+27 11 292 6000
saxon.co.za

**44 Stanley Ave**
Milpark
Johannesburg 2001
South Africa
+27 11 482 4444
44stanley.co.za

**The Apartheid Museum**
Northern Parkway
Gold Reef Road
Ormonde
Johannesburg 2001
South Africa
+27 11 309 4700
apartheidmuseum.org

**Constitution Hill**
1 Kotze St
Johannesburg 2001
South Africa
+27 11 381 3100
constitutionhill.org.za

**371**

**SHAMBALA PRIVATE
GAME RESERVE**

P.O. Box 567
Saxonworld 2196
+27 11 292 6030
Or
36 Saxon Road
Sandhurst, Johannesburg
South Africa
+27 22 292 6000
shambalagamereserve.co.za

**372**

**ROYAL MALEWANE**

Avoca Road
Off Orpen Gate Road
Hoedspruit 1390
South Africa
+27 15 793 0150
royalmalewane.com

**373**

**GRAN HOTEL LA FLORIDA
BARCELONA**

Crta. Vallvidrera al Tibidabo 83-93
08035 Barcelona, Spain
+34 93 259 30 00
hotellaflorida.com

**Papabubble**
Carrer Ample 28
Barcelona, Spain
+34 93 268 8625
papabubble.com

**Inopia**
Tamarit, 104
Barcelona, Spain
+34 93 424 52 31
barinopia.com

**374**

**CHALET HOTEL
HORNBERG**

Bahnhofstrasse 36
CH-3777 Saanenmöser
Gstaad, Switzerland
+41 33 748 66 88
hotel-hornberg.ch

**Restaurant Sonnenhof**
Gstaad 3792
+41 33 7441023
restaurantsonnenhof.ch

**375**

**THE DYLAN AMSTERDAM**

Keizersgracht 384
1016 GB Amsterdam
The Netherlands
+31 (0) 20 530 2010
dylanamsterdam.com

**Anne Frank House**
267 Prinsengracht
Amsterdam
The Netherlands
+31 20 556 7105
annefrank.org.uk

**Bussia**
Reestraat 28-30
Amsterdam
The Netherlands
+31 (0) 20 627 87 94
bussia.nl

**376**

**AMBERLEY CASTLE**

Nr Arundel
West Sussex BN18 9LT
United Kingdom
+44 (0)1798 831992
amberleycastle.co.uk

**Hot Airlines**
Little London
Ebernoe, Petworth
West Sussex GU28 9LF
United Kingdom
+44 (0) 1483 268934
hotairlinesballoonflights.co.uk

**Lurgashall Winery**
Lurgashall
West Sussex GU28 9HA
United Kingdom
+44 (0) 1428 707292
lurgashall.co.uk

**377**

**BUCKLAND MANOR**

Buckland
Gloucestershire WR12 7LY
United Kingdom
+44 (0)1386 852626
bucklandmanor.co.uk

**Hidcote Bartrim**
Nr Chipping Campden
Gloucestershire GL55 6LR
United Kingdom
+44 (0) 1386 438333
nationaltrust.org.uk

**Edward Sheldon Limited**
6 New Street
Shipston-on-Stour
Warwickshire CV36 5EN
United Kingdom
+44 (0) 1608 661409
edward-sheldon.co.uk

**378**

**HOTEL TRESANTON**

27 Lower Castle Road
St Mawes TR3 5DR
United Kingdom
+44 (0)1326 270055
tresanton.com

**St Maws Methodist Chapel**
United Kingdom
(organise through Hotel)

**379**

**HOTEL ENDSLEIGH**

Milton Abbot
Tavistock
Devon PL19 0PQ
United Kingdom
+44 (0)1822 870000
hotelendsleigh.com

**Endsleigh Fishing Club**
(book through Hotel)

**Tavistock Pannier Market**
Tavistock
Devon PL19 0AL
United Kingdom
+44 (0)1822 611003
tavistockpanniermarket.co.uk

**380**

**DEAN STREET
TOWNHOUSE**

69-71 Dean Street
London W1D 3SE
United Kingdom
+44 (0) 20 7434 1775
deanstreettownhouse.com

**The Ivy**
1-5 West Street
London WC2H 9NQ
United Kingdom
+44 (0) 20 7836 4751
the-ivy.co.uk

**Caprice**
Arlington House
25 Arlington Street, St James's
London SW1A 1RJ
United Kingdom
+44 (0) 20 7629 2239
le-caprice.co.uk

**Scotts**
20 Mount Street
London W1K 2HE
United Kingdom
+44 (0) 20 7495 7309
scotts-restaurant.com

**Cecconis**
5a Burlington Gardens
London W1S 3EP
United Kingdom
+44 (0) 20 7434 1500
cecconis.co.uk

**Pineapple Dance Studios**
7 Langley Street
Covent Garden
London WC2H 9JA
United Kingdom
+44 (0) 20 7836 4004
pineapple.uk.com

**381**

**THE HEMPEL**

31-35 Craven Hill Gardens
London W2 3EA
United Kingdom
+44(0)20 7289 9000
the-hempel.co.uk

**The Electric Cinema**
191 Portobello Raod
London W11 2ED
United Kingdom
+44 (0) 20 7908 9696
electriccinema.co.uk

**Ministry of Sound**
103 Gaunt Street
London SE1 6DP
United Kingdom
+44 (0)20 7740 8609
djacademy.ministryofsound.com

**382**

**BALFOUR CASTLE**

Balfour Estates
Shapinsay
Orkney KW17 2DY
United Kingdom
+44 (0)1856 711 282
balfourcastle.co.uk

**383**

**YNYSHIR HALL**

Eglwysfach
Machynllethy, Powys
Wales SY20 8TA
United Kingdom
+44 (0)1654 781209
ynyshirhall.co.uk

**Mecca Coffee House**
26 Chalybeate Street
Aberystwyth
Ceredigion SY23 1HX
United Kingdom
+44 (0)1970 612888

**THORNBURY CASTLE**

Castle Street
Thornbury
Gloucestershire BS35 1HH
United Kingdom
+44 (0)1454 281182
thornburycastle.co.uk

**Three Choirs Vineyard Estate**
Newent
Gloucestershire GL18 1LS
United Kingdom
+44 (0)1531 890223
three-choirs-vineyards.co.uk

**Cheltenham Racecourse**
Cheltenham
Gloucestershire GL50 4SH
United Kingdom
+44 (0)1242 513 014
cheltenham.co.uk

**STON EASTON PARK**

Ston Easton
Somerset BA3 4DF
United Kingdom
+44 (0)1761 241631
stoneaston.co.uk

**Berkeley Castle**
Berkeley
Gloucestershire GL13 9BQ
United Kingdom
+44 (0)1453 810332
berkeley-castle.com

**Wells Cathedral**
Cathedral Green
Wells
Somerset BA5 2UE
United Kingdom
+44 (0)1749 674483
wellscathedral.org.uk

**BABINGTON HOUSE**

Babington
Near Frome
Somerset BA11 3RW
United Kingdom
+44 (0) 1373 812266
babingtonhouse.com

**THE SAMLING**

Ambleside Road
Windermere
Cumbria LA23 1LR
United Kingdom
+44 (0)1539 431922
thesamlinghotel.co.uk

**Wainwright Guides**
amazon.co.uk

**Air Ventures Paragliding School**
+44 (0) 7830 281986
airventures.co.uk

**FOUR SEASONS CARMELO**

Ruta 21, Km 262
Carmelo
Dpto de Colonia
Uruguay
+598 (4542) 9000
fourseasons.com/carmelo

Book through:
**Dehouche**
Leblon
Rio de Janeiro 22431 050 – RJ
UK +44 (0) 871 284 7770
Rio +55 21 25123895
dehouche.com

**PLAYA VIK JOSÉ IGNACIO**

Playa Vik
Calle Los Cisnes y Los Horneros
Faro José Ignacio
Uruguay
+598 94 605 212/314
vikretreats.com

Book through:
**Dehouche**
Leblon
Rio de Janeiro 22431 050 – RJ
UK +44 (0) 871 284 7770
Rio +55 21 25123895
dehouche.com

**DUNTON HOT SPRINGS**

52068 West Fork Road
Dolores, CO
81323, USA
+1 970 882 4800
duntonhotsprings.com

**SOHO HOUSE NEW YORK**

29-35 Ninth Avenue
New York, NY
10014, USA
+1 212 627 9800
sohohouseny.com

**Kirna Zabete**
96 Greene Street
bt Prince & Spring Streets
New York, NY
10012, USA
+1 212 941 9656
kirnazabete.com

**Spotted Pig**
314 West 11th Street
@ Greenwich Street
New York, NY
10014, USA
+1 212 620 0393
thespottedpig.com

# Yacht charter with Yacht Masters
## '...superior to any 6-star hotel offering – and infinitely more exclusive'

Chartering is unquestionably the ultimate holiday experience, providing the utmost privacy and security. You and your guests will be free to enjoy sundecks, a personal Captain and crew, chef, jet-skis, scuba, snorkels and the like, 24 hours of every day.

Imagine the freedom to cruise and explore, waking up to a different view whenever you wish, without ever having to pack and unpack. Swimming in a secluded bay and being greeted with your favourite drink on your return, having your choice of music downloaded and cabins and Jacuzzi set at your required temperature, specific vintages of wine flown in, your favourite brand of water, even the way you like your bed made, all requirements ready for your arrival. It all adds up to a total flexibility of any number of delights, all tailormade for you – superior to any 6-star hotel offering – and infinitely more exclusive.

At Yacht Masters we are immensely proud of our bespoke and discreet service and pride ourselves on the fact that we are a smaller, privately owned, more intimate broker. With a combined experience of over 30 years and access to all charter yachts we'll help you decide upon your ideal yacht and cruising location.

Yacht Masters – quite simply raising the standard.

+44 (0)20 7099 0941
yachts@yachtmasters.com
www.yachtmasters.com

ALFA NERO
GEORGETOWN

EUROPE'S AIR TAXI SERVICE

*Blink – all the benefits of personal air travel but up to 50% cheaper than existing private jet services*

Blink is Europe's air taxi service. We make European private aviation more affordable and every journey more efficient, productive, flexible and enjoyable.

Carrying up to four passengers, our fleet of Blink jets provides unrivalled access to over 600 convenient destinations throughout Europe. Whether you pay as you go with our Blink Taxi service or buy in advance with the Blink Foresight Card, we have a range of value-for -money services to meet your specific European air travel needs.

You can now book online at www.flyblink.com where you will find our lowest taxi fares – guaranteed. Alternatively contact our Flight Services team – here to help 24 hours a day.

*London*
+44 (0)20 7199 1400

*Geneva*
+41 (0)22 592 75 77

*Email*
blink@flyblink.com

*Book online*
www.flyblink.com

# PremiAir

*PremiAir – unrivalled experience, exemplary service. We are, in short, experts in flight.*

Whether it's a short hop from the London Heliport to a shoot in Scotland, a skiing weekend with the boys or a family holiday to the south of France, PremiAir can ensure you arrive punctually, relaxed and in the most elegant way imaginable.

You'll travel in an aircraft picked from a wide range of executive helicopters and business jets. You'll enjoy a service that's been repeatedly recognised with prestigious travel awards; a service that regularly carries royalty and high-profile celebrities.

Charter with PremiAir and we'll organise every stage of your journey seamlessly – taking you, quite literally, from door to door. You can relax secure in the knowledge that you'll arrive in absolute safety, superb style, and on time.

You are in safe hands with PremiAir.

Call our Charter Services team:
+44 (0)1895 830900
charter@premiair-aviation.com
www.premiair.co.uk

# CREDITS

**Hotel Amigo**
Linda van Waesberge
Photographer
Loïc Delvaulx

**Hotel Excelsior**
Lokrum Island
Copyright Croatian
National Tourist Board

**Château de Bagnols**
Paul Bocuse
Photographer
Sebastien Veronese

**Hôtel Le Bristol**
Brasserie de L'ile St. Louis
Photographer
Paul Kappe

**Grand-Hôtel du Cap-Ferrat**
Ephrussi de Rothschild Villa
Copyright Culturespaces

**Hotel de Rome**
Bar Jeder Vernunft
Photographer
Jan Wirdeier

**Des McDonald**
Photographer
Philip Haynes

**Villa San Michele**
Loretta Caponi
Photographer
Loretta Caponi

**Grand Hotel a Villa Feltrinelli**
Verona Opera
Image courtesy
of Provincia di Verona

**Grand Hotel Timeo**
Polizzi Generosa
Copyright Mayor
Patrizio David

**Hotel Villa Magna**
Museo del Traje
Photographer Munio Rodil
Copyright Musea del Traje

**Hotel Puente Romano**
Picasso Museum Málaga
Photographer Bleday Rosa
Copyright Museo Picasso
Málaga

**Marbella Club Hotel**
Babylonia Palace
Photographer
Pablo Campbert

Marbella Vips
Photographer
Adam Winfield

**Gstaad Palace**
Lorenz Bach
Image courtesy
of Peter Rölli

Horse Sleighing
Image courtesy
of Gstaad Saanenland
Tourism

**Lower Slaughter Manor**
Cheltenham International
Jazz Festival
Image courtesy
of Cheltenham Festivals

**The Berkeley**
Regent's Park
Open Air Theatre
Photographer Alastair Muir

**Umaid Bhawan Palace
Jodhpur**
Bhangarh ruins
Image courtesy
of Incredible India
Tourist Board

**Taj Mahal Palace & Tower**
Enigma
Image courtesy
of Noelle Rocque

**Taj Lake Palace**
Ranthambore
National Park
Image courtesy
of Incredible India
Tourist Board

**Laura Morera**
Photographer
Bill Cooper

**One&Only Pamilla**
Hummer Adventure
Image courtesy
of Terramar Destinations

**The Setai**
Bin no 18
Image Courtesy
of Alfredo Patino

**The Pierre**
Birdland Club New York
Photographer
Ryan Paternite

**Aghios A, Casa Bianca
and La Quinta**
Image courtesy
of Unique Properties
& Events

**Tanya Rose**
Photographer
Ashton Keiditsch

# TANYA ROSE

Tanya Rose is one of the foremost authorities in the travel industry. As founder of respected sales and communication agency Mason Rose, Tanya is recognised as 'the voice of luxury travel'. Having been director of sales and marketing for the Savoy Group, Tanya saw a niche in the travel market for an agency that offered a different approach to representing luxury properties, and in 1993 she set up Mason Rose. Her foresight, understanding of travel trends and consumer insights have made Mason Rose the agency of choice for top hotels around the world. Over the years Tanya has become the trusted travel confidante of celebrities, business people and their families. With her insider access and unique knowledge of the best-kept travel secrets, Tanya ensures the perfect match of the right destination and the best place to suit each client. Educated at Gordonstoun, she is now a governor of the school and has previously held positions on the Development Boards of the Almeida, Clic Sargent and Wellchild. In addition to Tanya's passion for travel her interests include the opera, theatre and fashion. Tanya is married with one son.

# MARTIN TURNER

My great friend Martin has been travelling the world his whole life. A third birthday in the Panama Canal, school in Kent, North Queensland, and New York. He has spun through hundreds of hotels during a 25-year career in events and live communications. If he is not dancing at the Broadway Dance Center or Pineapple Studios in London, he is zooming down the ski slopes of Switzerland, Colorado or New Zealand. He may also be attending a screenplay workshop with Blake Snyder in Hollywood, guest-presenting at the Reebok Sports Club in NYC, lecturing at King's College, or volunteering for charity. Theatre, film and travel are his background and passion, as is his great love of writing. His sense of adventure, intimate knowledge of destinations, and great humour are evident in the writing of this book with me. We have spent many hysterical hours together laughing our way through the experience, and hope you enjoy reading this book as much as we have enjoyed writing it.

# MASONROSE
## PRIVATE

—

*Luxury travel*
*beyond your expectations*

Mason Rose Private is an elite bespoke travel service staffed
by a team of world travellers with the insider knowledge and
experience to make your next trip exceptional.

Catering to highly individual and discerning travellers,
Mason Rose Private gives clients assurance that properties
measure up to photography and descriptions. Our service extends
to providing chefs, masseurs, private jets and yachts. From an Italian
palace or an African safari lodge, to a private Indian Ocean island
hideaway or a chic city retreat, allow Mason Rose Private
to make your dreams become reality.

**Mason Rose Private**
Personal Consultant:
+44 (0)20 7201 8070

masonroseprivate.com